Violence, Trauma, and Memory

READING TRAUMA AND MEMORY

Series Editors: Aimee Pozorski, Central Connecticut State University and Nicholas Ealy, University of Hartford

Reading Trauma and Memory offers global perspectives on representations of trauma and memory while examining the tensions, limitations, and responsibilities that accompany the status of the witness. This series attempts to bridge the gap between trauma studies and new directions in the fields of memory studies, popular culture, and race theory and seeks submissions that closely read literature and culture for representations of traumatic wounding, the limits of memory, and the ethical duty to depict historical trauma and its effects.

Given its breadth, this series will appeal to scholars in a number of interdisciplinary fields; given the specific angle of trauma and memory, it will capture those who see ethics and responsibility as key factors in their scholarship. Such areas include: Holocaust studies; war trauma and PTSD; illness and disability; the trauma of migration and immigration; memory studies; race studies; gender and sexuality studies (which has recently had a resurgence with the #MeToo movement); studies in popular culture that take up television and films about witness; and the study of social and historical movements.

We are seeking projects that question how to honor the past through close readings of literature focused on trauma and memory—which would necessarily take on international perspectives. Examples include a consideration of literature, justice, and Rwanda through a postcolonial and trauma lens; recent thinking on the phenomenon of *American Crime Story* and the resurgence of interest in the O. J. Simpson trial that parallels the narrative of the Black Lives Matter movement; readings of the attempts of popular culture to address issues of historical injustice as exemplified by *12 Years a Slave* and HBO's *Westworld*.

Recent Titles in This Series

Violence, Trauma, and Memory: Responses to War in the Late Medieval and Early Modern World
    Edited by Nicholas Ealy and Alexandra Onuf
9/11 Gothic: Decrypting Ghosts and Trauma in New York City's Terrorism Novels

By Danel Olson
Philo-Semitic Violence: Poland's Jewish Past in New Polish Narratives
By Elżbieta Janicka and Tomasz Żukowski
Trauma in 20th Century Multicultural American Poetry: Unmuted Verse
By Jamie D. Barker
Ethics of Witness in Global Testimonial Narratives: Responding to the Pain of Others
By Kimberly A. Nance

Violence, Trauma, and Memory

Responses to War in the Late Medieval and Early Modern World

Edited by Alexandra Onuf and Nicholas Ealy

LEXINGTON BOOKS
Lanham • Boulder • New York • London

Published by Lexington Books
An imprint of The Rowman & Littlefield Publishing Group, Inc.
4501 Forbes Boulevard, Suite 200, Lanham, Maryland 20706
www.rowman.com

86-90 Paul Street, London EC2A 4NE

Copyright © 2022 by The Rowman & Littlefield Publishing Group, Inc.

All rights reserved. No part of this book may be reproduced in any form or by any electronic or mechanical means, including information storage and retrieval systems, without written permission from the publisher, except by a reviewer who may quote passages in a review.

British Library Cataloguing in Publication Information Available

Library of Congress Cataloging-in-Publication Data

Names: Onuf, Alexandra, 1974- editor. | Ealy, Nicholas, 1972- editor.
Title: Violence, trauma, and memory : responses to war in the late medieval and early modern world / edited by Alexandra Onuf and Nicholas Ealy.
Description: Lanham : Lexington Books, [2022] | Series: Reading trauma and memory | Includes bibliographical references and index. | Summary: "This volume examines late medieval and early modern warfare in France, the Hispanic World, and the Dutch Republic through the lens of trauma and memory studies. The essays, focusing on history, literature, and visual culture, demonstrate how people living with wartime violence processed and remembered the trauma of war"-- Provided by publisher.
Identifiers: LCCN 2022032164 (print) | LCCN 2022032165 (ebook) | ISBN 9781666914566 (cloth) | ISBN 9781666914580 (paperback) | ISBN 9781666914573 (ebook)
Subjects: LCSH: French literature--Early modern, 1500-1700--History and criticism. | Spanish literature--Early modern, 1500-1700--History and criticism. | Psychic trauma in literature. | Memory in literature. | Art, Dutch--16th century. | Psychic trauma in art. | Memory in art. | LCGFT: Essays.
Classification: LCC PQ239 .V46 2022 (print) | LCC PQ239 (ebook) | DDC 809/.93353 do23/eng/20220817
LC record available at https://lccn.loc.gov/2022032164
LC ebook record available at https://lccn.loc.gov/2022032165

Contents

List of Figures	ix
Acknowledgments	xiii
Introduction *Alexandra Onuf and Nicholas Ealy*	1

PART ONE: FRANCE — 21

Chapter One: Memorializing the Battle of Crécy: Colins de Beaumont's "On the Crécy Dead" as a Textual Monument for Processing Trauma — 23
Kimberly Lifton

Chapter Two: "Je hé guerre, point ne la doit prisier": Emotions, War, and Trauma in the Poetry of Charles of Orléans — 49
Charles-Louis Morand-Métivier

Chapter Three: Bringing up the Dead: The Grotesque in Literature after the French Wars of Religion — 67
Kathleen Long

PART TWO: THE HISPANIC WORLD — 95

Chapter Four: Desire, Trauma, and Warfare in Fernando de Rojas's *Celestina* — 97
Nicholas Ealy

Chapter Five: Violence in the Making: Remembering the Viceroy's Assassination during the Catalan Revolt of 1640 — 117
Ivan Gracia-Arnau

Chapter Six: Trauma and Postmemory in Martín Cortés's Uprising 135
Covadonga Lamar Prieto

PART THREE: THE DUTCH REPUBLIC 165

Chapter Seven: Hendrick Goltzius's *Lucretia* and the Eighty Years' War 167
Rachel Wise

Chapter Eight: Landscape and the Memory of Place in Claes Jansz. Visscher's Prints of Brabant 199
Alexandra Onuf

Index 233

About the Contributors 239

List of Figures

Figure 3.1: Hans Vredeman de Vries, *Caryatidum . . . sive Athlantidum multiformium*, plate 7, ca. 1565. Etching, 161 x 237 mm, Elisha Whittelsey Collection, Metropolitan Museum of Art, New York, accession number 66.545.4 (1–17). Image © by courtesy Metropolitan Museum of Art, New York.   69

Figure 3.2: After Hans Vredeman de Vries, *Diamond-shaped cartouche*, ca. 1547–1605. Engraving, 215 x 170 mm, bequest of Herbert Mitchell, Metropolitan Museum of Art, New York, inv. no. 2018.839.15. Image © by courtesy Metropolitan Museum of Art, New York.   75

Figure 3.3: Johannes or Lucas van Doetecum after Hans Vredeman de Vries, *Scenographiae sive perspectivae*, plate 16, 1563. Engraving, 209 x 256 mm, Rijksmuseum, Amsterdam, inv. no. BI-1897-A-972-18. Image © by courtesy Rijksmuseum, Amsterdam.   81

Figure 3.4: Johannes or Lucas van Doetecum after Hans Vredeman de Vries, *Scenographiae sive perspectivae*, plate 18, 1563. Engraving, 211 x 260 mm, Rijksmuseum, Amsterdam, inv. no. BI-1897-A-972-20. Image © by courtesy Rijksmuseum, Amsterdam.   83

Figure 7.1: Hendrick Goltzius, *The Banquet of Sextus Tarquinius*, plate 1 from *Lucretia* series, 1578–1580. Engraving, 209 x 247 mm, Rijksmuseum, Rijksprentenkabinet, Amsterdam, inv. no. RP-P-OB-10.085. Image © by courtesy Rijksmuseum, Amsterdam.   168

Figure 7.2: Hendrick Goltzius, *Lucretia and Her Handmaids Spinning*, plate 2 from *Lucretia* series, 1578–1580. Engraving,

210 x 249 mm, Rijksmuseum, Rijksprentenkabinet, Amsterdam, inv. no. RP-P-OB-10.086. Image © by courtesy Rijksmuseum, Amsterdam. 169

Figure 7.3: Hendrick Goltzius, *The Rape of Lucretia*, plate 3 from *Lucretia* series, 1578–1580. Engraving, 211 x 248 mm, Rijksmuseum, Rijksprentenkabinet, Amsterdam, inv. no. RP-P-OB-10.087. Image © by courtesy Rijksmuseum, Amsterdam. 170

Figure 7.4: Hendrick Goltzius, *The Suicide of Lucretia*, plate 4 from *Lucretia* series, 1578–1580. Engraving, 205 x 248 mm, Rijksmuseum, Rijksprentenkabinet, Amsterdam, inv. no. RP-P-OB-10.088. Image © by courtesy Rijksmuseum, Amsterdam. 171

Figure 7.5: Frans Hogenberg, *Death in Oudewater 1575*, 1574–ca. 1578. Etching, 214 x 274 mm, Rijksmuseum, Rijksprentenkabinet, Amsterdam, inv. no. RP-P-OB-78.785-89. Image © by courtesy Rijksmuseum, Amsterdam. 174

Figure 7.6: Dirck Volckertsz. Coornhert after Maarten van Heemskerck, *The Virtuous Woman Spins*, plate 1 from *Praise of the Virtuous Wife* series, 1555. Engraving, 251 x 203 mm, Rijksmuseum, Rijksprentenkabinet, Amsterdam, inv. no. RP-P-1894-A-18302. Image © by courtesy Rijksmuseum, Amsterdam. 178

Figure 7.7: Cornelis Cort after Titian, *Lucretia and Sextus*, 1571. Engraving, 371 x 266 mm, Rijksmuseum, Rijksprentenkabinet, Amsterdam, inv. no. RP-P-1951-541. Image © by courtesy Rijksmuseum, Amsterdam. 180

Figure 7.8: Titian, *Tarquin and Lucretia*, ca. 1571. Oil on canvas, 1889 x 1451 mm, Fitzwilliam Museum, Cambridge, inv. no. 914. Image © by courtesy Fitzwilliam Museum, Cambridge. 181

Figure 7.9: Detail of Figure 7.4. 184

Figure 7.10: Hans Collaert I after Ambrosius Francken, *Lament over the Desolation of the Netherlands*, ca. 1570–1580. Engraving, 434 x 572 mm, Museum Plantin-Moretus / Prentenkabinet, Antwerp, inv. no. PK.OP.18283. Image © by courtesy Museum Plantin-Moretus, Antwerp–UNESCO, World Heritage / Photo: Peter Maes. 185

List of Figures xi

Figure 7.11: Anonymous, *Maid of Holland and the Departure of the Duke of Alva from the Netherlands*, 1573. Copper, 30 mm diameter, Rijksmuseum, Amsterdam, inv. no. NG-VG-3-448. Image © by courtesy Rijksmuseum, Amsterdam. 186

Figure 8.1: Claes Jansz. Visscher, Title page to *Regiunculae, et Villae Aliquot Ducatus Brabantiae* . . . series, 1612. Etching, 100 x 155 mm, Andrew W. Mellon Fund, National Gallery of Art, Washington, D.C., inv. no. 1975.59.1. Image © by courtesy NGA Images. 199

Figure 8.2: Hans Collaert I after Ambrosius Francken, *Lament over the Desolation of the Netherlands*, ca. 1570–1580. Engraving, 434 x 572 mm, Museum Plantin-Moretus / Prentenkabinet, Antwerp, inv. no. PK.OP.18283. Image © by courtesy Museum Plantin-Moretus, Antwerp–UNESCO, World Heritage / Photo: Peter Maes. 203

Figure 8.3: Claes Jansz. Visscher, *Novissima, et Accuratissima Leonis Belgici* . . . , ca. 1611. Etching and engraving, 480 x 580 mm, The David Rumsey Map Collection, Stanford University, inv. no. G6011.A5 1611.V5. Image © by courtesy Stanford University. 205

Figure 8.4: Claes Jansz. Visscher, *Roode Poort*, no. 2 from *Regiunculae, et Villae Aliquot Ducatus Brabantiae* . . . series, 1612. Etching, 104 x 158 mm, Andrew W. Mellon Fund, National Gallery of Art, Washington, D.C., inv. no. 1975.59.2. Image © by courtesy NGA Images. 209

Figure 8.5 Frans Hogenberg, *Entrance of Prince William of Orange into Antwerp, 1577*, from Series 8 of *Nederlandse Gebeurtenissen, 1577–1583*, 1577–1579. Etching, 210 x 280 mm, Rijksmuseum, Amsterdam, inv. no. RP-P-OB-78.784-163. Image © by courtesy Rijksmuseum, Amsterdam. 210

Figure 8.6: Claes Jansz. Visscher, *Village Road*, no. 4 from *Regiunculae, et Villae Aliquot Ducatus Brabantiae* . . . series, 1612. Etching, 100 x 155 mm, Andrew W. Mellon Fund, National Gallery of Art, Washington, D.C., inv. no. 1975.59.4. Image © by courtesy NGA Images. 211

Figure 8.7: Claes Jansz. Visscher, *Country Village with Church and Bridge*, no. 15 from *Regiunculae, et Villae Aliquot Ducatus Brabantiae* . . . series, 1612. Etching, 99 x 155 mm, Andrew W.

Mellon Fund, National Gallery of Art, Washington, D.C., inv.
no. 1975.59.15. Image © by courtesy NGA Images. 211

Figure 8.8: Hans Collaert I after Hans Bol, *View of the Palace of Brussels*, no. 1 from *Environs of Brussels* series published by Claes Jansz. Visscher, ca. 1612. Engraving, 138 x 199 mm, Rijksmuseum, Amsterdam, inv. no. RP-P-1889-A-15012. Image © by courtesy Rijksmuseum, Amsterdam. 212

Figure 8.9: Hans Collaert I after Hans Bol, *View of Stal*, no. 15 from *Environs of Brussels* series published by Claes Jansz. Visscher, ca. 1612. Engraving, 138 x 199 mm, Rijksmuseum, Amsterdam, inv. no. RP-P-1889-A-15026. Image © by courtesy Rijksmuseum, Amsterdam. 213

Figure 8.10: Adriaen Collaert after Jacob Grimmer, *Landscape with Travelers*, no. 1 from the *By Antwerpen* series published by Claes Jansz. Visscher, ca. 1612. Engraving, 126 x 186 mm, Rijksmuseum, Amsterdam, inv. no. RP-P-1919-2072. Image © by courtesy Rijksmuseum, Amsterdam. 214

Figure 8.11: Adriaen Collaert after Jacob Grimmer, *Landscape with a River and a Windmill*, no. 8 from the *By Antwerpen* series published by Claes Jansz. Visscher, ca. 1612. Engraving, 124 x 184 mm, Rijksmuseum, Amsterdam, inv. no. RP-P-1919-2079. Image © by courtesy Rijksmuseum, Amsterdam. 214

Figure 8.12: Claes Jansz. Visscher, *Beacon at Zandvoort*, no. 2 from *Plaisante Plaetsen* series, ca. 1611–1613. Etching, 102 x 145 mm, Rijksmuseum, Amsterdam, inv. no. RP-P-1879-A-3463. Image © by courtesy Rijksmuseum, Amsterdam. 218

Figure 8.13: Claes Jansz. Visscher, *Huis ter Kleef*, no. 12 from *Plaisante Plaetsen* series, ca. 1611–1613. Etching, 103 x 158 mm, Rijksmuseum, Amsterdam, inv. no. RP-P-1879-A-3473. Image © by courtesy Rijksmuseum, Amsterdam. 219

Acknowledgments

We first thank all the contributors to this volume, without whom it would not have been possible. We would like to acknowledge Kate McGrath, who helped us formulate this project when it was in its early stages. We would also like to acknowledge the support received from the following people: Jenny Davis Barnett, Maria Esposito Frank, Aimee Pozorski, and Paul Watt.

We thank Lexington Books for producing this collection. Special recognition goes to Holly Buchanan and Megan White for keeping this project on track as we moved through its various stages. We also thank Amyrose McCue Gill and her team at TextFormations who did the copyediting for this volume.

Finally, we appreciate the financial support we received from two Cardin Grants through the College of Arts and Sciences. We also received funding through Faculty Development Grants from the Hartford Art School and Department of English and Modern Languages at the University of Hartford. Additionally, we thank the Renaissance Society of America for giving us the space and time in their 2021 Virtual Annual Conference to help get this project underway.

Introduction

Alexandra Onuf and Nicholas Ealy

WAR AND VIOLENCE

It is hardly an exaggeration to say that late medieval and early modern Europe experienced almost constant wars and the attendant violence and destruction they wrought. Wars were fought over territory and lines of succession, over religion, and over resources and power. There were localized uprisings, rebellions, and regional skirmishes. There were massive military mobilizations for the Crusades and later in the many wars against the Ottomans. There were peasant revolts and civil wars. Some conflicts were brief; others dragged on over decades, even centuries—most notably the Hundred Years' War between the kingdoms of France and England (1337–1453); the French Wars of Religion (1562–1598); the Eighty Years' War between the Netherlandish provinces and Spain (1568–1648); and the Thirty Years' War in the Holy Roman Empire (1618–1648). There were wars within wars; for instance, the War of the League of Cambrai was fought from 1508 to 1516 between France, the Papal States, and the Republic of Venice, alongside several other European forces, yet it was only one campaign within the extended Italian Wars, which were fought in successive periods lasting most of the sixteenth century and involved many other states (1494–1559). These conflicts touched every part of the continent, and indeed extended beyond it as conflicts begun in Europe spread to colonized territories in Asia and the New World.

The frequency and prolonged duration of these military encounters came at an enormous human cost. The fundamental mechanism of war is the application of violent force to inflict injury, pain, and death.[1] While medieval codes of chivalry had provided some parameters for how war ought to be conducted, new military tactics and technologies transformed the battlefield over the course of the late medieval and early modern periods, with gunpowder, artillery, and new bastion fortifications often supplanting and rendering obsolete not only traditional cavalry and castles but also the codes of honor by which aristocratic knights had long abided.[2] Even without the use of devastating modern military technologies, the estimated human toll from these premodern wars grew to staggering heights, with some battles resulting in tens of thousands of casualties. Rebellions were often suppressed with particularly brutal violence, as in the case of the German Peasants' Revolt of 1524–1525, during the course of which somewhere between 100,000 and 300,000 farmers and peasants were slaughtered.[3]

The effects of wartime violence and destruction spread far beyond the battlefield. Civilians were as much subject to the vicissitudes of war as were combatants; violent incursions permeated all social strata and all quarters, from country villages to major urban centers. Sieges and sacks of cities were regular and expected tactics of warfare, as were billeting and quartering of troops in both country and city. Towns and rural communities were often subject to pillaging and raids, especially when armies were released from duty or went unpaid. Famine and disease regularly followed in the aftermath of these military conflicts, leading to vast death tolls.[4] One estimate suggests that over the course of the Thirty Years' War, somewhere between four and eight million people perished, with some regions losing up to 50 percent of their populations, making it one of the most deadly and destructive European wars before the twentieth century.[5]

One might assume that people living through this seemingly endless succession of wars might become inured to their effects and consequences—war was simply a fact of life (and death). Premodern people did not have the extensive psychological language to express personal pain or trauma that modern people do. As a result, there are far fewer direct documentary records of the physical and psychic harm wrought by the violence of war on premodern populations that we have in such abundance for the modern period. However, in recent years scholars have sought to discern the emotional impacts of this violence, finding evidence in literary panegyrics, lyric poetry, war chronicles, pamphlets, broadsheets, prints, artwork, and songs of the nuanced ways late medieval and early modern people responded to the wars that raged around them.[6] What has emerged is an increasingly nuanced understanding of how the violence of war could result in traumatic wounds and enduring emotional distress, and in turn how this trauma could sometimes be transformed into more stabilizing forms of mourning and remembrance.[7] Most commonly, personal stories of pain, violence, and atrocities rely on the providential framing of horrific events as necessary parts of God's divine plan.[8] Beyond this, personal memories of painful events and experiences were often deployed much later to authenticate communal narratives that supported specific religious or political framings of past suffering and violence.[9] The chapters of this book offer specific case studies that showcase how late medieval and early modern peoples experienced and processed the atrocities and traumas of war.

TRAUMA

Since the 1990s, trauma as a cultural and critical theory has risen in prominence throughout the humanities, due primarily to the work of scholars such as Cathy Caruth, Shoshana Felman, and Dori Laub, who began to investigate the confluence of language, literature, testimony, and history, and their relation to traumatic experiences.[10] Stemming in part from neurobiology, psychology, Holocaust studies, and the Yale School of deconstructive theory, trauma studies have gained even more prominence in the public consciousness due to the unprecedented 9/11 terrorist attacks on US soil and the COVID-19 pandemic two decades later. Over the years, the field has widened its scope to include not only the effects of catastrophic events but also contemporary issues related to intergenerational violence, crises in human subjectivity, ecocide, and the legacy of societal inequities.[11] Linking the threads of these various discourses, however, is the way these events and experiences investigate notions of injury—inflicted upon individuals and groups—as having the potential to cause both physical and (more importantly for trauma scholars) psychical harm. True to its etymology, the term "trauma," from the related Greek words τραύμα (traúma) and τιτρπσχω (titrpscho)—"wound" and "piercing," respectively—has been used since ancient times to reference "an injury where the skin is broken as a consequence of external violence."[12] This notion of a wound caused by a harmful disturbance thus implies that trauma is something carried within the psyche and/or upon the body in a way that exposes the human subject's vulnerability, denies it a sense of wholeness, and bears witness to the lingering effects of the initial violence.

In such a manner, this volume posits that trauma is not a phenomenon limited to the modern period, as psychological wounding—and the witnessing that comes from it in literature, visual culture, and historical records—transcends time and place. Scholars have often assumed that medieval and early modern societies were so bellicose as to be immune to the consequences of trauma, or that they simply had no framework for processing its impacts. Scholarship during the 2010s, however, began to reveal how the fields of trauma theory and memory studies can be fruitfully applied to the study of medieval and early modern communities. Donna Trembinski, for instance, has posited that discussions of "melancholia" in premodern medical literature, a condition whose genealogy can be traced as far back as the ancient

Mediterranean world, display many similarities to what we consider to be trauma today.[13] Similarly, scholars including Zackariah C. Long have formulated theoretical models of trauma by looking at early modern cultural production as a type of "early modern psychology," examining how it uncovers notions of a "wounded consciousness."[14] Along these lines, Wendy J. Turner and Christina Lee posit that although the "physical trauma of a body is more in line with what the term 'trauma' meant for the premodern world: a wound," nonetheless "in the Middle Ages, traumatic events, as defined today, were in abundance. There is evidence of trauma experienced by many parts of the population.... The evidence of individual psychological trauma and social trauma in poetry and literature, of mental and physical trauma in court records, of blunt and sharp force trauma on medieval skeletons is varied and rich."[15]

Any discussion of trauma—particularly within the context of war and, perhaps surprisingly, medieval history and early modern literature as well—cannot be had without mention of Freud's seminal work *Beyond the Pleasure Principle* (1920), considered by many in trauma studies to be the field's foundational text. Shaped by the aftermath of World War I, Freud explores here the neurosis from which shell-shocked war veterans were suffering, an enigmatic form of psychological wounding that he likens to hysteria, hypochondria, melancholia, and "a general enfeeblement and disturbance of mental capacities."[16] Arising from the fright of being unprepared for and overwhelmed by danger or a near-death experience, trauma, as Freud recognized from his patients, presents what theorists would later see as a complication of how we might interpret an event that seemingly happens in a specific time and place. This complication, in turn, upsets traditional understandings of both memory and history. For trauma, he observes, is not something that remains in the past, circumscribed by the temporality specific to the event in which it emerges, but rather is a phenomenon, not understood or assimilated—*unknown*—in its occurrence, that perplexingly and persistently returns. Experiencing such repetitions, for instance, in dreams, hallucinations, and flashbacks, the traumatized patients are put back into the moment of trauma, as each repetition places them within yet "another fright."[17] This notion of a continuous wounding, inserting itself in unforeseen ways, consequently poses an enigma in its repetition, creating a narrative where the traumatic event gives way to what Cathy Caruth calls a "history . . . grasped only in the very inaccessibility of its occurrence."[18]

To explain the inaccessible nature of the history that trauma causes, Freud turns to a pair of episodes from Torquato Tasso's early-modern epic *Jerusalem Delivered* (*Gerusalemme liberata*, 1591) which, he claims, gives "the most moving poetic picture of such a [traumatic] fate."[19] Tancred, the work's hero, unknowingly kills his beloved Clorinda, disguised in the black armor of a rival knight, in battle during the First Crusade (1096–1099). Later, while traveling through an enchanted forest, he encounters a large cypress and: "Pur tragge al fin la spade, e con gran forza / percote l'alta pianta. Oh meraviglia! / manda fuor sangue la recisa scorza, / e fa la terra intorno a sé vermiglia" (ultimately draws his sword, and with great strength / strikes the tall tree. O marvel! / it bleeds through its severed bark / and makes the earth around it red).[20] From the slashed tree, however, emerges Clorinda's voice, whose soul has been housed there, informing Tancred that he has unwittingly harmed her yet again: "Ahi! troppo . . . / m'hai tu, Trancredi, offeso; / . . . Dopo la morte gli aversari tuoi, / crudel, ne' lor sepolcri offender vuoi?" (Ay! Too much . . . / have you injured me, Tancred / . . . After the death of your adversaries, / cruel one, you want to damage their graves?).[21]

In this scene of piercing, of trauma, Tancred's action recalls not simply the original killing, but turns this fatal deed, here in this new iteration, into a continued wounding. Clorinda's accusation, crying out from the slashed bark, that Tancred has "offeso" (offended) and wants to "offender" (offend), from the Latin *offendere* (to receive an injury and suffer damage), only serves to reinforce this point. As such, Clorinda's voice emerging from the wound sends an appeal that, according to Caruth, asks Tancred to be "witness to a truth that [he] cannot fully know," and yet the appeal, nonetheless, asks him *to know*, to understand, to hear the voice of this other speaking to him.[22] Clorinda's voice, in other words, carries with it the memory of wounding and of its repetition, and attempts to retell it in a manner that puts trauma, history, and language—and literary language at that—into conversation. As Caruth states, Freud's use of Tasso's epic forces us to think of history "around the site of a wound," a history bound to "trauma's irreducible delay" and its "endlessly repeated departure" in ways that may—or may not—render witnessing, remembrance, and memorialization successful.[23] And the cultural products of such a history—the literature, visual culture, and historiographical documents examined in this volume—represent, we argue, such a repetition, speaking to the ways late medieval and early modern people experienced and then attempted to process the trauma of war into personal and collective memory and remembrance.

MEMORY

Like trauma theory, the field of memory studies has blossomed since the 1990s. From the outset it has been an interdisciplinary undertaking, involving academic fields as diverse as sociology, psychology, neuroscience, and the humanities, particularly history, philosophy, archaeology, literary studies, art history, and visual and media studies. Collaborations across these disciplines have allowed for flexible and useful new understandings of how cultural remembering takes place and contributes to both personal and collective identities.[24] The study of memory has become especially crucial in recent decades as new technologies have enabled unprecedented levels of data storage: What and how will we actively remember when massive agglomerations of data are relegated to and stored in digital archives? At the same time, scholars across disciplines have also turned to memory studies in an effort to elucidate many of the same historical events that trauma theory also seeks to grapple with, particularly the Holocaust, the end of the Cold War, truth and reconciliation efforts, and the events of 9/11. The connections between trauma and memory have thus been fundamental and formative for both fields.

The development of the field of memory studies in the 1990s springs from the earlier work of the French philosopher and sociologist Maurice Halbwachs, who in 1925 published *Les cadres sociaux de la mémoire*.[25] In this text, he argues that an individual's memories are in fact entwined with and indeed dependent upon larger social contexts, coining the phrase "collective memory" to describe the way personal memories are generated and operate within sociocultural frameworks. Around the same time, art and cultural historian Aby Warburg developed a related notion of how cultural memory can be transmitted across time and cultures through affective visual symbols that serve as storehouses of collective cultural memory. Warburg focuses on distinctively visual and material forms as constitutive agents and receptacles of cultural memory, which he termed *Bildgedächtnis*, or iconic memory.[26] Taken together, the twinned activities of social and material remembering provide access to shared knowledge and experience, and fulfill a fundamental role in the processes of identity formation. Moreover, both authors demonstrate that the processes of memory actively construct relationships to the past, prefiguring the poststructuralist theories of the constructed nature of reality that emerged in the late 1960s. Far from being fixed or objective, memories are the product of shifting social and cultural contexts and therefore offer, as Judith Pollmann has put it, "ever-changing representations of the past."[27] The processes of remembering are dynamic, and the constructed (or reconstructed) memories they produce are neither static nor objective, but rather actively and newly negotiated with every act of remembrance. As Astrid Erll has summarized, "versions of the past change with every recall, in accordance with the changed present situation. Individual and collective memories are never a mirror image of the past, but rather an expressive indication of the needs and interests of the person or group doing the remembering in the present."[28]

Pierre Nora is probably the single most influential scholar to have taken up the ideas of collective memory that Halbwachs first initiated. In his monumental seven-part *Les lieux de mémoire*, published between 1984 and 1992, and especially in his introductory text "Between Memory and History," Nora laid out his concept of the modern French *lieux de memoire*, or sites of memory, which he argues serve as repositories and placeholders for a lost collective living memory.[29] For him, these *lieux de mémoire* are loci or markers that signal the end of active practices and communities of memory, or *milieux de mémoire*. He assumed this transformation in communities' relationships with the past to be specific to the ruptures of modernity and globalization. This fundamental distinction between active lived memory environments versus fixed loci of memory has generated several related but more nuanced and flexible frameworks that scholars have applied to a broader range of contexts, especially Aleida and Jan Assmann's dyad of communicative versus cultural memory, as well as their more specific formulations of working versus archival memory and hot versus cold memory.[30]

One of the important correctives to Nora's model of (modern) memory has been put forth by Anne Rigney, who posits that *lieux de mémoire* might themselves be less stable entities than Nora assumed.[31] She argues that *lieux de mémoire* might more profitably be understood as dynamic processes rather than fixed artifacts or vessels of memory, and that they are therefore subject to change and reinvestment through time. In other words, these sites of memory can be reactivated and reanimated according to new social and cultural needs, much as Warburg had argued for the active reanimation of material and visual symbolic forms across cultures over time. This more dynamic understanding of the processes by which memory and meaning are invested into literary, material, and metaphorical loci informs more than one of the chapters in this volume.

Another important corrective to the field of memory studies—and the one perhaps most pertinent to this volume—has come in the last decade, as scholars have looked beyond the modern world to examine how memory was practiced in earlier periods of time. Until quite recently, the manifold branches of the field of memory studies have largely been instigated by and preoccupied with modern events and the conditions of modernity, with scholars like Nora presuming the "rupture" ushering in the modern world to be a prerequisite for the sorts of memory formation they observed. In recent years, however, Erika Kuijper, Judith Pollmann, and others have brought to light ample evidence that premodern peoples generated and deployed practices of memory well before 1800, and did so in ways that often continue in the memory practices of the modern age.[32] Drawing on many sources of evidence from the premodern world, scholars have detected the formation and expression of personal and public memories, and have assessed the uses to which these memories were put. Many premodern scholars have focused on the particularly volatile circumstances of war and violence to understand "how early modern memories of (civil) war and persecution affected future generations."[33] This "growing interest in memories of violence, in texts, rituals, images, and public spaces" has led to an increasingly nuanced picture of early modern memory across local, regional, and national contexts.[34] This volume attempts to add to this growing body of work on premodern memory, memorial practices, and processes of remembering.

Two key insights emerge from the theorization of memory and practices of remembering that are of particular relevance to the present volume. The first is the recognition that memory is always inextricably paired with its inverse, namely forgetting and oblivion.[35] If memory is constructed through every act of remembering, it is by its very nature selective and subjective, omitting or actively suppressing certain aspects of the past in order to forge memories into coherent and meaningful narratives in the present. Passive forgetting or active suppression of elements of past experiences also relates directly to the processes of traumatic memory and the unbidden, recursive return of the past in the present, wherein memory as such is often complicated and curtailed. Indeed, the particularly unstable nature of traumatic memory highlights the mutability of all memory processes more generally. The second insight, corollary to the first, is that selective, mutable memory-making often leads to highly contested and even contradictory versions of the past, raising the specter of "memory wars" as different individuals or groups seek to shore up their version of the past to justify or authenticate their present cultural, social, or political agendas.[36] The late medieval and early modern disputes over memories and the selective invocations and interpretations of past events highlighted in the chapters that follow showcase just what a powerful tool memory was across premodern contexts.

ABOUT THIS VOLUME

This volume is not, and cannot present, a comprehensive or systematic overview of trauma and memory in the late medieval and early modern world. Rather, it brings together a collection of case studies that we hope overlap and speak to one another in productive ways. Both the chronological and geographical scopes of the volume are broad, with the idea that we can discern both the sustained impacts of traumas connected to the violence of war and the memory practices that emerged from those traumas over time and space, as well as recognize the specific ways trauma was experienced and memory practices were adapted and transformed in the particular circumstances—historical, political, and geographic—of each case.

This volume as a whole, and the individual chapters it contains, take up the intertwined themes of violence, trauma, and memory. Each chapter examines late medieval and early modern responses to war in the broadest sense, discerning moments of traumatic wounding, processes of grief and mourning, and how memory could be deployed in processes of identity formation and communal or political mobilization. Taken together, one can discern just how linked processes of trauma and memory often were. If traumatic events call into question the possibility of creating stable memories or narratives, late medieval and early modern people developed a rich array of mechanisms—performative, textual, literary, and visual—through which to process the effects of violence and atrocities into meaningful memory, often in order to shape or contest the status of the past.

In this volume, we have organized the contributors' works into three parts according to region. The first part is focused on France and contains three chapters, each of which explores how authors in the medieval and early modern periods attempted to come to terms with, give a language to, and seek healing from the psycho-physiological effects of trauma resulting from violence and warfare. These chapters include studies on Colins de Beaumont's "On the Crécy Dead," written after the Battle of Crécy (1346); Charles of Orléans's poetry after the Battle of Agincourt (1415); and the literature of the French Wars of Religion (1562–1629). Part 2 is dedicated to the Hispanic world, with three chapters that focus on how authors framed war as a cultural tool and how memories of war could be deployed in highly contested and unstable ways. These chapters focus on the bellicose imagery and nature of Fernando de Rojas's *Celestina* (1499), the written accounts surrounding the viceroy's assassination in the Catalan Revolt (1640), and the literature resulting from Martín Cortés's failed uprising against the Spanish Crown in Mexico (1566). Finally, part 3 turns to the nascent Dutch Republic during the Eighty Years' War (1568–1648), with two studies on the printmakers Hendrick Goltzius (1558–1617) and Claes Jansz. Visscher (1587–1652) and the ways their print series served as tools of collective or cultural memory that aimed to forge new narratives of cultural identity and political meaning out of past violence.

Opening the part on France, Kimberly Lifton's "Memorializing the Battle of Crécy: Colins de Beaumont's 'On the Crécy Dead' as a Textual Monument for Processing Trauma" traces a course through one attempt to resolve trauma with narrative. In this chapter, Lifton looks at Colins de Beaumont's poem "On the Crécy Dead," a dream vision and dialogic work that memorializes the Battle of Crécy (1346), one of the decisive conflicts of the Hundred Years' War where the English massacred countless French soldiers. Analyzing the poem, Lifton studies how the dream vision genre, along with its use of allegorical figures who debate the value of death in battle, allows Beaumont to formulate a discourse on grief capable of articulating trauma. Outlining how the poem most likely had a public—and performative—component, serving as a mortuary roll to be read aloud in a manner that allowed the community to memorialize the dead, she argues that the poem allowed listeners to react to the trauma of war by creating a space for mourning. Ultimately, Lifton demonstrates how literature can intersect with the emotions of a specific community, allowing for the making of collective and communal memorialization.

Along similar lines, Charles-Louis Morand-Métivier in "'Je hé guerre, point ne la doit prisier': Emotions, War, and Trauma in the Poetry of Charles of Orléans" writes about how literary expression might resolve trauma through political and personal alliances. Here, he analyzes the poetry of Charles of Orléans, nephew of the king of France, who spent twenty-five years imprisoned in England after English troops captured and slaughtered French soldiers at the Battle of Agincourt (1415) during the Hundred Years' War. Exploring the trauma of Charles's separation from his homeland in his poetry as "emotional autobiography," Morand-Métivier speaks to how it reflects the development of a deeply emotional stance toward imprisonment. Removed from France and forced into exile, Charles lived between two languages, literary traditions, and courts—the duality of which, Morand-Métivier posits, opened a wound that comes to be repeated in the "present absence" and "absent presence" of memorialized references to France in his poetry. To help ease this separation from his home, Charles began an epistolary relationship with Philip III, Duke of Burgundy, through his poetry, something which Morand-Métivier argues links the political to the personal in a way that lessened the trauma of his captivity. The creative process of poetic composition, in other words, can be the locus where the wounds of trauma, although ever-present, might begin their healing.

Conversely, Kathleen Long, in "Bringing up the Dead: The Grotesque in Literature after the French Wars of Religion," demonstrates how artistic and literary attempts to depict loss related to the French Wars of Religion (1562–1629) struggled to find meaning in the memory of such unspeakable trauma. Working against and around royal commands that sought to maintain control by banning direct portrayals of these wars, authors employed the grotesque as a central means of articulating the difficulty in representing the catastrophes of battle. In her analysis of Théodore Agrippa d'Aubigné's epic *Les Tragiques* (1616) and the anonymous *L'Isle des hermaphrodites* (*The Island of Hermaphrodites*, 1605), Long explores how the proliferation of grotesque images (such as dehumanizing depictions of Catherine de' Medici's body and iterations of truncated bodies) in these literary works exposed the religious violence they were forbidden to discuss, all the while pointing, nonetheless, to the very impossibility of transmitting a meaning that fully grasped the traumatic losses from these wars. Using the imagery of Hans Vredeman de Vries and the concept of the *parergon* (the margin that frames, and therefore indexes, the center) as guides, she argues that the grotesque not only exposes the dystopian world that war creates but ultimately can point to how better worlds might appear when we realize that we are not that distinct from those around us.

Opening the volume's middle part on the Hispanic world, Nicholas Ealy's "Desire, Trauma and Warfare in Fernando de Rojas's *Celestina*" establishes notions of trauma within a traditional theoretical context by exploring the brutal nature of desire in one of the most authoritative literary texts from early modern Spain. Reflecting the interreligious warfare and anti-Semitism of fifteenth-century Iberia, *Celestina* presents a worldview where the human condition is simultaneously defined by persistent bellicosity and the onslaught of uncontrollable longing. With special attention given to Cupid, Ealy establishes how this figure, as the son of the gods of war and desire, traumatizes the victims he catches unaware, putting them in the position of not understanding the wounds caused by his arrows. As such, Ealy argues that *Celestina*, with its focus on inter- and intrapersonal battles, war, and savagery, establishes a notion of bellicose desire that approaches contemporary understandings of trauma: it is unassimilated in the moment of its occurrence, a wound that causes a crisis in human subjectivity, and a phenomenon that repeats, with each iteration an appeal for its victims to understand its puzzling nature. In the process, he reveals that the battle with Cupid, which *Celestina* manifests as a general paradigm for the human condition, ultimately questions notions of agency and free will while revealing a desire to suppress and forget desire's harrowing violence upon the self and its place within history.

In contrast to the ultimately unresolvable nature of trauma that Ealy's chapter explores, Ivan Gracia-Arnau's chapter, "Violence in the Making: Remembering the Viceroy's Assassination during the Catalan Revolt of 1640," examines how a traumatic event, in this case the assassination of the Spanish viceroy in Catalonia, could become a site of contested political interpretation and meaning. This assassination was the trigger for a military conflict between the Spanish Crown and the joined forces of Catalan institutions and the French monarchy. During the first years of the war, printed pamphlets, official chronicles, and political writings sought to construct a cohesive explanation for the traumatic events that had led Catalonia into a civil war. However, different accounts interpreted the viceroy's death in antithetical ways, leading to a textual and rhetorical battle over how those events were to be both remembered *and* forgotten, according to the political interests of their authors and patrons. Gracia-Arnau's chapter analyzes the narrative schemes and rhetorical devices used in these accounts to show how they both memorialize the assassination and resulting insurrection and deploy them as key tools within the contested political discourse surrounding the revolt more broadly.

Covadonga Lamar Prieto's contribution "Trauma and Postmemory in Martín Cortés's Uprising" traces ideas of memory into postmemory—the emotional reworking of traumatic memory across generations into a new "official narrative"—in two key texts that detail the aftermath of the failed uprising (1566) in New Spain (present-day Mexico) by the sons of the conquistadores against the Spanish crown. Led by Martín Cortés (the son of Hernán Cortés) and the Ávila brothers, the rebellion over disputes related to property and labor rights was met with an immediate and violent suppression by the monarchy, with the uprising's leaders imprisoned and executed. Lamar Prieto examines Juan Suárez de Peralta's *Tratado del descubrimiento de las Indias* (*Treatise on the Discovery of the Indies*, 1579), positing that the traumatic memories it records became a postmemory for the next generation of Spanish descendants in Luis de Sandoval Zapata's *Relación fúnebre a la infeliz trágica muerte de dos caballeros* (*Funeral Relation to the Unhappy, Tragic Death of Two Gentlemen*, ca. 1645). Lamar Prieto explores how the psychic wounds maintained by such postmemory forced a reconsideration of the Spanish descendants' role within the larger context of the monarchy and contributed to a collective imagination that spurred the later independence movement in Mexico. Through her analysis, Lamar Prieto documents how this ongoing process of political identity formation ultimately springs from the cultural negotiation between memory and postmemory.

The final part shifts focus to the Dutch Republic, with two chapters that likewise take up the question of how trauma and memory contribute to the formation of new collective identities across generations. Over the course of the Eighty Years' War (1568–1648), seven Northern Netherlandish provinces rebelled against the Spanish Crown, ultimately establishing a new independent polity. In the process, however, these seven provinces were cleaved from the ten Netherlandish provinces to the south, which remained under Spanish Catholic rule, leading to the emergence of two distinct political, religious, and cultural states, and the massive displacement of southerners who emigrated to the nascent Dutch Republic in pursuit of religious freedom and economic prosperity.

Rachel Wise's chapter, "Hendrick Goltzius's *Lucretia* and the Eighty Years' War," studies how visual imagery could help define and justify this act of rebellion and the violence it engendered. She focuses on the engraved series *Lucretia* (ca. 1578–1580) made by the virtuoso printmaker Hendrick Goltzius, who had settled in Haarlem just five years after the Siege of Haarlem in 1572. This is the first and only Netherlandish series to represent the full narrative of this ancient Roman heroine's life, rather than just her act of suicide. In particular, Goltzius focuses visual attention on her violent rape by Tarquin and the later display of her body to the Roman people, an act that incites the Romans to overthrow their tyrant kings and establish the Roman Republic. Wise argues that this visual narrative served as a political allegory of the Eighty Years' War. Goltzius produced the series of four prints around the time of the Union of Utrecht in 1579, one of the first important steps toward the founding of the Dutch Republic. The artist localizes the ancient Roman tale to Holland, and more specifically Haarlem, validating a reading of Lucretia as a symbol of the founding of the republic and as Belgica, the personification of the Netherlands. In so doing, Goltzius deploys the ancient story of the rape and eventual suicide of Lucretia as a corollary to the memory of the assault of the Spanish against the Dutch, and as justification for the emerging autonomy of the Northern provinces.

Alexandra Onuf's chapter, "Landscape and the Memory of Place in Claes Jansz. Visscher's Prints of Brabant," explores how less overtly political or propagandistic printed imagery could likewise contribute to the complex negotiation of identity and community, particularly among displaced populations of southern Netherlanders who emigrated north during the course of the war. Her chapter focuses on three sets of landscape prints that Claes Jansz. Visscher published in the years just after the Twelve Years' Truce in 1609, all of which were reprinted or copied editions of earlier Brabantine landscape print series depicting the rural areas around the southern cities of Antwerp and Brussels. The chapter grapples with how Visscher's audiences—both "native" Northerners and Southern émigrés from the very locales the prints depict—might have responded to these Brabantine views. It contends that these prints offered loci for the dynamic construction of historical memory during the fraught political period of the Twelve Years' Truce (1609–1621). Collectively, the views preserve a memory of the Brabantine countryside that no longer existed after the long decades of violent revolt. However, at the same time that the prints functioned as sites of memory, they were also active agents in the reinvention of the past in the present, envisioning both rupture and continuity between Brabant and Holland. In registering the nuances and specifics of places now distant both in time and space, Visscher's reissued Brabantine prints were both retrospective and generative, affording audiences in seventeenth-century Holland a visual medium through which to reshape past experiences of trauma and displacement wrought by the Revolt into new narratives of political and geographic identity.

Over the course of these chapters, several main concepts emerge. All examine, for instance, the problematic nature of wartime violence and its lingering traumatic effects upon communities and individuals who then feel compelled to memorialize it through cultural production and narrative. This violence, central here, takes place in conversation with the literary, visual, and historiographical models articulated throughout this volume. Within this framework, we see a focus, especially in the contributions by Long and Ealy, on how literature can simultaneously depict and occlude representations of trauma's unassimilated and unknown nature. Lifton and Morand-Métivier, on the other hand, examine how literature can trace a course through the very thing that trauma might resist—a resolution in language and narration. Along these lines, the chapters by Gracia-Arnau, Lamar Prieto, Wise, and Onuf explore the formation of a new consciousness built upon the trauma of war and how memory can lead to identity formation, resistance, and nation-building. Lamar Prieto, in particular, brings this trajectory into notions of postmemory, looking at how fragments of memory, with emotive force, can be reconstituted as a new narrative for subsequent generations.

Essential to these discussions are questions about how the trauma of warfare can be grasped, understood, and "worked through"; whether it is doomed to repeat its violent structures; and whether memorialization can serve as an adequate means of closing wounds and addressing grief—both public and private, personal and communal—as well as appeals for justice and redress. Throughout this volume, we therefore repeatedly see the centrality of humanistic discourse—of literature, the visual arts, and historiography—as a privileged space employed to represent and bear witness to the horrors of violence and bellicosity. And bearing witness, as Shoshana Felman reminds us, is always more involved than the mere reporting of events; it is, instead, a use of memory, the narrating of events from the personal to the universal, that always addresses *another*.[37] This notion of audience, of *address*, at the heart of many of the chapters in this volume, speaks to how art and literature do the work of witnessing history, taking responsibility for truth itself. It is our hope, therefore, that these chapters, in a real sense, can help bring such testimony to light.

WORKS CITED

Anderson, Thomas P. *Performing Early Modern Trauma from Shakespeare to Milton*. Burlington, VT: Ashgate, 2006.

Assmann, Aleida. *Erinnerungsräume: Formen und Wandlungen des kulturellen Gedächtnisses*. Munich: Beck, 1999.

Assmann, Jan. "Communicative and Cultural Memory." In *A Companion to Cultural Memory Studies*, edited by Astrid Erll and Ansgar Nünning, 109–18. Berlin: De Gruyter, 2010.

———. *Das kulturelle Gedächtnis: Schrift, Erinnerung und politische Identität in frühen Hochkulturen*. Munich: Beck, 1992.

Bak, Janos, ed. *The German Peasant War of 1525*. New York: Routledge, 2013. First published 1976 by F. Cass (London).

Blickle, Peter. *The Revolution of 1525: The German Peasants' War from a New Perspective*. Translated by Thomas A. Brady Jr. and H. C. Erik Midelfort. Baltimore: Johns Hopkins University Press, 1981.

Bond, Lucy, and Stef Craps. *Trauma*. New York: Routledge: 2020.

Broomhall, Susan, and Sarah Finn, eds. *Violence and Emotions in Early Modern Europe*. London: Routledge, 2016.
Bussmann, Klaus, and Heinz Schilling, eds. *1648: War and Peace in Europe*. 3 vols. Münster: Westfälisches Landesmuseum für Kunst und Kultergeschichte Münster, 1998.
Caruth, Cathy. "Trauma and Experience: Introduction." In *Trauma: Explorations in Memory*, edited by Cathy Caruth, 3–12. Baltimore: Johns Hopkins University, Press, 1995.
———. *Unclaimed Experience: Trauma, Narrative, and History*. Baltimore: Johns Hopkins University Press, 2016. First published 1996.
Davis, Colin, and Hanna Meretoja, eds. *The Routledge Companion to Literature and Trauma*. New York: Routledge, 2020.
Deseure, Brecht, and Judith Pollmann. "The Experience of Rupture and the History of Memory." In Kuijpers et al., *Memory before Modernity*, 315–29.
Downes, Stephanie, Andrew Lynch, and Katrina O'Loughlin, eds. *Writing War in Britain and France, 1370–1854: A History of Emotions*. London: Routledge, 2018.
Erll, Astrid. "Cultural Memory Studies: An Introduction." In *A Companion to Cultural Memory Studies*, edited by Astrid Erll and Ansgar Nünning, 1–15. Berlin: De Gruyter, 2010.
———. *Memory in Culture*. Translated by Sarah B. Young. New York: Palgrave Macmillan, 2011.
Felman, Shoshana, and Cathy Caruth. "A Ghost in the House of Justice: A Conversation with Shoshana Felman." In *Listening to Trauma: Conversations with Leaders in the Theory and Treatment of Catastrophic Experience*, edited by Cathy Caruth, 321–53. Baltimore: Johns Hopkins University Press, 2014.
Felman, Shoshana, and Dori Laub. *Testimony: Crises in Witnessing in Literature, Psychoanalysis, and History*. New York: Routledge, 1992.
Fishman, Jane Susannah. *Boerenverdriet: Violence between Peasants and Soldiers in Early Modern Netherlands Art*. Ann Arbor, MI: UMI Research Press, 1982.
Freud, Sigmund. "Beyond the Pleasure Principle." In *The Standard Edition of the Complete Works of Sigmund Freud*, vol. 18, translated and edited by James Strachey, 7–64. London: Hogarth, 1955.
Gombrich, Ernst H. *Aby Warburg: An Intellectual Biography*. 2nd ed. Chicago: University of Chicago Press, 1986.
Gutmann, Myron. *War and Rural Life in the Early Modern Low Countries*. Princeton, NJ: Princeton University Press, 1980.
Guynn, Noah, and Zrinka Stahuljak, eds. *Violence and the Writing of History in the Medieval Francophone World*. Woodridge, Suffolk: D. S. Brewer, 2013.
Halbwachs, Maurice. *On Collective Memory*. Translated by Lewis Coser. Chicago: University of Chicago Press, 1992.
Hale, J. R. *War and Society in Renaissance Europe 1450–1620*. New York: St. Martin's Press, 1985.
Kuijpers, Erika. "The Creation and Development of Social Memories of Traumatic Events: The Oudewater Massacre of 1575." In *Hurting Memories and Beneficial Forgetting: Posttraumatic Stress Disorders, Biographical Developments, and*

Social Conflicts, ed. Michael Linden and Krzysztof Rutkowski, 191–201. Amsterdam: Elsevier, 2013.

———. "Trauma, Memories and Emotions in Early Modern Europe." Unpublished manuscript.

Kuijpers, Erika, and Cornelis van der Haven, eds. *Battlefield Emotions, 1500–1800: Practices, Experience, Imagination*. London: Palgrave Macmillan, 2016.

Kuijpers, Erika, Judith Pollmann, Johannes Müller, and Jasper van der Steen, eds. *Memory before Modernity: Practices of Memory in Early Modern Europe*. Leiden: Brill, 2013.

Kunzle, David. *From Criminal to Courtier: The Soldier in Netherlandish Art 1550–1672*. Leiden: Brill, 2002.

Kurtz, J. Roger, ed. *Trauma and Literature*. Cambridge: Cambridge University Press, 2018.

LaPlanche, Jean, and Jean-Bertrand Pontalis. *The Language of Psychoanalysis*. Translated by Donald Nicholson-Smith. New York: W. W. Norton, 1973.

Long, Zackariah C. "Toward an Early Modern Theory of Trauma: Conscience in 'Richard III.'" *Journal of Literature and Trauma Studies* 1, no. 1 (2012): 48–72.

Martines, Lauro. *Furies: War in Europe, 1450–1700*. New York: Bloomsbury, 2013.

Nicholson, Helen. *Medieval Warfare: Theory and Practice of War in Europe, 300–1500*. New York: Palgrave Macmillan, 2003.

Nora, Pierre. "Between Memory and History: *Les lieux de mémoire*." Translated by Marc Roudebush. *Representations* 26 (1989): 7–24.

———, ed. *Les lieux de mémoire*. 3 vols. Paris: Gallimard, 1984–92.

———, ed. *Realms of Memory: The Construction of the French Past*. 3 vols. Revised and abbreviated translation of *Les lieux de mémoire* by Arthur Goldhammer. Edited by Lawrence D. Kritzman. New York: Columbia University Press, 1996–98.

Parker, Geoffrey, ed. *The Cambridge Illustrated History of Warfare: The Triumph of the West*. 2nd ed. Cambridge: Cambridge University Press, 2022.

———. *The Thirty Years' War*. 2nd ed. New York: Routledge, 1987.

Peters, Erin, and Cynthia Richards. "Reading Historical Trauma: Moving Backwards to Move Forwards." In *Early Modern Trauma: Europe and the Atlantic World*, edited by Erin Peters and Cynthia Richards, 3–28. Lincoln: University of Nebraska Press, 2021.

Pollmann, Judith. *Memory in Early Modern Europe, 1500–1800*. Oxford: Oxford University Press, 2017.

Rigney, Ann. "The Dynamics of Remembrance: Text between Monumentality and Morphing." In *A Companion to Cultural Memory Studies*, edited by Astrid Erll and Ansgar Nünning, 345–53. Berlin: De Gruyter, 2010.

———. "Plenitude, Scarcity and the Circulation of Cultural Memory." *Journal of European Studies* 35, no. 1 (2005): 11–28.

Scarry, Elaine. *The Body in Pain: The Making and Unmaking of the World*. New York: Oxford University Press, 1985.

Spinks, Jennifer, and Charles Zika, eds. *Disaster, Death and the Emotions in the Shadow of the Apocalypse, 1400–1700*. London: Palgrave Macmillan, 2016.

Tallett, Frank. *War and Society in Early Modern Europe, 1495–1715*. New York: Routledge, 1992.
Tasso, Torquato. *Gerusalemme liberata*. Edited by Lanfranco Caretti. Milan: Mondadori, 1957.
Taylor, Craig. "Chivalry and the Ideals of Knighthood in France during the Hundred Years' War." In *Chivalry and the Ideals of Knighthood in France during the Hundred Years' War*, 54–90. Cambridge: Cambridge University Press, 2013.
Thompson, Ann. *The Art of Suffering and the Impact of Seventeenth-Century Anti-Providential Thought*. Burlington, VT: Ashgate, 2003.
Trembinski, Donna. "Comparing Premodern Melancholy/Mania and Modern Trauma: An Argument in Favor of Historical Experiences of Trauma." *History of Psychology* 14, no. 1 (2011): 80–99.
Turner, Wendy J., and Christina Lee. "Conceptualizing Trauma for the Middle Ages." In *Trauma and Medieval Society*, edited by Wendy J. Turner and Christina Lee, 3–12. Leiden: Brill, 2018.
Van der Steen, Jasper. *Memory Wars in the Low Countries, 1566–1700*. Leiden: Brill, 2015.
Walsham, Alexandra. *Providence in Early Modern England*. New York: Oxford University Press, 1999.
Warburg, Aby, Roberto Ohrt, and Axel Heil. *Aby Warburg: Bilderatlas Mnemosyne; The Original*. Berlin: Hatje Cantz, 2020.

NOTES

1. Elaine Scarry, "The Structure of War: The Juxtaposition of Injuring Bodies and Unanchored Issues," in *The Body in Pain: The Making and Unmaking of the World* (New York: Oxford University Press, 1985), 60–157.

2. On medieval warfare, see Helen Nicholson, *Medieval Warfare: Theory and Practice of War in Europe, 300–1500* (New York: Palgrave Macmillan, 2003). On chivalric codes, see Craig Taylor, "Chivalry and the Ideals of Knighthood in France during the Hundred Years' War," in *Chivalry and the Ideals of Knighthood in France during the Hundred Years' War* (Cambridge: Cambridge University Press, 2013), 54–90. On the shifting nature of war over the early modern period, see J. R. Hale, *War and Society in Renaissance Europe 1450–1620* (New York: St. Martin's Press, 1985); Frank Tallett, *War and Society in Early Modern Europe, 1495–1715* (New York: Routledge, 1992); Geoffrey Parker, ed., *The Cambridge Illustrated History of Warfare: The Triumph of the West*, 2nd ed. (Cambridge: Cambridge University Press, 2022).

3. On this revolt, see Peter Blickle, *The Revolution of 1525: The German Peasants' War from a New Perspective*, trans. Thomas A. Brady Jr. and H. C. Erik Midelfort (Baltimore: Johns Hopkins University Press, 1981); Janos Bak, ed., *The German Peasant War of 1525* (New York: Routledge, 2013). First published 1976 by F. Cass (London).

4. For multifaceted perspectives on the conduct and impacts of war in early modern Europe, see Klaus Bussmann and Heinz Schilling, eds., *1648: War and Peace in Europe*, 3 vols. (Münster: Westfälisches Landesmuseum für Kunst und Kultergeschichte Münster, 1998). On the particularly heavy toll paid by rural communities in the Netherlands, see Myron Gutmann, *War and Rural Life in the Early Modern Low Countries* (Princeton, NJ: Princeton University Press, 1980). For the representation of this violence, see Jane Susannah Fishman, *Boerenverdriet: Violence between Peasants and Soldiers in Early Modern Netherlands Art* (Ann Arbor, MI: UMI Research Press, 1982); David Kunzle, *From Criminal to Courtier: The Soldier in Netherlandish Art 1550–1672* (Leiden: Brill, 2002). For a more general survey, see Lauro Martines, *Furies: War in Europe, 1450–1700* (New York: Bloomsbury, 2013).

5. Geoffrey Parker, *The Thirty Years' War*, 2nd ed. (New York: Routledge, 1987).

6. There is a burgeoning literature in this field. See, for example, Jennifer Spinks and Charles Zika, eds., *Disaster, Death and the Emotions in the Shadow of the Apocalypse, 1400–1700* (London: Palgrave Macmillan, 2016); Susan Broomhall and Sarah Finn, eds., *Violence and Emotions in Early Modern Europe* (London: Routledge, 2016); Stephanie Downes, Andrew Lynch, and Katrina O'Loughlin, eds., *Writing War in Britain and France, 1370–1854: A History of Emotions* (London: Routledge, 2018).

7. See, for example, Thomas P. Anderson, *Performing Early Modern Trauma from Shakespeare to Milton* (Burlington, VT: Ashgate, 2006); Erika Kuijpers, "The Creation and Development of Social Memories of Traumatic Events: The Oudewater Massacre of 1575," in *Hurting Memories and Beneficial Forgetting: Posttraumatic Stress Disorders, Biographical Developments, and Social Conflicts*, ed. Michael Linden and Krzysztof Rutkowski (Amsterdam: Elsevier, 2013), 191–201; Noah Guynn and Zrinka Stahuljak, eds., *Violence and the Writing of History in the Medieval Francophone World* (Woodridge, Suffolk: D. S. Brewer, 2013); Erika Kuijpers and Cornelis van der Haven, eds., *Battlefield Emotions, 1500–1800: Practices, Experience, Imagination* (London: Palgrave Macmillan, 2016); Erika Kuijpers, "Trauma, Memories and Emotions in Early Modern Europe" (unpublished manuscript).

8. See, for example, Alexandra Walsham, *Providence in Early Modern England* (New York: Oxford University Press, 1999); Ann Thompson, *The Art of Suffering and the Impact of Seventeenth-Century Anti-Providential Thought* (Burlington, VT: Ashgate, 2003).

9. Erika Kuijpers et al., eds., *Memory before Modernity: Practices of Memory in Early Modern Europe* (Leiden: Brill, 2013); Judith Pollmann, "Remembering Violence: Trauma, Atrocities, and Cosmopolitan Memories," in *Memory in Early Modern Europe, 1500–1800* (Oxford: Oxford University Press, 2017), 159–85.

10. Cathy Caruth, *Unclaimed Experience: Trauma, Narrative, and History* (1996; Baltimore: Johns Hopkins University Press, 2016); Shoshana Felman and Dori Laub, *Testimony: Crises of Witnessing in Literature, Psychoanalysis, and History* (New York: Routledge, 1992). For excellent volumes on trauma in literary studies, see J. Roger Kurtz, ed., *Literature and Trauma* (Cambridge: Cambridge University Press, 2018); Colin Davis and Hanna Meretoja, eds., *The Routledge Companion to Literature and Trauma* (New York: Routledge, 2020).

11. For an in-depth discussion of the history and scope of trauma studies, see Lucy Bond and Stef Craps, *Trauma* (New York: Routledge, 2020).

12. Jean LaPlanche and Jean-Bertrand Pontalis, *The Language of Psychoanalysis*, trans. Donald Nicholason-Smith (New York: W. W. Norton, 1973), 465.

13. Donna Trembinski, "Comparing Premodern Melancholy/Mania and Modern Trauma: An Argument in Favor of Historical Experiences of Trauma," *History of Psychology* 14, no. 1 (2011): 80–99.

14. Zackariah C. Long, "Toward an Early Modern Theory of Trauma: Conscience in 'Richard III,'" *Journal of Literature and Trauma Studies* 1, no. 1 (2012): 49–72.

15. Wendy J. Turner and Christina Lee, "Conceptualizing Trauma for the Middle Ages," in *Trauma and Medieval Society*, ed. Wendy J. Turner and Christina Lee (Leiden: Brill, 2018), 8. For an introduction to trauma and the early modern period, see Erin Peters and Cynthia Richards, "Reading Historical Trauma: Moving Backwards to Move Forwards," in *Early Modern Trauma: Europe and the Atlantic World*, ed. Erin Peters and Cynthia Richards (Lincoln: University of Nebraska Press, 2021), 3–28.

16. Sigmund Freud, "Beyond the Pleasure Principle," in *The Standard Edition of the Complete Works of Sigmund Freud*, vol. 18, trans. and ed. James Strachey (London: Hogarth, 1955), 12.

17. Freud, "Beyond," 13.

18. Cathy Caruth, "Trauma and Experience: Introduction," in *Trauma: Explorations in Memory*, ed. Cathy Caruth (Baltimore: Johns Hopkins University Press, 1995), 8.

19. Freud, "Beyond," 22. Caruth, who explores Freud's use of Tasso in the introduction to the 1996 edition of *Unclaimed Experience*, has since written more extensively on it in the book's 2016 edition. Cathy Caruth, "Addressing Life: The Literary Voice in the Theory of Trauma," in *Unclaimed Experience*, 116–39.

20. Torquato Tasso, *Gerusalemme liberata*, ed. Lanfranco Caretti (Milan: Mondadori, 1957), 404. Translation ours.

21. Tasso, *Gerusalemme liberata*, 404–5. Translation ours.

22. Caruth, *Unclaimed Experience*, 2–3.

23. Caruth, *Unclaimed Experience*, 121–22.

24. For an excellent summary of the state of the field of memory studies, see Astrid Erll, "Cultural Memory Studies: An Introduction," in *A Companion to Cultural Memory Studies*, ed. Astrid Erll and Ansgar Nünning (Berlin: De Gruyter, 2010), 1–15; Astrid Erll, *Memory in Culture*, trans. Sarah B. Young (New York: Palgrave Macmillan, 2011).

25. Partially translated in Maurice Halbwachs, *On Collective Memory*, trans. Lewis Coser (Chicago: University of Chicago Press, 1992).

26. Ernst H. Gombrich, *Aby Warburg: An Intellectual Biography*, 2nd ed. (Chicago: University of Chicago Press, 1986); Aby Warburg et al., *Aby Warburg: Bilderatlas Mnemosyne; The Original* (Berlin: Hatje Cantz, 2020).

27. Pollmann, *Memory in Early Modern Europe*, 3.

28. Erll, *Memory in Culture*, 8.

29. Pierre Nora, ed., *Les lieux de mémoire*, 3 vols. (Paris: Gallimard, 1984–92). See also Pierre Nora, ed., *Realms of Memory: The Construction of the French Past*, 3 vols., rev. and abbr. trans. of *Les lieux de mémoire* by Arthur Goldhammer, ed. Lawrence D. Kritzman (New York: Columbia University Press, 1996–98). For his introductory text, see also Pierre Nora, "Between Memory and History: *Les lieux de mémoire*," trans. Marc Roudebush, *Representations* 26 (1989): 7–24.

30. Aleida Assmann, *Erinnerungsräume: Formen und Wandlungen des kulturellen Gedächnissess* (Munich: Beck, 1999); Jan Assmann, *Das kulturelle Gedächtnis: Schrift, Erinnerung und politische Identität in frühen Hochkulturen* (Munich: Beck, 1992); Jan Assmann, "Communicative and Cultural Memory," in *A Companion to Cultural Memory Studies*, ed. Astrid Erll and Ansgar Nünning (Berlin: De Gruyter, 2010), 109–18.

31. Ann Rigney, "The Dynamics of Remembrance: Text between Monumentality and Morphing," in *A Companion to Cultural Memory Studies*, ed. Astrid Erll and Ansgar Nünning (Berlin: De Gruyter, 2010), 345–53. See also Ann Rigney, "Plenitude, Scarcity and the Circulation of Cultural Memory," *Journal of European Studies* 35, no. 1 (2005): 11–28.

32. For a clear articulation of the continuities between and evolution of premodern and modern memory practices, see Brecht Deseure and Judith Pollmann, "The Experience of Rupture and the History of Memory," in Kuijpers et al., *Memory before Modernity*, 315–29.

33. Pollmann, *Memory in Early Modern Europe*, 7.

34. Pollmann, *Memory in Early Modern Eruope*, 7–8. See esp. 7n27 for extensive additional literature.

35. Erll, *Memory in Culture*, 8–9; Pollmann, "Acts of Oblivion," in *Memory in Early Modern Europe*, 140–58.

36. For an extensive analysis of one such early modern example of "memory wars," see Jasper van der Steen, *Memory Wars in the Low Countries, 1566–1700* (Leiden: Brill, 2015).

37. Shoshana Felman and Cathy Caruth, "A Ghost in the House of Justice: A Conversation with Shoshana Felman," in *Listening to Trauma: Conversations with Leaders in the Theory and Treatment of Catastrophic Experience*, ed. Cathy Caruth (Baltimore: Johns Hopkins University Press, 2014), 322.

PART ONE
France

Chapter One

Memorializing the Battle of Crécy

Colins de Beaumont's "On the Crécy Dead" as a Textual Monument for Processing Trauma

Kimberly Lifton

> Hé Diex! tant estoie esperdus,
> Que tant d'enseignes là véoie,
> Et riens qui fust n'i congnoissoie,
> Fust pauoncel ou fust banière,
> Targe, tunicle ou archounière,
> Tout despairé et tout déroupt.
>
> Ah, Lord! I was so anguished
> That I was seeing so many insignia there
> And none that I could recognize,
> Whether it were a little pennant or a standard,
> A shield, a surcoat, or a pommel ornament:
> All were dismantled and all were broken.[1]

Looking out upon the dreamscape of the Crécy battlefield, author and herald Colins de Beaumont, narrator of "On the Crécy Dead," visually takes in the expanse of destruction in this elegiac dream vision. Here, he composes a narrative abstraction of the enumeration ritual to process trauma in a way that resists direct representation. Fallen shields, surcoats, and other heraldic ornaments are scattered across the landscape, representing the fallen bodies that discarded them. Synecdoche enables the author to focus on the trauma of loss through inanimate objects, which soften the psychological impact of seeing mounds of fresh corpses. Colins's anguish derives from the debilitating loss of the noblemen who owned such items of heraldic display and bore them while fighting at the Battle of Crécy.[2] This was one of the decisive battles of the Hundred Years' War between France and England over the rightful heir to the French crown. The battle took place at Crécy in northern France during August of 1346; Philip VI commanded the French army while Edward III commanded the English army. England's use of the longbow caused immense bloodshed, enabling the English to win despite being vastly outnumbered.[3]

The battle ultimately constituted a crushing defeat for the House of Valois and its allies. Many members of the French nobility died that day, thinning France's ruling class. It is the bodies of these men that Colins counts. Assuming the duties of a herald following a battle, Colins begins to catalog the dead.[4] In assembling a death register following a battle, heralds set in motion a process of memorialization for the English and the French, as both sides needed to know who had fallen in battle from their ranks. The enumeration of the dead, however, ws only the beginning of the mourning process—a process that Colins de Beaumont, herald to Jean de Beaumont (1288–1356), parses in his poem "On the Crécy Dead."

"On the Crécy Dead," which Colins de Beaumont wrote shortly following the battle, sometime before the end of 1346, constitutes an affective object that both affects the reader and consolidates affects through prescription, communicated by way of emotional prototypes, into grief.[5] Scholars have paid the text virtually no attention despite the wealth of insight it offers into the history of emotions during the Hundred Years' War.[6] "On the Crécy Dead" is rare within the genre that Helen Swift terms "epitaph fiction" because it memorializes multiple individuals instead of only one.[7] The poem captures the collective fatality of a battle and not the personalized postmortem identity of one deceased participant, thereby formulating a monolithic postmortem identity framed around a single event that encapsulates all of those aligned with the French king who fell on the battlefield at Crécy. This provokes the question: How does Colins de Beaumont manipulate the literary conventions that he deploys in "On the Crécy Dead" to provide a framework for making sense of the emotional implications that the Battle of Crécy had for those who supported the French cause?

In this chapter, I argue that the poem's materiality, composite dream vision–dialogue form, allegorical emotional prototypes, fictional architecture, and sensory imagery work together to evoke emotional responses of which "On the Crécy Dead" then seeks to make sense through the "chivalric economy of honor."[8] The text references a traumatic event in the collective consciousness of its audience, presenting it in a way that mitigates excessive emotional responses. By rationalizing death through the economy of honor, where war is not zero sum but an arena in which individuals from both the losing and winning sides can gain honor, the deaths of those who fell at Crécy are given meaning.[9] Those who fell on the battlefield did not incur a total loss—they gained honor. However, honor could only be accrued through the act of witnesses spreading word of honorable actions; by way of this public talk, one's *fama* (reputation) was inducted into the consciousness of a community.[10]

"On the Crécy Dead" is a form of disseminating the postmortem *fama* of notable individuals and of the collective French army that fell at Crécy, allowing the dead to live on in the audience's historical consciousness. Although making sense of death in battle through the context of the medieval economy of honor is not necessarily unique to the text, the way in which "On the Crécy Dead" acts as a witness that deliberately frames loss to influence how viewers interpret the affects it elicits is unique. The circulation of this epitaph fiction engendered what Barbara Rosenwein terms an "emotional community": a group in which "people adhere to the same norms of emotional expression and value—or devalue—the same or related emotions."[11] Here, a community remembers the *fama* of those who died fighting for the French king.

The emotional community for which Colins de Beaumont wrote consisted of nobles in the Low Countries who were allies of King Philip VI of France during the Hundred Years' War. The text disseminates the trauma of Crécy to readers that likely did not experience it by enabling them to engage with the traumatic event while also regulating their reaction to it by modeling an appropriate gendered performance of mourning. The homodiegetic narrator or narrating "je" (the "I" of the poem) renders subjective the experience of reading or hearing the work, inviting the reader to identify as the subject and allowing affect to travel between the text and the reader. Within his dream vision, the narrator witnesses a dialogue between feminized allegorical figures who, via their representation of chivalric virtues, provide the reader with both an emotional lexicon through their use of "emotives"—claims of emotion that translate internal feelings into words—and a framework for understanding death in war, the economy of honor.[12] Beaumont deploys dialogue for decidedly undialogic ends: to respond to threats that recent military innovations posed to the long-established honor system. His poem both borrows from and perpetuates chivalric discourse at a time when men like Geoffroi de Charny, alongside King John II of France, sought to reform chivalry by sounding "a clarion call for an augmented display of prowess and loyalty."[13]

This chapter brings models that medieval scholars originally designed for religious affect together with frameworks recently developed in cognitive studies to bear upon a heraldic text. Dismantling the divide between secular and religious genres is necessary for understanding discourses on trauma in medieval Europe because the brutalized body of Christ constituted the ultimate trauma that guided how people thought about other traumas. By bringing it into conversation with modern studies on cognitive emotions, existing work on trauma in medieval writing can be further extended to consider the emotional resonances that secular texts on death had for audiences. "On the Crécy Dead" constitutes a significant example of how a "textual community" and an "emotional community" could intersect in the form of an "emotional script" to aid with the communal memorialization of trauma into collective memory.[14]

I adopt Kathy Charmaz and Melinda J. Milligan's definition of grief as the subjective emotion elicited from an involuntary loss that is acted out through physical, social, and mental manifestations.[15] In the instance of the Battle of Crécy, the loss is both France's devastating defeat in a pivotal battle and the destruction of human life. Grief is "historically, culturally, and socially inscribed," meaning that the performance of grief differs from historical epoch to epoch.[16] It is an emotion, although not the sole emotion, of trauma—a response to a distressing event.[17] What constitutes psychological trauma, or traumatic memories more specifically, in the Middle Ages is a difficult question with which to grapple. The American Psychological Association defines trauma as "experiences that result in significant fear, helplessness, dissociation, confusion, and other disruptive feelings" that influence an individual's emotional perception of the world and/or the self.[18] Locating reactions to this broad definition of trauma in the Middle Ages is complicated because sources do not capture the complete range, depth, and duration of the emotions of trauma.

Teasing out psychological responses from sources that record acts of violence—excavating trauma, even if an incomplete picture of it—is, however, possible. I contend that a narrative of trauma can be detected in a source that attaches at least one emotion of trauma, in this instance grief, to the recollection of a violent event. For instance, drawing on fourteenth- and fifteenth-century French remission letters, Aleksandra Pfau determines that the prolonged warfare instigated by the Hundred Years' War constituted a traumatic event for those Frenchmen who fought in it based on mental illnesses reported in the letters.[19] Although flawed in its broadness, my parameter for classifying a medieval document as a narrative is likely the closest scholars will come to locating expressions of psychological trauma that no longer survive in living minds. Historically, communities have tended to process intergenerational trauma by reenacting it through transforming the memory into something more accessible, in this instance a dream-vision poem.[20] "On the Crécy Dead" is a locus of mourning that promotes the collective emotional expression of grief across generations, controls the narrative of trauma, and retains loss in a society's collective memory.[21] Unlike conventional memorials situated in churches—tombs, stained glass windows, chantry foundations, wall paintings, etc.—or liturgical *memoria*, the form of "On the Crécy Dead" enabled it to circulate amongst a broader audience less constrained by geography.[22]

Unfortunately, the original manuscript for "On the Crécy Dead" does not survive. Instead, the text comes down to us in Gilles li Muisis's *Chronicon majus*. I rely on the version in Brussels at the Bibliothèque Royale de Belgique (MS 16604 XVIII) but five other manuscripts of the chronicle exist. Only Muisis's preface to the text and the title he gives it—*Tenor et copia rotuli* (Contents and Copy of a Roll)—provide evidence for its status as a type of secular mortuary roll. While *rotulus* signifies that the poem first appeared on a roll, Michael Livingston's suggestion that it served as a mortuary roll carried between "monasteries and other places of worship" makes a tenuous assumption about the intended audience grounded solely in the word *rotulus*.[23] The text, which would have made up the encyclical of a traditional mortuary roll, does not follow the conventional format and formulaic language of the genre.[24] Instead, the poem borrows from both the material context of the religious mortuary roll and the tropes of the "literary epitaph" genre to form a hybrid document that could have been passed between a broader audience of lay and clerical communities as a newsletter or secular bede-roll.[25] Several examples of such newsletters circulated in England and France after the Battle of Agincourt (1415), one of which—a Latin ballad account in the ledger book of the city of Salisbury that dedicates several lines to the dead—is strikingly similar to Colins de Beaumont's text. Anne Curry postulates that the Salisbury ballad was originally composed in a vernacular, either English or Anglo-Norman, for the secular community of Salisbury.[26] The existence of such documents intended for laypeople and the lack of religious references in Colins de Beaumont's poem are strong indicators that he wrote "On the Crécy Dead" for a primarily secular audience.

The community for which Jean de Beaumont, Seigneur of Beaumont and Count of Soissons, intended "On the Crécy Dead" when he commissioned the poem from Colins de Beaumont is difficult to pinpoint due to the Avesnes dynasty's fractured political landscape, making the parameters of the emotional community that the poem sought to engender equally difficult to distinguish. During the thirteenth and fourteenth centuries, the House of Avesnes ruled Hainault, Holland, and Zeeland.[27] Several prominent members of the house—including William I, Count of Hainault, and Jean de Beaumont, his younger brother—helped depose Edward II and place Edward III on the English throne. William I further strengthened the English alliance by marrying his daughter, Philippa of Hainault, to Edward III and by supporting Edward III's claim to the French crown. Upon succeeding his father, William II joined the Flemish-Brabantine alliance in the Low Countries, which included Edward III and opposed French subjugation. William II later died without an heir while campaigning in Friesland, leaving Margaret II, his sister, to succeed him. She began The Hook and Cod Wars against her son, William III, when she attempted to sell Holland and Zeeland to Edward

III. William III defeated his mother and the English forces in a 1351 naval battle at Zwartewall. Despite aligning with Margaret II in the wars, Edward III promptly allied with William III—an alliance that was consolidated when William III married Matilda of Lancaster, the daughter of Henry of Lancaster. The marriage heralded a period of close collaboration between Edward III and William III.[28]

Although the Counts of Hainault were relatively loyal to their English allies, the cadet branch under Jean de Beaumont defected. After years of serving Edward III since leading the expedition to place him on the throne in 1327, Jean de Beaumont was persuaded to join the French forces on July 21, 1346, by Louis II, Count of Blois, who was married to Jean de Beaumont's daughter, Jeanne of Hainault. Jean de Beaumont fought on the side of France during the Battle of Crécy, where his son-in-law, Louis II, died.[29] At the court of Margaret I, Countess of Burgundy, Jean de Beaumont and his household stimulated literary activity through commissioning works such as Jean le Bel's chronicle and *Voeux du Héron*.[30] It is likely that Jean de Beaumont brought Colins de Beaumont with him from Hainault as part of his entourage and commissioned him to write "On the Crécy Dead" for a circle of like-minded nobles ruling the Low Countries who were sympathetic to France's cause and wanted peace in their realms.

The text evidently reached an ecclesiastical audience in the form of Gilles li Muisis's Latin chronicle. Muisis (1272–1353) was the abbot of St. Martin's Abbey, Tournai, a region that supported Philip VI as King of France.[31] In Muisis's chronicle, after a stark account of the Battle of Crécy, he prefaces the literary epitaph with a short attribution and his reasoning for including a vernacular poem:

> Notandum igitur quod quidam familiaris domino Johanni de Hannonia domino de Byaumont, confecit in metro gallico quemdam rotulum de supradicto bello et de morte proborum et nobilium virorum, cujus tenorem feci inserere in praesenti opusculo, ad memoriam et solamen futurorum.

> Consequently, it should be noted that for the lord John of Hainaut lord of Beaumont he [Colins de Beaumont] prepared in a French meter a certain roll concerning the aforementioned war and concerning the death of virtuous and noble men, of which I have included a copy in the present little work, for the memory and the consolation of future generations.[32]

Muisis may have borrowed the original roll from Jean de Beaumont. The chronicler saw value in the poem's contribution to the "collective memory" of the region. His deployment of the word "solamen" (consolation) implies that the Battle of Crécy constituted a generational trauma that the community must process through the repeated reiteration of the memory. The text thereby acts as a repository for an emotional history on which the Low Countries communities allied with France could draw to understand the reverberations of the trauma caused by the deadly battle.

"On the Crécy Dead," which Colins de Beaumont may have composed only days after the battle, recounts its fictional aftermath in the form of a dream vision narrated by Colins.[33] Instead of recounting the battle, the author utilizes a composite genre of dream vision and dialogue to process the trauma in a form that resists direct articulation, as trauma tends to do.[34] Dream vision is a subgenre of visionary narrative that allows an author to explore the interior experience of a narrator through a subjective dream that ultimately provides readers insight into the human condition.[35] Whereas the chronicle presents death in stark terms that are devoid of emotiveness—a symptom of the genre—the liminal space of the dream vision allows for a more emotional engagement with the theme of death, which may have been why Muisis included it in his own chronicle.[36] Other medieval authors also realized the utility of the dream vision in framing elegiac narratives, for instance in *Pearl*, *The Book of the Duchess*, and *Li Regret Guillaume*. Although "On the Crécy Dead" draws from the same tradition as these texts, it does something that tends to be exclusive to the chronicle—that is, it records a multitude of deaths in a single battle. The emotionality of the literary epitaph in dream-vision form affords Colins de Beaumont the ability to craft his writing into a narrative of trauma that avoids the emotional sterilization of a conventional chronicle entry.[37]

The narrative begins with Colins, the character, falling asleep in the dead of winter. He dreams of a "chastel gasté" (ruined castle) in which he meets Renom, who is unable to speak because of his "duel" (grief).[38] Impatient to find the source of such grief, Colins searches the barren castle hall until he comes upon the closed door of a room, outside which he listens to Proesce (Prowess), Largesse (Largesse), Loyautés (Loyalty), Joie (Joy), Courtoisie (Courtesy), and Nature (Nature) blame one another as they grieve the death of many noblemen, John of Bohemia in particular. These allegorical figures of chivalric virtues bring their case to their sovereign, Honnour (Honor), who rules that none should grieve because the men who died at Crécy gained great honor by their deaths. She then calls upon Renom "dire los de ceuls qui mors sont" (to speak praise of those who died); in turn, he commissions Colins to set down an account of the dream vision in rhyme.[39] Invited into the room, Colins sees a pile of shields, standards, and coats of arms cast upon the floor, echoing a battlefield. He is tasked with identifying, by their heraldry, those who fell and then writes the story of their deaths, a ceremonial process pictured in The Hague's Koninklijke Bibliotheek, MS 72 A 24, fol. 144r.[40] Upon awakening, he hastily composes his vision in verse and presents it to the reader with the words "si les ay mis en general" (thus I offer a more general account).[41]

The homodiegetic "je" of the dream vision is determined by genre and, in the case of "On the Crécy Dead," invites the reader to imagine him- or herself as the narrator moving through the literary landscape. A. C. Spearing identifies the homodiegetic narrative—where "je" gives an account of a past event in which the experiencing "je" participated—as a convention of the dream-vision genre.[42] The "narrating self" and the "experiencing self," which take the form of a character, are separate despite their personal connection because the narrator must have experienced the events in the past to recount them in the present.[43] The two temporalities of the narrator—the fictitious *then* of the dream and the theatrical *now*—are separate subjectivities between which the dreamer mediates to form his fragmented voice.[44]

While the narrative point of view is first person, rendering the experience subjective, the character of Colins lacks depth and personalization. This absence of characterization shapes the individual into "an inflection of the universal."[45] Colins de Beaumont thereby deploys a convention common in poems of affective devotion like *Off alle women* to achieve the same ends, invoking an inward experience.[46] The effect is that the characters' experiences join them to, rather than divide them from, the audience, providing readers the opportunity to experience grief in a mediated way. A similar phenomenon occurs to the one Christine Libby identifies in mystic texts where affect travels between the text and the reader, reproducing the emotional experience in the reader.[47] From the first-person perspective, Colins de Beaumont intends his audience to experience grief in a collective sense by empathizing with the characters as the narrator does in his single emotive: "Là-dedens oy une dame / Plaindre, plourer, et grant duel faire, / Dont forment me devoit desplaire" (Inside I heard a lady / Lamenting, weeping, and despairing greatly, / Which constrained me to suffer profoundly).[48]

Colins de Beaumont individualizes the character Colins in a single instance, which is a choice motivated by self-promotion perhaps prompted by the competitiveness of his office. The Hundred Years' War provided a stimulus for the use of heralds in ceremonial and diplomatic scenarios, a development that precipitated the granting of titles or offices to previously anonymous heralds.[49] While heralds like Colins de Beaumont worked under a specific nobleman, they could be commissioned by other noblemen. Dedicating five lines to himself at the end of "On the Crécy Dead," therefore may have acted as an advertisement. Colins is only introduced by Renom in line 409 of the 566-line poem, briefly personalizing his character:

> Et il y a ci un ménestrel
> Qui ne sert les hauls hommes d'el.

Colins a nom, de Hénaut nés,
Que par pluseurs fois s'est pénés
Du bien des bons amentevoir.

And there is a court musician here,
Who serves high-born men in exactly this.
Colins is his name, born of Hainaut
And he has many a time exerted great effort
To commemorate the good of good men.[50]

Prior to these lines, the character goes unnamed. Colins de Beaumont intentionally delays doing so in order to maintain the effect of the unindividualized "je." His use of the term "ménestrel" may signify that the office of the herald had not fully developed in the Low Countries during the mid-fourteenth century or was preferable to "héraut" because Honnour demands that the account "fust mise en rime, non en prose" (be set in rhyme, not in prose).[51] In referencing his former work commemorating noblemen, Colins de Beaumont foregrounds his professional experience and bolsters the reliability of the narrator. The five lines are a product of self-interest and, due to their location in the text, do not detract from the generalization of the experiencing "je." By not fully developing his characters—either Colins or the allegorical figures—Colins de Beaumont universalizes the interior, personal, and subjective. At the same time, controlling the reader's perspective through the narrating "je" enables the text to elicit a specific individualized emotion. Reading the text, therefore, becomes a ritualized action analogous to a more emotionally provocative *memoria*.[52] The subjectivity of the text serves to more poignantly preserve both the memory of dead individuals and the trauma of the tragic event in the collective memory of the community that engaged with it.

"On the Crécy Dead" textually establishes a discourse on and lexicon of grief, which the audience is meant to draw upon to perform a culturally sanctioned form of mourning. "Duel" (grief) is central to the text and occurs, along with the related form "dolour" (grief), fifteen times. Colins de Beaumont provides his readers with emotional prototypes through the voices of the allegorical personifications. These models consist of verbal and nonverbal vocalizations that readers could mimic, enabling the text to script how the audience processes the trauma that the battle and its poetic depiction provokes.[53] To accomplish this objective, he deploys "emotives" in the dialogue as well as descriptive terms for embodiments of grief.[54] The lexicon of physicality is made up of variants on only a few verbs and adjectives: "plaindre" (lamenting), "plourant" (weeping), "grant duel faire" (despairing greatly), "voix mate" (dejected voice), "lermoi" (sob), "mates" (saddened), "palles" (pale), "mornes" (mournful), "afflicttes" (afflicted). Such terms inform the reader of the cultural expectation for their embodiment of grief.[55] The allegorical figures also verbally name their emotions in order to consolidate their affects, declaring phrases such as: "Tant ai au cuer et duel et ire" (I have so much grief and pain in my heart); "J'ai de mon duel assés à faire" (I am preoccupied enough with my own grief); and "Je lermoi / De duel, et bien y a raison" (I am weeping / From mourning and for good reason).[56] By naming and embodying "duel," the allegorical figures provide readers with the conceptualization of an emotion around which readers can then build an emotional community by following the prototyped performances—performances that were distinctly gendered to pertain to men and women, who both had the capacity to experience loss on the battlefield at Crécy.

Since the embodiment of emotions is intimately connected with the gendered body, specific emotions were performed differently according to gender across the late medieval Low Countries.[57] Colins de Beaumont uses the term "duel" to describe the grief experienced by both men and women, but how characters perform their grief is rooted in "gendered signs."[58] It is necessary to note that Colins de Beaumont writes his "emotional script" from the perspective of a herald, a male-dominated occupation deeply entwined with chivalric culture. His social situation and his patron Sir Jean de Hainault, Lord of Beaumont, inform his representation of both feminine and masculine displays of grief.[59] The way in which the poem's various gendered allegorical figures embody their emotions circumscribes how individual men and women who read the text processed their feelings.

The female allegorical figures enact a communal performance of "dolour commune" (shared grief) that, as they grieve collectively in an enclosed room, is physically separated from that of their male counterparts. The segregation of female expressions of grief stems from what Katherine Goodland, in relation to morality plays, identifies as the "underlying paradox that women's tears are not only excessive and subversive but also necessary and efficacious."[60] Colins de Beaumont, as a product of his society, sees a value in women's ritual lament, but mitigates its potential to disturb the community by situating the female allegorical figures in "une cambre . . . close" (a closed chamber) down a "trouvai qui n'estoit pas moult lée" (hallway that was not very wide).[61] When he approaches the door to the chamber, Colins claims that "je ne poi entrer dedens" (I could not go inside), likely because of the excessive feminine grief the room contained.[62] Neither he nor Renom, the only two male characters, are able to enter the room without an express invitation from those inside. In the literary blueprint of the castle, the women consequently occupy an architecturally marginal space set apart from the "sale"—a place of "power, justice and council" in a French palace as well as the locus of the court where meals and entertainment took place.[63] The "sale," in other words, constituted a male-dominated public space where late medieval society deemed excessive performances of female grief to be transgressive, as mourning fundamentally undermined the dominant Christian belief in eternal life for those of faith.[64] Colins disaligns the allegorical women's performances of grief with biblical women's performances of grief:

> Ke Lamech, Racel, ne Judée.
> Quant leur vie fu affineé,
> De Josué, leur très-boin roy,
> Ne firent onques tel desroi
>
> That neither Lamech, Rachel, nor Judith
> When their life was deprived
> Of Joshua, their excellent king,
> Ever made such an outcry[65]

In comparing the allegorical figures to celebrated women from the Old Testament, their grieving becomes contradictory to a biblical tradition of female mourning. Significantly, the poem reveals that fourteenth-century noble society in the Low Countries controlled female grief by containing it through normalizing the importance of privacy and restrained bodily performances of emotion.

While Colins de Beaumont genders female the majority of the allegorical figures in the poem, he genders Renom male. Notably, Renom is a masculine noun in French that embodies the core purpose of the herald: to publicize *fama* verbally or textually, as signified by the character's status as a "varlet" (page) in the text.[66] The chivalric economy of honor could not exist without *fama* because obtaining honor depended on the collective's knowledge of an individual's honorable deeds.[67] Compared to that of the female allegorical figures, Renom's emotional state receives little attention. He grieves alone. This solitary expression of grief may have been a product of attitude changes toward male demonstrations of grief in the late Middle Ages. Several scholars have observed that late medieval French society increasingly viewed violent or excessive emotional expressions from men as disruptive and "feminine," unlike during the high Middle Ages when epic laments were part of chivalric culture.[68] Mia Korpiola and Anu Lahtinen observe that medieval French and English societies restrained men's public grief by institutionalizing highly scripted mourning rituals and encouraging men to embody their grief in seclusion.[69] Colins de Beaumont affords Renom's embodiment of emotion a brief description at the beginning:

> Et je croi bien que il ne pot,
> Car de duel estoit si estains,
> Que ses vis ert de lermes tains

> Et pallis, que bien l'apiercui.
>
> Indeed I believe he was unable to speak,
> For he was so destroyed with grief
> That his face was bathed with tears
> And pale, as I clearly perceived.[70]

The physicality of grief expressed by Renom does not differ substantially from that of the female allegorical figures, whom Colins de Beaumont describes as "palles" (pale) and "pleurant" (weeping).[71] However, the greatest contrast is Renom's inability to speak. His "duel" isolates him in a way that female "duel" does not fully isolate the individual women who partake in "dolour commune."[72] While the embodiment of emotions is not vastly different between genders in the text, gender determines the environment in which characters express emotions and the degree to which they are able to express them. The cultural work done by "On the Crécy Dead," therefore, reinforces late medieval gendered assumptions about how emotion was to be performed among the nobility of the Low Countries, providing historical insight into the matter. However, a question remains: Where were such gendered expressions of emotion performed?

The literary landscape of the dream vision acts as a stage for embodied performances of grief, portraying it as a sensory experience that engages sight, smell, and hearing. The tumbledown castle symbolizes the state of France's nobility. As Robert Rouse observes, the ruin is "a cultural *memento mori*";[73] it is a signifier of loss, making the castle an ideal setting for a narrative of grief. The cultural function of a castle thus makes Colins de Beaumont's choice of location even more poignant in relation to the trauma it memorializes. Jim Bradbury, for instance, describes the medieval castle as an expression of "power which might be royal, comital, seigneurial or castellan, in other words, the castle did not represent any one of the layers of social and political power in this age but all of them."[74] A deteriorating castle, therefore, signifies a loss of political power—and, in this instance, the loss of a large fraction of the ruling class at the Battle of Crécy. Within the castle, the hall stands remarkably vacant, which is only accentuated by it being "moult . . . grande" (very large).[75] The abandoned hall, which at one point would have functioned as a lively court, is haunted by the disappearance of its former purpose. The Battle of Crécy left counties, duchies, and entire kingdoms without a ruler or a noble class to cultivate them. In effect, the trauma of the battle was social, economic, and political for the French and their allies.

The poem's central action takes place in an enclosed room that becomes both a tomb monument and an arena for processing grief. Colins de Beaumont, the author, subsequently shapes this room into a sensory experience for

Colins, the character. Since the door to the room is shut and Colins cannot enter a space of female grieving without invitation, his first perceptions of it are through sound and scent:

> Moult scenti grant oudour d'encens,
> Souef flairant et de dous basme
> Là-dedens oy une dame
> Plaindre, plourer et grant duel faire.
>
> I smelled a strong scent of incense
> Softly fragrant and full of sweet balm.
> Inside I heard a lady
> Lamenting, weeping, and despairing greatly.[76]

The incense that he smells evokes that used for the embalming of bodies.[77] Similar fragrances emanating from the dead appear in hagiography and romance to indicate the purity or sanctity of the soul of the deceased. For instance, an odor of sanctity comparable to that of flowers is reported to have emanated from the tomb of Thomas Becket, and Thomas Malory describes Launcelot's corpse as having "the swettest savour aboute hym that ever they felte" in *Le Morte d'Arthur*.[78] Colins also hears audible embodiments of mourning, stimulating another sense. The chamber becomes a figurative tomb for the fallen knights that functions as a location for mourning the dead through sensory experiences.

Colins de Beaumont architects a multisensory experience upon which his audience can meditate.[79] To accomplish this, he exploits the standard model of cognitive processing established in the twelfth and thirteenth centuries, as elucidated in the pseudo-Augustinian *Liber de spiritu et enima*: "Cum ab inferioribus ad superiora volumus ascendere, prius occurrit nobis sensus, deinde imaginatio, postea ratio, intellectus et intelligentia, et in summo est sapiential" (When the mind wants to rise up from lower to higher things, we first meet with the sense, then imagination, then reason, intellection and understanding, and at the top is wisdom).[80] Sensory language such as this subsequently appeals to the imagination by means of similitude and engages with affections to elicit an emotional response.[81] According to William of Auvergne, bishop of Paris in the thirteenth century, emotions contained a passive dimension that reacted to the stimulation of the senses.[82] Therefore, poetry is an apt form for an "emotional script" in medieval medical philosophy because it targets the senses and cognitive functions that medieval societies believed to influence the audience's understanding. In appealing to the sensorium through language, Colins de Beaumont stimulates an interiority that enables the reader to experience emotion. He is able to curate the audience's cognitive process in a progression from the senses to the imagination, fantasy, and finally memory.[83]

When Renom invites Colins into the chamber, sight transforms the space into a pseudo-battlefield during the enumeration of the dead ritual. Michael Livingston suggests that the room could represent King Edward III's pavilion, attested to in the *Chronique de l'Abbaye de Saint Trond*: "Et y eult de tournicles en la tente du roy, où on les apporta, ce tesmoignèrent ceulx qui les virent et regardèrent, bien .xxii.c. et plus" (And the surcoats were placed in the tent of the king, where they had been carried, those witnessing these things and regarded them, over 2,200 and more).[84] The contents of the room parallel the chronicle's description of the event after the Battle of Crécy. On first seeing the heap of armor taken from the dead, Colins describes his affective experience:

> Là vi-je gésir enmi l'aire
> Tante banière deschirée
> Et mainte coste deffoulée,
> Et tant escu desroupt, despaint,
> Qu'il n'I paroit couleur ne taint'
> Dont au cuer moult courrouciés fui.
> Les viij banières bien congnui
> D'un roi, d'un duc et de vj contes,
> Pour qui mémoire est fait cil contes.
>
> There I saw cast in the middle of the floor
> Many a ragged standard
> And many a befouled coat,
> And many a shield so shattered and so scratched
> That no color nor hue appeared upon them,
> And all of this greatly saddened my heart.
> I clearly recognized the eight standards
> Of a king, a duke and six counts,
> In memory of whom this account has been produced.[85]

The standards, coats, and shields become material monuments attesting, through their mutilation, to the death of those who owned them. The objects induce affects in Colins that are consolidated into an emotive with the verb "courroucer" (to enrage). Loss provokes an anger in him that operates as a primary emotive driver of his grief, a complex emotion consisting of multiple other emotions and affects.[86] Almost immediately, he begins his task as a herald by identifying noblemen based on their armor, listing their names and honorable deeds as he does so. The surreal enumeration ritual encompasses the herald's entire process of constructing a textual monument after a battle, beginning with identification on the battlefield and ending with the narrator writing the poem. The moment invites the reader to reflect on how a memorial is made to induce an affective response through sympathy by way of the herald's personal suffering.

The dialogue between allegorical personifications presents the audience with a framework for processing these emotions and affects by rationalizing death in battle as a coping mechanism. Whereas ecclesiastical authors tended to use the notion of the apocalypse as consolation for death, Colins de Beaumont turns to the chivalric economy of honor.[87] In the text, eternal life is gained through postmortem *fama*, not faith. He writes a dialogue that is intentionally undialogic to perpetuate the notion that death in battle is the most honorable of chivalric acts and should be celebrated as such. The dialogue mediates among the multiple voices in the text to form a cohesive message for the audience, in the process exposing the author's own voice.[88] While the debate between Proesce, Largesse, Loyautés, Joie, Courtoisie, and Nature as to who is to blame for the traumatic event initially appears to be an attack on Prowess, the resolution only affirms its supremacy in the hierarchy of chivalric virtues. When the allegorical figures approach Hounour, their "royne" (queen), the narrator then deems Nature's emotional response "cruel duel" (unrestrained mourning), marking a transition in which grief becomes culturally transgressive in its excessiveness.[89] Hearing their case, Honnour rules that "estre ne puet plus noble fins" (there can be no more noble end).[90] Since honor acted as a type of social currency that expressed the value of one's identity, dying in battle enhanced one's *fama* immensely. Honour's emotives qualify her grief according to her ideological framework: "De leur mort sui molt courroucie / Mais sachiés que je sui moult lie / De ce qu'il sont mort en tel guise" (I am greatly afflicted by their death, / But may you know that I am greatly joyful / That they died in such a manner).[91] In voicing her emotions, she behaves as the final emotional prototype that the audience is meant to interpret as the socially correct performance. The two dichotomous emotions of grief and joy paradoxically coexist as an emotional response to trauma. It is the framework of chivalry's economy of honor that consoles the audience's grief though the justification of death in battle and enables them to feel a duality of emotions.

In drawing on the honor system as a framework for understanding the trauma of war, Colins de Beaumont participates in a wider movement within the French nobility to reform chivalry during the Hundred Years' War. Developments in weaponry, military organization, and strategy widened the gap between the laws of chivalric warfare and the realities of contemporary Anglo-French warfare. Nigel Saul posits that, based on the brutal tactics of the English in warfare against the French, chivalry began deteriorating or at least mutating as early as the 1340s. In particular, the Battle of Crécy was a bloodbath where the English took few prisoners and, according to Michael de Northburgh's estimation, 1,542 French knights and men-at-arms were killed.[92] The introduction of the longbow, the more common invocation of *guerre mortelle*, the escalating importance of specialist footmen, and the increased use of siege warfare as well as *chevauchée* undermined the chivalric code of violence.[93] In his chronicles, Froissart, a foremost chronicler of the fourteenth century, notes how maladapted the chivalric code was to the new realities of the battlefield.[94] During the fourteenth and fifteenth centuries, the French royal armies suffered a series of defeats and marauding soldiers ravaged the countryside, bringing the "moral fibre of the military classes" into question.[95] The circumstances of the time prompted writers to engage in debates on the nature of chivalric knighthood, the majority supporting the Valois monarchy's reforms.[96] Geoffroi de Charny, a renowned French knight, identified a diminishing of prowess in the nobility as France's central military plight. His reform plan, set out in his *Livre de chevalerie*, is simple: an augmented emphasis on prowess as a chivalric virtue. Richard Kaeuper observes that Charny's book was part of a larger "royal campaign for reform of governance in the interest of unity" under John II.[97] I posit that Colins de Beaumont's "On the Crécy Dead" buttressed this reform discourse early in its conception. The interrogation of Proesce in the dialogue and her ultimate vindication in the final judgement foreground the primacy of prowess as a chivalric virtue. Furthermore, the 164-line lament for John of Bohemia is selective in the characteristics it presents, dwelling mainly on the king's prowess in spite of his blindness and revealing that the author's principles of selection were driven by his desire to laud prowess.[98] Ultimately, the text responds to the Battle of Crécy's blow to chivalry through the celebration of prowess's place in the honor economy. It is a herald's thinly veiled attempt to reassert the relevance of prowess at a time when France's chivalric code was in flux.

While there is a vast amount of scholarship on the Hundred Years' War, very little of it explores the emotional consequence that prolonged war had on the societies it affected. "On the Crécy Dead" constitutes a material point of contact for an emotional community that is unique in how it deploys literary conventions to structure emotional responses. Since it is a product of the historical moment and geographical location in which Colins de Beaumont wrote, the narrative of trauma provides a window into how a well-connected poet sought to script what might have otherwise registered as an unmitigated disaster. Via the poem's circulation, it engendered an emotional community—consisting of both lay and clerical members in the upper strata of society—that reinforced culturally determined performances of emotion. As Gilles le Muisis's preface suggests, the trauma of the Battle of Crécy lingered in collective memory of northern France and the Low Countries and required means of communal processing—one of those means being precisely "On the Crécy Dead."

WORKS CITED

Akehurst, F. R. P. "Good Name, Reputation, and Notoriety in French Customary Law." In Fenster and Smail, *Fama*, 75–94.
APA Dictionary of Psychology. Accessed March 12, 2022. https://dictionary.apa.org /trauma.
Arblaster, Paul. *A History of the Low Countries.* 3rd ed. London: Red Globe Press, 2019.
Badham, Sally. *Seeking Salvation: Commemorating the Dead in the Late-Medieval English Parish.* Donington: Church Archaeology, 2015.
Baker, Denise N. "Julian of Norwich and the Varieties of Middle English Mystical Discourse." In *A Companion to Julian of Norwich*, edited by Liz Herbert McAvoy, 53–63. Cambridge: D. S. Brewer, 2008.
Beaumont, Colins de, "On the Crécy Dead." In Livingston and DeVries, *Battle of Crécy*, 26–51. Liverpool: Liverpool University Press, 2015.
Beyer, Hartmut. "*Tituli—Versus*—Epitaphs: The Form and Topology of Mortuary Roll Poems." In *Bruno the Carthusian and His Mortuary Roll: Studies, Text, and Translations*, edited by Hartmut Beyer, Gabriela Signori, and Sita Steckel, 25–45. Turnhout: Brepols, 2014.
Boldrick, Stacy. "Speculations on the Visibility and Display of a Mortuary Roll." In *Continuous Page: Scrolls and Scrolling from Papyrus to Hypertext*, edited by Jack Hartnell, 102–21. London: Courtland Institute of Art, 2020.
Boquet, Damien, and Piroska Nagy. "Medieval Sciences of Emotions during the Eleventh to Thirteenth Centuries: An Intellectual History." *Osiris* 31, no. 1 (2016): 21–45.
Bradbury, Jim. *The Medieval Siege.* 1992. Reprint, Woodbridge: Boydell, 1998.
Charmaz, Kathy, and Melinda J. Milligan. "Grief." In *Handbook of the Sociology of Emotions*, edited by Jan E. Stets and Jonathan H. Turner, 516–43. New York: Springer, 2007.
Chaucer, Geoffrey. *The Book of the Duchess.* In *The Riverside Chaucer*, edited by Larry D. Benson, 330–46. Boston: Houghton Mifflin, 1987.
Cherewatuk, Karen. "The Saint's Life of Sir Launcelot: Hagiography and the Conclusion of Malory's 'Morte Darthur.'" *Arthuriana* 5, no. 1 (1995): 62–78.
Clarke, Catherine. "Signs and Wonders: Writing Trauma in Twelfth-Century England." *Reading Medieval Studies* 35 (2009): 55–77.
Curry, Anne. *The Battle of Agincourt: Sources and Interpretations.* Woodbridge: Boydell Press, 2000.
Delogu, Daisy. "'Ala grant temps de douleur languissant': Grief and Mourning in Girart d'Amiens' *Istoire le Roy Charlemaine*." *Speculum* 93, no. 1 (2018): 1–26.

Devaux, Jean. "From the Court of Hainault to the Court of England: The Example of Jean Froissart." In *War, Government and Power in Late Medieval France*, edited by Christopher Allmand, 1–20. Liverpool: Liverpool University Press, 2000.

Devereaux, Rima. *Constantinople and the West in Medieval French Literature: Renewal and Utopia*. Cambridge: D. S. Brewer, 2012.

The de Wit Collection of Medieval Coins. Osnabrück: Fritz Rudolf Künker, 2008.

Encyclopedia of the Medieval Chronicle Online. Leiden: Brill. https://referenceworks.brillonline.com/subjects.

Fenster, Thelma, and Daniel Lord Smail, eds. *Fama: The Politics of Talk and Reputation in Medieval Europe*. Ithaca, NY: Cornell University Press, 2003.

Froissart, Jean. *Chroniques*. MS 72 A 24. Koninklijke Bibliotheek, The Hague. https://galerij.kb.nl/kb.html#/en/froissart/page/156/zoom/5/lat/-66.02694736625703/lng/4.02099609375.

Gagné, John. "Counting the Dead: Traditions of Enumeration and the Italian Wars." *Renaissance Quarterly* 67, no. 3 (2014): 791–840.

Gillespie, Vincent. "The Senses in Literature: The Textures of Perception." In *A Cultural History of the Senses in the Middle Ages*, edited by Richard G. Newhauser. 2 vols. London: Bloomsbury Academic, 2014.

Gobodo-Madikizela, Pumla. *Breaking Intergenerational Cycles of Repetition: A Global Dialogue on Historical Trauma and Memory*. Opladen: Barbara Budrich, 2016.

Goodland, Katharine. "'Us for to wepe no man may let': Resistant Female Grief in the Medieval English Lazarus Plays." In Perfetti, *Representation of Women's Emotions*, 90–118.

Gordon, Bruce, and Peter Marshall. *The Place of the Dead: Death and Remembrance in Late Medieval and Early Modern Europe*. Cambridge: Cambridge University Press, 2000.

Harvey, Susan Ashbrook. *Scenting Salvation: Ancient Christianity and the Olfactory Imagination*. Berkeley: University of California Press, 2006.

Hodapp, William F. "The Real and Surreal in Medieval Dream Vision: The Case of James I's *Kingis Quair*." *Journal of the Midwest Modern Language Association* 42, no. 1 (2009): 57–76.

Jacobsen, Michael Hviid, and Anders Petersen, eds. *Exploring Grief: Towards a Sociology of Sorrow*. London: Routledge, 2019.

Jean de la Mote. *Li Regret Guillaume, comte de Hainaut*. Edited by August Scheler. Louvain: J. Lefever, 1882.

Kaeuper, Richard. *Chivalry and Violence in Medieval Europe*. Oxford: Oxford University Press, 2001.

Karnes, Michelle. *Imagination, Meditation, and Cognition in the Middle Ages*. Chicago: University of Chicago Press, 2011.

Kerth, Sonja. "Narratives of Trauma in Medieval German Literature." In *Trauma in Medieval Society*, edited by Wendy J. Turner and Christina Lee, 274–97. Leiden: Brill, 2018.

Korpiola, Mia, and Anu Lahtinen. *Cultures of Death and Dying in Medieval and Early Modern Europe*. Helsinki: Helsinki Collegium for Advanced Studies, 2015.

Lawton, David. *Voice in Later Medieval English Literature: Public Interiorities.* Oxford: Oxford University Press, 2017.
Libby, Christine. "The Object of His Heart: Subjectivity and Affect in Mystic Texts." *Literature Compass* 13, no. 6 (2016): 362–71.
Livingston, Michael, and Kelly DeVries, eds. *The Battle of Crécy: A Casebook.* Liverpool: Liverpool University Press, 2015.
Marchant, Alicia. "Narratives of Death and Emotional Affect in Late Medieval Chronicles." *Parergon* 31, no. 2 (2014): 81–98.
Mayo, James M. "War Memorial as Political Memory." *Geographical Review* 78, no. 1 (1988): 62–75.
McNamer, Sarah. *Affective Meditation and the Invention of Medieval Compassion.* Philadelphia: University of Pennsylvania Press, 2011.
Muisis, Gilles li. *Corpus Chronicorum Flandriae, sub Auspiciis Leopoldi Primi, Serenissimi Belgarum Regis.* Edited by Joseph Jean de Smet. 3 vols. Brussels: Bruxellis Ex Officina, 1841.
Nieuwenhove, Rik Van, Robert Faesen, and Helen Rolfson. *Late Medieval Mysticism of the Low Countries.* New York: Paulist Press, 2008.
Perfetti, Lisa. *The Representation of Women's Emotions in Medieval and Early Modern Culture.* Gainesville: University Press of Florida, 2005.
Pfau, Aleksandra. "Warfare, Trauma, and Madness in French Remission Letters of the Hundred Years' War." In *The Hundred Years' War (Part III)*, edited by L. J. Andrew Villalon and Donald J. Kagay, 437–55. Leiden: Brill, 2013.
The Poems of the Pearl Manuscript: Pearl, Cleanness Patience, Sir Gawain and the Green Knight. Edited by Malcolm Andrew and Ronald Waldron. Liverpool: Liverpool University Press, 2008.
Reedy, William M. "Against Constructionism: The Historical Ethnography of Emotions." *Current Anthropology* 38, no. 3 (1997): 327–51.
———. "Emotional Liberty: Politics and History in the Anthropology of Emotions." *Cultural Anthropology* 14, no. 2 (1999): 256–88.
Riegel, Christian. "The Fraught Work of Mourning in Fiction." In *Exploring Grief: Towards a Sociology of Sorrow*, edited by Michael Hviid Jacobsen and Anders Petersen, 104–20. London: Routledge, 2019.
Rollo-Koster, Joelle. *Death in Medieval Europe.* Abingdon: Routledge, 2016.
Rosenwein, Barbara H. *Emotional Communities in the Early Middle Ages.* Ithaca, NY: Cornell University Press, 2006.
Rouse, Robert. "Reading Ruins: Arthurian Caerleon and the Untimely Architecture of History." *Arthuriana* 23, no. 1 (2013): 40–51.
Salisbury Ledger book A (G23/1/1). Wiltshire County Record Office, Trowbridge.
Saul, Nigel. *Chivalry in Medieval England.* Cambridge, MA: Harvard University Press, 2011.
Saunders, Corinne. "Mind, Body and Affect in Medieval English Arthurian Romance." In *Emotions in Medieval Arthurian Literature: Body, Mind, Voice*, edited by Frank Brandsma, Carolyne Larrington, and Corinne Saunders, 31–46. Cambridge: D. S. Brewer, 2015.

Schönfelder, Christa. *Wounds and Words: Childhood and Family Trauma in Romantic and Post-modern Fiction.* Bielefeld: Verlag, 2013.
Spearing, A. C. *Textual Subjectivity: The Encoding of Subjectivity in Medieval Narratives and Lyrics.* Oxford: Oxford University Press, 2005.
Spinks, Jennifer, and Charles Zika. *Disaster, Death and the Emotions in the Shadow of the Apocalypse, 1400–1700.* London: Palgrave, 2016.
Sposato, Peter, and Samuel Claussen. "Chivalric Violence." In *A Companion to Chivalry*, edited by Robert W. Jones and Peter Coss, 99–117. Woodbridge: Boydell Press, 2019.
Stanzel, F. K. *A Theory of Narrative.* Cambridge: Cambridge University Press, 1984.
Stevenson, Katie. *The Herald in Late Medieval Europe.* Woodbridge: Boydell, 2009.
Swift, Helen. "Posthumous Reputation Unraveled in Sixteenth-Century Epitaph Fictions." *Early Modern French Studies* 40, no. 1 (2018): 11–24.
———. *Representing the Dead: Epitaph Fictions in Late-Medieval France.* Cambridge: D. S. Brewer, 2016.
Taylor, Craig. *Chivalry and the Ideals of Knighthood in France during the Hundred Years' War.* Cambridge: Cambridge University Press, 2013.
Thiry-Stassin, Martine. "Jean de Hainaut, comte de Beaumont et de Chimay, entre Jean le Bel et Jean Froissart." In *Autour du XV siècle: Journées d'étude en l'honneur d'Alberto Vàrvaro*, edited by Paola Moreno and Giovanni Palumbo, 229–40. Liège: Presses Universitaires de Liège, 2008.
Thornbury, Emily V. "Lyric Form, Subjectivity and Consciousness." In *A Companion to British Literature.* Vol. 2, *Early Modern Literature 1450–1660*, edited by Robert Demaria Jr., Heesok Chang, and Samantha Zacher, 30–47. Malden: Wiley Blackwell, 2014.
Trigg, Stephanie. "Introduction: Emotional Histories—Beyond the Personalization of the Past and the Abstraction of Affect Theory." *Exemplaria* 26, no. 1 (2014): 3–15.
Warner, Angela. "'Doel' in Situ: The Contextual and Corporeal Landscape of Grief in *La Chanson de Roland*." In *Affective and Emotional Economies in Medieval and Early Modern Europe*, edited by A. Marculescu and C. L. Morand Métivier, 211–26. London: Palgrave, 2018.
Wheeler, Bonnie. "Grief in Avalon: Sir Palomydes' Psychic Pain." In *Grief and Gender 700–1700*, edited by Jennifer C. Vaught and Lynne Dickson Bruckner, 65–80. London: Palgrave, 2003.
Whetham, David. "The English Longbow: A Revolution in Technology?" In *The Hundred Years' War (Part II): Different Vistas*, edited by Andrew Villalon and Donald Kagay, 213–32. Leiden: Brill, 2008.
Woolgar, C. M. *The Senses in Late Medieval England.* New Haven, CT: Yale University Press, 2006.
Zink, Michel. *Froissart et le temps.* Paris: Presses Universitaires de France, 1998.

NOTES

1. Edition and translation from Colins de Beaumont, "On the Crécy Dead," in *The Battle of Crécy: A Casebook*, ed. Michael Livingston and Kelly DeVries (Liverpool: Liverpool University Press, 2015), 46–47.
2. I refer to the character as Colins and the author as Colins de Beaumont to differentiate between the two. Christa Schönfelder, *Wounds and Words: Childhood and Family Trauma in Romantic and Post-modern Fiction* (Bielefeld: Transcript Verlag, 2013), 31.
3. David Whetham, "The English Longbow: A Revolution in Technology?," in *The Hundred Years' War (Part II): Different Vistas*, ed. Andrew Villalon and Donald Kagay (Leiden: Brill, 2008), 213–32.
4. John Gagné, "Counting the Dead: Traditions of Enumeration and the Italian Wars," *Renaissance Quarterly* 67, no. 3 (2014): 802.
5. In this chapter, I adopt Stephanie Trigg's definition of "affect" as "an unconscious, pre-discursive bodily response." Emotions are secondary consolidations of affects. Stephanie Trigg, "Introduction: Emotional Histories—Beyond the Personalization of the Past and the Abstraction of Affect Theory," *Exemplaria* 26, no. 1 (2014): 5–6; see also Christian Riegel, "The Fraught Work of Mourning in Fiction," in *Exploring Grief: Towards a Sociology of Sorrow*, ed. Michael Hviid Jacobsen and Anders Petersen (London: Routledge, 2019), 108–9; Christine Libby, "The Object of His Heart: Subjectivity and Affect in Mystic Texts," *Literature Compass* 13, no. 6 (2016): 369.
6. Beaumont, "On the Crécy Dead," 26–51. "On the Crécy Dead" has received no attention from scholars beyond Livingston and DeVries's *The Battle of Crécy: A Casebook* and *Medieval Warfare: A Reader*. The latter contains an excerpt of the poem from the former.
7. See Helen Swift, *Representing the Dead: Epitaph Fictions in Late-Medieval France* (Cambridge: D. S. Brewer, 2016); Helen Swift, "Posthumous Reputation Unraveled in Sixteenth-Century Epitaph Fictions," *Early Modern French Studies* 40, no. 1 (2018): 11–24.
8. I adopt the term "chivalric economy of honor" from Peter Sposato and Samuel Claussen, "Chivalric Violence," in *A Companion to Chivalry*, ed. Robert W. Jones and Peter Coss (Woodbridge: Boydell Press, 2019), 107.
9. For more on honor, see Craig Taylor, "Chivalry and the Ideals of Knighthood in France during the Hundred Years' War," in *Chivalry and the Ideals of Knighthood in France during the Hundred Years' War* (Cambridge: Cambridge University Press, 2013), 54–90.
10. *Fama* encompasses "rumor," "the things people say," "reputation," and "memory." Here I define it as the image formed of a person by the talk spread about him or her. Thelma Fenster and Daniel Lord Smail, eds., *Fama: The Politics of Talk and Reputation in Medieval Europe* (Ithaca, NY: Cornell University Press, 2003), 1–2, 4.
11. Barbara H. Rosenwein, *Emotional Communities in the Early Middle Ages* (Ithaca, NY: Cornell University Press, 2006), 2.

12. William M. Reedy, "Against Constructionism: The Historical Ethnography of Emotions," *Current Anthropology* 38, no. 3 (1997): 332–34.

13. Richard Kaeuper, *Chivalry and Violence in Medieval Europe* (Oxford: Oxford University Press, 2001), 228.

14. This phrase is inspired by Sarah McNamer's concept of "affective scripts." I use the term "emotion" because "On the Crécy Dead" consolidates the affects it provokes into an emotion. Sarah McNamer, *Affective Meditation and the Invention of Medieval Compassion* (Philadelphia: University of Pennsylvania Press, 2011); Libby, "The Object of His Heart," 363.

15. Kathy Charmaz and Melinda J. Milligan, "Grief," in *Handbook of the Sociology of Emotions*, ed. Jan E. Stets and Jonathan H. Turner (New York: Springer, 2007), 518–19.

16. "Feeling rules" are socially sanctioned rules that determine how and whom one grieves. Michael Hviid Jacobsen and Anders Petersen, eds., *Exploring Grief: Towards a Sociology of Sorrow* (London: Routledge, 2019), 2.

17. Jacobsen and Petersen, *Exploring Grief*, 524.

18. *APA Dictionary of Psychology*, s.v. "trauma," accessed March 12, 2022, https: //dictionary.apa.org/trauma.

19. Aleksandra Pfau, "Warfare, Trauma, and Madness in French Remission Letters of the Hundred Years' War," in *The Hundred Years' War (Part III)*, ed. L. J. Andrew Villalon and Donald J. Kagay (Leiden: Brill, 2013), 437–55.

20. Pumla Gobodo-Madikizela, *Breaking Intergenerational Cycles of Repetition: A Global Dialogue on Historical Trauma and Memory* (Opladen: Barbara Budrich, 2016), 2–3.

21. Charmaz and Milligan, "Grief," 524; James M. Mayo, "War Memorial as Political Memory," *Geographical Review* 78, no. 1 (1988): 62–65.

22. Sally Badham, *Seeking Salvation: Commemorating the Dead in the Late-Medieval English Parish* (Donington: Church Archaeology, 2015), 46–49; Bruce Gordon and Peter Marshall, *The Place of the Dead: Death and Remembrance in Late Medieval and Early Modern Europe* (Cambridge: Cambridge University Press, 2000), 4.

23. Michael Livingston and Kelly DeVries, eds., *The Battle of Crécy: A Casebook* (Liverpool: Liverpool University Press, 2015), 340.

24. Stacy Boldrick, "Speculations on the Visibility and Display of a Mortuary Roll," in *Continuous Page: Scrolls and Scrolling from Papyrus to Hypertext*, ed. Jack Hartnell (London: Courtland Institute of Art, 2020), 107.

25. Swift, *Representing the Dead*, 25–45; Hartmut Beyer, "*Tituli—Versus*—Epitaphs: The Form and Topology of Mortuary Roll Poems," in *Bruno the Carthusian and His Mortuary Roll: Studies, Text, and Translations*, ed. Hartmut Beyer, Gabriela Signori, and Sita Steckel (Turnhout: Brepols, 2014), 25–45.

26. Salisbury Ledger book A (G23/1/1), fol. 55, Wiltshire County Record Office, Trowbridge; Anne Curry, *The Battle of Agincourt: Sources and Interpretations* (Woodbridge: Boydell Press, 2000), 263–64.

27. Paul Arblaster, *A History of the Low Countries*, 3rd ed. (London: Red Globe Press, 2019), 79.

28. Arblaster, 84–85; *The de Wit Collection of Medieval Coins* (Osnabrück: Fritz Rudolf Künker, 2008), 239–40.
29. Martine Thiry-Stassin, "Jean de Hainaut, comte de Beaumont et de Chimay, entre Jean le Bel et Jean Froissart," in *Autour du XV siècle: Journées d'étude en l'honneur d'Alberto Vàrvaro*, ed. Paola Moreno and Giovanni Palumbo (Liège: Presses Universitaires de Liège, 2008), 229–40.
30. Jean Devaux, "From the Court of Hainault to the Court of England: The Example of Jean Froissart," in *War, Government and Power in Late Medieval France*, ed. Christopher Allmand (Liverpool: Liverpool University Press, 2000), 4–6.
31. "Giles Li Muisis," in *Encyclopedia of the Medieval Chronicle*, accessed November 23, 2020, https://referenceworks.brillonline.com.
32. Translation my own using the edition Gilles li Muisis, *Corpus Chronicorum Flandriae, sub Auspiciis Leopoldi Primi, Serenissimi Belgarum Regis*, ed. Joseph Jean de Smet, 3 vols. (Brussels: Bruxellis Ex Officina, 1841), 2:246.
33. Livingston and DeVries, *Battle of Crécy*, 340.
34. Catherine Clarke, "Signs and Wonders: Writing Trauma in Twelfth-Century England," *Reading Medieval Studies* 35 (2009): 56.
35. William F. Hodapp, "The Real and Surreal in Medieval Dream Vision: The Case of James I's *Kingis Quair*," *Journal of the Midwest Modern Language Association* 42, no. 1 (2009): 62.
36. Alicia Marchant, "Narratives of Death and Emotional Affect in Late Medieval Chronicles," *Parergon* 31, no. 2 (2014): 82.
37. For a discussion of the implication of genre on a text's ability to act as a "narrative of trauma," see Sonja Kerth, "Narratives of Trauma in Medieval German Literature," in *Trauma in Medieval Society*, ed. Wendy J. Turner and Christina Lee (Leiden: Brill, 2018), 276.
38. Beaumont, "On the Crécy Dead," lines 15, 27.
39. Beaumont, "On the Crécy Dead," line 390.
40. In the Koninklijke Bibliotheek copy of Jean Froissart's *Chroniques*, the illuminator—the Virgil Master (active ca. 1410)—depicts the commencement of a memorialization process after the Battle of Crécy (1346) headed by a rubrication reading: "Comment le Roy Eangleterre fist nombres les mors et pius sen party de Crécy" (How the King of England had the dead counted and then left Crécy). The crowned figure standing in front of the English forces wearing the armorial bearings of England represents Edward III's King of Arms counting the dead with his pointed finger. My translation, from MS 72 A 24, fol. 144r, Koninklijke Bibliotheek, The Hague, https://galerij.kb.nl/kb.html#/en/froissart/page/156/zoom/5/lat/-66.02694736625703/lng/4.02099609375.
41. Beaumont, "On the Crécy Dead," line 560.
42. A. C. Spearing, *Textual Subjectivity: The Encoding of Subjectivity in Medieval Narratives and Lyrics* (Oxford: Oxford University Press, 2005), 148.
43. F. K. Stanzel, *A Theory of Narrative* (Cambridge: Cambridge University Press, 1984), 210.
44. David Lawton, *Voice in Later Medieval English Literature: Public Interiorities* (Oxford: Oxford University Press, 2017), 20, 34, 104.

45. Emily V. Thornbury, "Lyric Form, Subjectivity and Consciousness," in *A Companion to British Literature*, vol. 2, *Early Modern Literature 1450–1660*, ed. Robert Demaria Jr., Heesok Chang, and Samantha Zacher (Malden: Wiley Blackwell, 2014), 31.

46. Thornbury, "Lyric Form," 44.

47. Libby, "The Object of His Heart," 362.

48. Beaumont, "On the Crécy Dead," line 52–54.

49. Katie Stevenson, *The Herald in Late Medieval Europe* (Woodbridge: Boydell, 2009), 3–4.

50. Beaumont, "On the Crécy Dead," lines 407–11.

51. Beaumont, "On the Crécy Dead," line 404.

52. *Memoria* is a collective term for the liturgical and social acts connecting the living and the dead. Badham, *Seeking Salvation*, 46.

53. Lawton, *Voice in Later Medieval English*, 104–5.

54. William M. Reedy, "Emotional Liberty: Politics and History in the Anthropology of Emotions," *Cultural Anthropology* 14, no. 2 (1999): 256–88.

55. Beaumont, "On the Crécy Dead," lines 53, 81, 102, 264, 422.

56. Beaumont, "On the Crécy Dead," lines 104, 185, 265.

57. Lisa Perfetti, *The Representation of Women's Emotions in Medieval and Early Modern Culture* (Gainesville: University Press of Florida, 2005), 5.

58. Bonnie Wheeler, "Grief in Avalon: Sir Palomydes' Psychic Pain," in *Grief and Gender 700–1700*, ed. Jennifer C. Vaught and Lynne Dickson Bruckner (London: Palgrave, 2003), 66.

59. Livingston and DeVries, *Battle of Crécy*, 340.

60. Katharine Goodland, "'Us for to wepe no man may let': Resistant Female Grief in the Medieval English Lazarus Plays," in Perfetti, *Representation of Women's Emotions*, 112.

61. Beaumont, "On the Crécy Dead," lines 46, 40.

62. Beaumont, "On the Crécy Dead," line 49.

63. Rima Devereaux, *Constantinople and the West in Medieval French Literature: Renewal and Utopia* (Cambridge: D. S. Brewer, 2012), 84.

64. Goodland, "'Us for to wepe no man may let,'" 93.

65. Beaumont, "On the Crécy Dead," lines 59–62.

66. Beaumont, "On the Crécy Dead," line 17.

67. F. R. P. Akehurst, "Good Name, Reputation, and Notoriety in French Customary Law," in Fenster and Smail, *Fama*, 78.

68. Mia Korpiola and Anu Lahtinen, *Cultures of Death and Dying in Medieval and Early Modern Europe* (Helsinki: Helsinki Collegium for Advanced Studies, 2015), 3–4; Daisy Delogu, "'Ala grant temps de douleur languissant': Grief and Mourning in Girart d'Amiens' *Istoire le Roy Charlemaine*," *Speculum* 93, no. 1 (2018): 1–26; Angela Warner, "'Doel' in Situ: The Contextual and Corporeal Landscape of Grief in *La Chanson de Roland*," in *Affective and Emotional Economies in Medieval and Early Modern Europe*, ed. A. Marculescu and C. L. Morand Métivier (London: Palgrave, 2018), 211–26.

69. Korpiola and Lahtinen, *Cultures of Death and Dying*, 3–4.

70. Beaumont, "On the Crécy Dead," lines 26–29.
71. Beaumont, "On the Crécy Dead," lines 28–29.
72. Beaumont, "On the Crécy Dead," line 79.
73. Robert Rouse, "Reading Ruins: Arthurian Caerleon and the Untimely Architecture of History," *Arthuriana* 23, no. 1 (2013): 40–51, 41.
74. Jim Bradbury, *The Medieval Siege* (1992; repr., Woodbridge: Boydell, 1998), 76.
75. Beaumont, "On the Crécy Dead," line 38.
76. Beaumont, "On the Crécy Dead," lines 50–53.
77. Joelle Rollo-Koster, *Death in Medieval Europe* (Abingdon: Routledge, 2016), 172–73.
78. C. M. Woolgar, *The Senses in Late Medieval England* (New Haven, CT: Yale University Press, 2006), 125; Karen Cherewatuk, "The Saint's Life of Sir Launcelot: Hagiography and the Conclusion of Malory's 'Morte Darthur,'" *Arthuriana* 5, no. 1 (1995): 72. For more on the odor of sanctity, see Susan Ashbrook Harvey, *Scenting Salvation: Ancient Christianity and the Olfactory Imagination* (Berkeley: University of California Press, 2006).
79. Corinne Saunders, "Mind, Body and Affect in Medieval English Arthurian Romance," in *Emotions in Medieval Arthurian Literature: Body, Mind, Voice*, ed. Frank Brandsma, Carolyne Larrington, and Corinne Saunders (Cambridge: D. S. Brewer, 2015), 34; Rik Van Nieuwenhove, Robert Faesen, and Helen Rolfson, *Late Medieval Mysticism of the Low Countries* (New York: Paulist Press, 2008), 206; Denise N. Baker, "Julian of Norwich and the Varieties of Middle English Mystical Discourse," in *A Companion to Julian of Norwich*, ed. Liz Herbert McAvoy (Cambridge: D. S. Brewer, 2008), 57.
80. Michelle Karnes, *Imagination, Meditation, and Cognition in the Middle Ages* (Chicago: University of Chicago Press, 2011), 26.
81. Vincent Gillespie, "The Senses in Literature: The Textures of Perception," in *A Cultural History of the Senses in the Middle Ages*, ed. Richard G. Newhauser, 2 vols. (London: Bloomsbury Academic, 2014), 2:156.
82. Damien Boquet and Piroska Nagy, "Medieval Sciences of Emotions during the Eleventh to Thirteenth Centuries: An Intellectual History," *Osiris* 31, no. 1 (2016): 39.
83. Gillespie, "The Senses in Literature," 173.
84. Livingston and DeVries, *Battle of Crécy*, 210.
85. Beaumont, "On the Crécy Dead," lines 424–32.
86. Charmaz and Milligan, "Grief," 517.
87. Jennifer Spinks and Charles Zika, *Disaster, Death and the Emotions in the Shadow of the Apocalypse, 1400–1700* (London: Palgrave, 2016), 3–4.
88. Lawton, *Voice in Later Medieval English*, 104–30.
89. Beaumont, "On the Crécy Dead," line 359.
90. Beaumont, "On the Crécy Dead," lines 348, 378.
91. Beaumont, "On the Crécy Dead," lines 371–73.
92. Nigel Saul, *Chivalry in Medieval England* (Cambridge, MA: Harvard University Press, 2011), 348–49.

93. *Guerre mortelle* was indicated by the unfurling of the Oriflamme, signalling that prisoners would not be taken. Saul, 355; Kaeuper, *Chivalry and Violence*, 172.

94. Michel Zink, *Froissart et le temps* (Paris: Presses Universitaires de France, 1998), 52.

95. Taylor, *Chivalry and the Ideals of Knighthood*, 12.

96. Taylor, *Chivalry and the Ideals of Knighthood*, 276.

97. Kaeuper, *Chivalry and Violence*, 286–88.

98. Beaumont, "On the Crécy Dead," lines 87–251.

Chapter Two

"Je hé guerre, point ne la doit prisier"

Emotions, War, and Trauma in the Poetry of Charles of Orléans

Charles-Louis Morand-Métivier

Many tragic events marked the reign of Charles VI of France (1368–1422, crowned in 1380); among them were the massacre of French knights at Nicopolis[1] in 1396 as they attempted to prevent the advance of the Ottoman armies and the defeat of the French army on French soil by the English troops of Henry V at Agincourt in 1415. Those who did not die were brought to England as prisoners, and many never returned to France. The kingdom was also in a long-standing conflict with the Catholic Church, as the Great Schism (1378–1417) was tearing Christianity in two, with one pope in Rome and the other, recognized by France, in Avignon.[2] Lastly, starting in 1392, King Charles VI began suffering bouts of madness that would last until his death. The crisis of governance brought about by his disease eventually devolved into a civil war between the Armagnacs (supporters of Louis of Orléans, brother of the king) and the Burgundians (supporters of Philip of Burgundy, one of the most powerful uncles of Charles VI and the Duke of Burgundy). This war escalated until the assassination of Louis of Orléans on November 23, 1407, a murder ordered by John the Fearless, who had become the new Duke of Burgundy when his father died in 1404.[3]

Charles of Orléans (1394–1465), the son of Louis of Orléans, was among the many knights captured at Agincourt.[4] He spent twenty-five years in detention in England, only released in 1440.[5] If his years in prison put an end to his political aspirations, they were fertile for his literary creation. In this chapter, I will focus on how Charles of Orléans inscribed the emotions linked to the trauma of his forced exile in his poetry, where he created an emotional landscape of England and France, and thus restructured the traumatic experiences of his forced captivity. Even before he was made prisoner, the life of Charles of Orléans had been eventful and highly emotional. He was only thirteen when his father was killed. His mother, Valentina Visconti, was not only completely devastated by her husband's death[6] but was also slandered by many, who saw her as a witch responsible for the king's disease.[7] As a result, she and Charles quickly moved out of Paris, a decision that could very well be perceived as self-imposed exile.[8] These traumatic events had a deeply emotional impact on the young prince. Furthermore, to Charles's frustration, Charles VI never pushed the Duke of Burgundy to apologize for his role in the death of Louis of Orléans.[9]

What did twenty-five years of captivity do to Charles? His time in prison did not, per se, start his literary career.[10] It was, however, an activity that developed tremendously during his stay in England, as most of his ballads were written during his captivity. Prison writing, as Joanna Summers argues, presents the prisoner-author with "a shared experience of alienation"; another important element in the development of their persona is the uncertainty of their fate: "The prisoner is objected to, subject to, and opposed by others who may decide his fate."[11] Jean-Marc Varant underlines how detention is, by definition, considered detrimental to the idea of creation: "Le poète en prison est affronté à une situation qui est par nature contraire à celle où la création poétique peut naître et s'épanouir" (the poet in prison is exposed to a situation that is inherently contrary to the natural condition for poetic composition).[12]

Charles's imprisonment came after the traumatic defeat at Agincourt, nearly twenty years after another tremendous military defeat for the French troops at Nicopolis. The whole population felt the repercussions of the Nicopolis massacre.[13] The *Chronique du religieux de Saint Denis*, for instance, covers the aftermath of the battle in many chapters, and emphasizes how it shocked both the population and the king.[14] The Bourgeois de Paris, in his *Journal*, explains that the battle was the most terrible debacle ever for France: "Oncques puis que Dieu fut né ne fut faite telle prise en France par Sarrasins ni par autres" (never, since God was born, was such an action committed by the Saracens or any others).[15] Likewise, Enguerrand de Monstrelet, in his *Chroniques*, stresses that the battle "laisse les François en grand' douleur et tristesse pour la perte et destruction de leurs gens" (leaves the French in great pain and sadness following the destruction of their fellow French people).[16] Monstrelet also provides a long list of the most important princes who died or who were made prisoners following the "piteuse et douloureuse journée" (pitiful and sad day).[17] These authors stress the emotional toll on the whole population, and how the French were profoundly saddened and disgusted by the defeat. I would argue that the battle of Agincourt likewise induced a response that could be considered trauma, as it was felt by and had repercussions for a large majority of the population. Whether trauma can be applied to past events, and whether the use of the word in its modern sense is possible and acceptable, has been debated. Wendy J. Turner and Christina Lee have demonstrated that we can view the past through the modern lens of trauma.[18] Jenny Edkins furthermore explains that trauma could be defined as a set of violent actions imposed on groups or people sharing the same norms (whether emotional, societal, religious, etc.).[19] I have previously argued for the use of trauma, based on its very etymology of "wound,"[20] as a term to address painful experiences in the Middle Ages.[21] I understand trauma as the direct, longing responses that occur after a momentous event—in Charles's case, one that was horrendously violent and horrific in nature—disrupts life as it was supposed to occur. Jeffrey C. Alexander argues that trauma occurs "when members of a collectivity feel they have been subjected to a horrendous event that leaves indelible marks upon their group consciousness, marking their memories forever and changing their future identity in fundamental and irrevocable ways."[22] These traumatic events, then, disrupt what should have been "normal" lives, thus unnerving those who suffer them: "Human beings need security, order, love, and connection. If something happens that sharply undermines these needs, it hardly seems surprising . . . that people will be traumatized as a result."[23] The events of the late fourteenth and early fifteenth centuries in which Charles found himself embedded offer a framework for the analysis of trauma as presented in his poetry. Indeed, the whole kingdom was traumatized on the macro level by the terrible massacre that happened at Agincourt, with most people knowing someone who died or was made prisoner. Through his imprisonment, Charles's poetry proposes the representation, on his micro level, of the trauma experienced by the kingdom, and installs the conditions for a traumatic understanding of Charles's experience in England. This trauma is represented in his poetry (mainly the ballads) by the highly emotional development of his daily experience, through which he narrates the evolution of his imprisonment. The traumatic wound that is at the core of his poetry, then, is presented as both that of the lost battle itself as well as the actual imprisonment. The two aspects of his traumatic experience complement and feed each other, and are the main fuel for Charles's poetic creation.

Scholarship on Charles of Orléans and (as well as in) captivity is abundant. Jean-Marc Varaut, while arguing that his poetry cannot be considered jail poetry, nevertheless underlines the important themes of regret, complaint, and frustration.[24] Catherine Atwood explains that the parallel between prison of love and prison of war, a common trope in medieval literature, is an important trope in Charles's poetry.[25] For Jean-Claude Mühlethaler, the ballads written in captivity are infused with the experience of jail; however, he argues that they are still primarily courtly ballads.[26] Céline Cecchetto believes that Charles of Orléans's poetry of exile demonstrates how the poet expresses his forced detachment from his location; she nevertheless argues that this poetry is not aggressive.[27] I will direct my analysis to the emotions of his poetry; however, I will not focus on his love poetry. Rather, I examine how Charles presents his feelings about his captivity. Although most of his works have no direct references to his exile and imprisonment, his whole poetic œuvre in England is obviously laden with many events from his life in France. His poems, and specifically his ballads, are an opportunity for him to express his traumatic experiences and create a narrative of his bereavement in England.

MISSING FRANCE AND THE TRAUMA OF DISTANCE

The life of Charles of Orléans fed his poetic experience. However, rarely does he directly inscribe in words the various events that affected his life in his poetry. Where and how, then, is trauma to be found in his poetry? First, Charles introduces himself, by name and by action, in his works; he is "Charles, Duc d'Orlians" (Charles is his name, the Duke of Orléans).[28] He also stresses that he is a member of the French royal family and that he composed numerous ballads dedicated to friends and cousins, such as the duke of Nevers (Burgundy).[29] Charles, in his works, presents two personae. On the one hand, he is a traditional love poet, who continued to compose in captivity the courtly poetry he had been writing since the *Retenue d'amours*; on the other, he is also a poet who wrote more personal, political pieces, in which he discusses his imprisonment and his longing for France. Likewise, the emotions that Charles presents are twofold: those traditionally associated with courtly love (love, sadness, melancholy) and those he felt more deeply, echoing his situation as a prisoner. Pilar Boué underlines the importance of the "nostalgie de la patrie" (nostalgia for the fatherland) that she argues Charles reinforced and made more personal when he associated it with the traditional trope of the lovelorn poet.[30] As a knight and a member of the royal family, his life and essence were naturally linked to the very fact of "being" France. Captivity tore apart this secular relationship and, I believe, wounded the very essence of Charles's connection to France. The kingdom is indeed what fuels his poetic persona; due to his forced stay in England (Mary-Jo Arn underscores that England was not keen on freeing such an important prisoner)[31] and as the result of being torn between two languages, two literary traditions, and two courts (one he had been forced to leave and one where he was forced to be a guest), France became both a memory filled with longing for what was and what could have been as well as a utopia. This duality is represented in what I would coin the "absent presence" or "present absence" of France and of any reference to Agincourt in his poems; a melancholic remembrance of what the kingdom was and was not, a kingdom completely out of reach for the poet and which, henceforth, feeds the voice of his trauma.[32] The relative lack of any mention of France makes its rare appearances particularly important. Indeed, once France is mentioned, like in the "Complainte de France," the emotionality of the *ressenti*—or, that which is felt by the poet—is heightened, because the emotional impact of the poetry is direct, total, and frankly transmits Charles's emotional reality.

In its first stanza, the "Complainte de France" unfolds the emotionality of Charles's relation to France and England:

> En regardant vers le païs de France
> Un jour m'avint a Dovre sur la mer
> Qu'il me souvint de la *doulce plaisance*
> Que souloye ou dit paÿs trouver
> Si commençay de *cueur* a *souspirer*
> Combien certes que *grant bien* me faisoit
> De voir France que *mon cueur amer* doit.[33]

> While gazing toward the country of France
> One day at Dover by the sea
> I recalled a *sweet pleasure*
> I used to find in that country
> And so from the heart I began to *sigh*
> Even though it certainly did me *much good*
> To look at France, which *my heart should love*.[34]

Remembrance, the core of this poem, is crucial to consider here in order to understand how Charles develops notions of longing. What he remembers from the kingdom does not bring him solace but rather amplifies the sadness and unrest he feels, reminding him that his home is very close but also that it is where his life changed for the worse. Dover was a major port of entry to England; Charles arrived there, as a prisoner, on November 16, 1415.[35] When he was taken back to Dover—in 1433, when the "Complainte de France" was written—he had been a prisoner for eighteen years. Dover could then be considered a pathway from and to a different life. The rhyme between "païs de France" (country of France) and "doulce plaisance" (sweet pleasure), for instance, exemplifies his relation to France: it is very close, both physically and mentally, yet also very far. He is faced with the memories of his arrival and also with the physical presence of France.[36] The "Complainte," I believe, proposes a representation of what could be defined as "wistful happiness," as presented in the last three verses. The happiness and joy upon seeing France ("*grant bien* me faisoit" [it did me much good]) also gave him much sadness ("de *cueur* a *souspirer*" [sighing from the heart]). The trauma of the absence is made even worse by the fact that Charles himself realizes that thinking about France is not healthy for him: "Ie m'avisay que c'estoit non savance / De telz souspirs dedens mon cueur garder" (I realized that it was not wise / To keep such woes inside my heart). The "Complainte" then slowly changes into a more general plea for peace, around which Charles develops his ideas. Peace is presented as the grand scheme toward which Charles must strive; he seems to allude to the fact that his longing for France is therefore problematic for the realization of this ultimate goal. The ballad that follows (ballad 115) is a strong appeal to the Virgin Mary for peace: "Priés pour paix, douce Vierge Marie" (Pray for peace, sweet Virgin Mary).[37] In it, all are criticized for their lack of action to end the war: the prelates (stanza 2), princes and royals (stanza 3), and the people (stanza 4); the final stanza focuses on lovers and demonstrates the adverse impact that war can have on their lives, notably leaving them in dire straits ("Guerre vous tient la bourse degarnie!" [War empties your pockets!]).[38] Charles chastises all the components of the body politic because their actions—or lack thereof—prevent the Virgin from aiding the achievement of peace, as exemplified in the refrain. The stanza that focuses on lovers here is particularly interesting. Charles explains that war will eventually distract the wives and companions of those who fight away from them: "Qui maintesfoiz fait leurs vouloirs tourner" (Which changes their minds many times).[39] From the king to the simple lover, all have their responsibility, himself included. Indeed, in his reference to the lovers, it is hard not to see a nod to his own condition as a courtly poet. In these two poems, Charles therefore proposes a double emotional take on his exile. On the one hand, as a man who is far from his country, he feels a profound sadness and longing when he returns to the place that first marked the location of his exile; on the other, he also recognizes the need to push his own emotions and problems aside in order to put the greater good and, most notably, the greater necessity of the time—peace between the two kingdoms—above anything else. Emotions are moderated from the micro level (his own personal reaction to his exile) to the macro level (the need to push personal problems aside in order to prioritize peace over personal issues). Carole Bauguion has demonstrated how Charles diverts the tropes of courtly love for his own interests;[40] likewise, I believe that the traditional tropes of most of his poems serve as gateways to his own emotional poetry about his time in captivity. The appeals to peace, where Charles puts all his focus, are soon replaced by ballads in which his emotions are far less mitigated.

Charles's imprisonment, nonetheless, should not be considered through the eyes of a twenty-first-century reader. The medieval prison for nobles, as an institution that prevented an individual from enjoying freedom, should also not be seen as the same institution as the Foucauldian space of punishment. Many scholars have described it as a place—both temporal and locational— in which Charles had to remain, and which he tried to make as bearable as possible. He was authorized to receive visitors, could communicate with outsiders, had servants, and had his precious library with him, as it had been sent to him from France in the early years of his imprisonment. Charles argued that his many years in England had caused him to speak better English than French when he was eventually freed. However, the calls and pleas for freedom should not be considered the ultimate truth that Charles wished to convey. As the poems were written during his stay in England, I believe that they represent a wide array of his emotional reactions to his captivity; just as his own emotions fluctuated, their representation in his poems also shifts.

POETRY OF NATIONAL AND PERSONAL POLITICS

Even though he was a captive, Charles was also a royal prince of France, born to be a figure of authority. While his captivity prevented him from actively participating in the political life of the kingdom, his poems were nevertheless conceived as a way to remain present as a political figure, even though he was physically absent. In ballad 122, Charles reminds everyone that he is not dead, despite rumors that might have said otherwise: "Nouvelles ont courru en France / Par mains lieux que j'estoye mort. . . . Si fais a toutes gens savoir / Qu'encore est vive la souris!" (The news in France was / That I was dead. . . . But I want to let everyone know / That the mouse is alive and well!).[41] This reminder (directed toward those who wished or believed he was dead) is central to the first stanzas of the ballad. There, he opposes those who had pleasure in thinking he was dead ("Dont avoient peu desplaisance / Aucuns qui me hayent fort" [And this gave but little displeasure / To some who unjustly despise me]) with those who had empathy for him and were relieved and full of joy that he was alive ("Autres en ont eu desconfort / Qui m'ayment de loyal vouloir / Comme mes bons et vrais amis" [Some were distressed / Those who love me with a faithful will / Like my fine and true friends]).[42] He is doing very well ("Je n'ay eu ne mal ne grievance / Dieu mercy, mais suis sain et fort" [I've had neither ill nor pain / Thank God, but am healthy and strong])[43] and is still young and vigorous—despite the fact that he is aging: "Ieunesse sur moy a puissance / Mais vieillesse fait son effort / De m'avoir en sa gouvernance" (Youth has power over me / But old age makes an effort / To keep me under her power).[44]

This poem, even though it is meant to prove that Charles is still present in the world of politics, is nevertheless also a statement of the implacable weight of time. This Pyrrhic victory of sorts—as he is still "dead" because of his absence and cannot have any impact on the politics of France—is central to a group of "political" poems such as ballad 124. The emotions of the envoy of the poem (its final stanza), although largely positive, nevertheless also imply that the end of his imprisonment will not be immediate:

> Resveillez vous en *joyeux* souvenir,
> Car j'ay *espoir* qu'encore je vous voye
> Et moy aussi, en *confort* et *Plaisir*
> Par bonne pay que brief Dieu nous envoye.
>
> Awaken yourself to joyful memory,
> For I have hope to see you again,
> And me as well, in comfort and pleasure
> With good peace—may God send it soon.[45]

Charles is hopeful that a potential return to France would allow him to see his friends again. Such a return would be a healing touch that would finally soothe the many years of trauma from both the defeat and the imprisonment. However, because the wounds of Agincourt and prison are deeply ingrained in him, he also considers that he might yet again be disappointed; he wants his friends and family to think about their happy memories ("joyeux souvenirs") of him, which similarly expresses the uncertainty of his return.

During his captivity, Charles conversed with Philip III, Duke of Burgundy, through poems. It may seem incongruous that Charles developed such an epistolary relationship with Philip. He was indeed the son of John the Fearless, who was directly responsible for the death of his father. However, the civil war in France ended in 1435, when Philip signed the Treaty of Arras with King Charles VII.[46] Pierre Champion, for instance, has examined the political dimension of the poems that Charles and Philip exchanged as the former was trying to persuade the latter to use his power and connections to have him freed from England.[47] Because the traumatic experience of Charles's imprisonment in England was caused by the war between France and England, trying to find a peaceful solution to it could not only lead to his eventual liberation from jail but also (and more importantly) operate as a sort of closure that would ease the pain of all his years in captivity, an assuaging of the great anguish of imprisonment. Even though their ballads unfurl around political questions, their exchange is quite emotional, and both men turn to their feelings when writing to one another, addressing each other in overtly sentimental terms. In ballad 127 Philip is hailed by Charles as "mon compaignon, frere et cousin" (my companion, brother, and cousin);[48] in ballad 131, he reiterates that he is "mon frère et mon compaignon" (my brother and my companion).[49]

Likewise, Philip designates Charles in ballad 127 as "mon maistre et amy sans changier" (My master and friend beyond any alteration).[50] Coming from Charles, this could be seen as a classic example of encomiastic poetry; he needed as much help as he could get from powerful allies in order to find a solution to his imprisonment. Philip is equally invested in presenting Charles as someone with whom he feels connected. The men were first cousins once removed; their relationship, as exposed in their back-and-forth discussion in the ballads, thus demonstrates a profoundly shared bond between them. Charles, for instance, acknowledges himself as Philip's vassal, even though his imprisonment prevents him from truly being Philip's vassal. During all the ballads of his "conversation" with Philip, his tone turns increasingly emotional, wholly devoting himself to him, as in ballad 129: "Comme tout vostre entierement / De cueur, de corps et de puissance" (As someone entirely yours / With heart, body, and might).[51] His dedication to the duke is so profound that he gives him his heart: "Et sans plus despendre langage / A cours mots, plaise vous penser / Que vous laisse mon coeur en gage / Pour tousjours, sans jamais fausser" (And without spending more speech / My words brief, may you be pleased to think / I leave my heart with you as a warrant / For always, never proving false).[52] The heart, the center of emotions, is naturally associated with love; by dedicating it to Philip, Charles shows him how devoted he is to Philip's service, as well as to him personally. Charles, in other words, gives his all to Philip, so much so that Charles's allegiance has shifted: "Tout Bourgongnon sui vrayement / De cueur, de corps et de puissance" (I am truly all Burgundian / With heart, body, and might).[53] Allegiances in the Middle Ages were powerful, and not made in vain. The emotional bond that is present in this dialogue should be seen as such, and not as a mere attempt to garner the good will of the powerful Duke of Burgundy, who himself also offers vivid evidence of his sentimental bond with Charles.

Philip was a powerful man; Burgundy had been an important actor in the Hundred Years' War and had shared interests with both France and England. During the reigns of Charles VI and Charles VII, Philip II and John, respectively the grandfather and the father of Philip III, were crucial figures in the life of the kingdom. Philip III's tenure, however, was not as interventionist as those of his forebears.[54] As such, his reaction to the poems addressed to him by Charles is warm, and echoes the emotional pleas of his cousin. In his response to ballad 128 (the first sent by Charles), Philip immediately explains that he will do his best to get Charles out of prison as soon as possible: "Je vous asseure, pour tout voir / Qu'en vo fait n'auroit nul dangier / Mais par deça, sans atatrgier / Vous verroye hors de prison / Quitte du tout" (I assure you, in all truth / You would be facing no threat / For on this side, with no delay / I should see you out of prison / Free from everything).[55] In ballad 130, Philip's response directly echoes the previous ballad by starting it with the sentence that finishes the previous one: "De cueur, de corps et de puissance" (By heart, body, and power). Philip is as devoted to Charles as Charles is to him; this devotion can be seen through an allusion to France by the Duke of Burgundy. He urges Charles not to forget the disastrous state of the kingdom:

> Ne mectés point en oubliance
> L'estat et le gouvernement
> De la noble maison de France
> Qui se maintient piteusement.
>
> Do not forget in the least
> The state and condition
> Of the noble house of France,
> Which is in a pitiful state.[56]

France, in dismal condition, is defended here by a person who represented not long ago one of its strongest enemies. The emotional bond he shares with Charles extends to France, and he insists on the necessity of lasting peace between both kingdoms and England in order to enable the return of prisoners. However, he also puts a direct emotional reference to his cousin in the envoy of the ballad:

> Or prions Dieu, par sa doulceur,
> Qu'a vous delivrer se dispose,
> Car trop avez souffert douleur
> Quoy que nul dye ne depose.
>
> Now let us pray that God in His grace
> Determines to deliver you,
> For you have suffered too much grief,
> No matter what anyone says or affirms.[57]

Two emotional ideas are opposed here: the benevolence and love of God, and Charles's pain in captivity. Philip knows how Charles suffers, and makes himself a witness to this fact, whatever people may say otherwise. Charles was very aware of the powerful response he received from Burgundy, and that Philip was one of the people who could truly enable him to recover his freedom. Ballad 135, the last he wrote in England as a prisoner, is dedicated to his benefactor, where Charles acknowledges Philip and his role in Charles's release: "Beau frere, je vous remercie, / Car aidié m'avez grandement" (Fair brother, I thank you / For you have given me much help) and Charles later emphasizes his emotional dedication to his benefactor: "Et desserviray loyaument / A ceulx qui m'ont de bon courage / Aidié" (And I will faithfully serve / Those who, with a good heart, have / Helped me).[58] But it is a ballad, written after Charles's return, that contains the most intense examples of his emotional commitment to Philip.

Ballad 136 was written as Charles had finally been freed from his twenty-five years of incarceration. He admits that his freedom and return to France have put him in a situation where he is now, as he says to Philip: "Avec la gent vostre ennemie" (Among the people of your enemies).[59] The whole ballad is organized around the opposing themes of dissimulation and truth; Charles reveals that he will have to present a double emotional personality. Because he is a member of the royal family, he must officially not show any sign of friendship for the Duke of Burgundy. Indeed, he must pretend to hate the duke ("Faignant que ne vous aiyme mie" [Feigning I love you not at all]), slandering his name in order to please Charles's entourage ("Tous maulx de vous je voiz disant / Pour aveugler leur faulse envye" [I go about only speaking ill of you / In order to block their false envy]).[60] He advises Philip to behave likewise: "Faignez envers moy mal talent" (Pretend you think ill of me).[61] Two emotional behaviors are opposed here: on the one hand, feigned hatred, and on the other, benevolence and even love. Indeed, Charles clearly indicates that his true feelings for the duke are very strong: "Faignant que je vous ayme mye" (Feigning I love you not at all); "Que je seray toute ma vye / Vostre loyaumant, sans faulser" (That all my life I will be / Yours faithfully, never to prove false) (this last line is the refrain of the ballad); "Je vous ayme tant" (I love you so much); "A celle fin que nul n'espye / Nostre amour" (So that no man might sense / Our love); "Faictes que Bonne Foy lye / Nos cuers" (Yet make certain that Good Faith binds / Our hearts).[62] This abundance of words referring to love leaves no doubt about Charles's profound attachment. He also swears on his honor that he will always be faithful to Philip, as he explains in the envoy:

> Dieu me fiere d'espidimie
> Et ma part es cieulx je renye,
> Se jamais vous povez trouver
> Que me faigne par tromperie,
> Vostre loyaumant, sans faulser.
>
> May God strike me with sickness,
> Even as I renounce my place in heaven,
> If you are ever able to discover
> That, intending to deceive, I am pretending to be
> Yours faithfully, never to prove false.[63]

Calling on God, Charles presents his feelings as completely faithful. Philip and he share the same blood, the same bond to France. Even though he is back from his quarter century in prison, I believe that, through these lines, Charles shows us how profoundly traumatic this experience was for him, as he feels a need to express his loyalty and love to his cousin for fear that Charles might be considered, because of his long time in England, not totally French. Even at home, England remains deeply present in his political works; now that he is back in France, the trauma experienced throughout those years could be seen, I believe, as some sort of PTSD.

Ballad 76 was written after Charles returned to France. Indeed, the sentence "Et t'a rendu Guyenne et Normandie" (And returned both Guyenne and Normandy to you)[64] makes it clear that the ballad dates from after 1453. After the Battle of Castillon (July 17, 1453) and the defeat of the English armies, their territorial possessions, including Guyenne, were returned to France.[65] Back in France, far from his years in prison, Charles is nevertheless still emotionally connected to that time, and presents his reaction toward England in this ballad. Here, the English have "plus couraige ne puissance" (no power or might left); their behavior is impious, as they behave like witches on the Sabbath: "Et les Anglois menoient leur sabat / En grans pompes, baubans et tiranie" (And the English wreaked their havoc / With great pomp, pride, and tyranny). They are also known to be traitors: "N'ont pas Anglois souvent leurs roys traÿs?" (Have not the English often betrayed their kings?). The emotional description of the English is thus negative, as they are presented as mean, hateful, and treacherous; the rhyme between "mauvais langaige" [ugly tongue] and "oultraige" [do . . . wrong] reinforces this poor image. They do not respect their sovereign, and even God has a strong aversion to them: "On apparçoit que de Dieu sont haÿs" (It is evident that they are hated by God). In this poem, the moderation and calls for peace are gone; the encomiastic dimension of this ballad is predominant. The English, portrayed as evil and hated by God, are placed in opposition to those who are powerful and loved by God, that is, the King of France. Indeed, God himself is responsible for the change in the king's fortune. Previous attacks by the king were unsuccessful because of his behavior; he was a sinner ("Lors estoies ainsi que fut Taÿs / Pecheresse" [Then you were like Thaïs, / A sinner]) and was punished by God himself ("Enclouse fut par divine ordonance" [Was shut in by divine command]). Due to his own actions, the king's emotional state was despondent, but his return to God granted him joy once again: "Or a tourné Dieu ton dueil en esbat" (Now God has changed your suffering to joy).[66] Even though this ballad was written many years after Charles had returned to France, he still maintains strong memories from his imprisonment in England. The king's glorification and Charles's strong revulsion for the English shows how his poems are cast under an emotional veil that fluctuates greatly. Charles's emotional state—as either free or captive—and his locale, as a captive throughout his time in England or in France, are intertwined in the writing of his poetry.

Charles of Orléans reimagines the traditional trope of love poetry as a testimony of his own life in detention. From the sadness of distance to the hope of potential resolution, from love for his benefactor to his anger against England, Charles presents an emotional autobiography that does not so much describe the events he experienced in captivity as explore how the emotions of his captivity affected his life and his writing. From trauma to relief, these twenty-five years, if they did not "create" his poetic persona, nevertheless molded it profoundly.

WORKS CITED

Alexander, Jeffrey C. *Trauma: A Social Theory*. Cambridge: Polity Press, 2012.
Arn, Mary-Jo. "Manuscrit français, manuscrit anglais: De la ductilité du propos poétique." In *Lectures de Charles d'Orléans: Les ballades*, edited by Denis Hüe, 19–42. Rennes: Presses universitaires de Rennes, 2010.
Atiya, Aziz. *The Crusade of Nicopolis*. London: Methuen, 1934.
Atwood, Catherine. "Prison d'amour, prison de guerre: Service ou servage? L'exemple de Charles d'Orléans." In *Être poète au temps de Charles d'Orléans (XVe siècle)*, edited by Hélène Basso and Michèle Gally, 210–22. Avignon: Éditions universitaires d'Avignon, 2012.
Bauguion, Carole. "Charles d'Orléans: La plume et l'épée; Étude des métaphores toponymiques rimées par le prisonnier d'Azincourt en exil à Albion." *Dalhousie French Studies* 104 (Winter 2014): 45–60.
Blumenfeld-Kosinski, Renate. *Poets, Saints, and Visionaries of the Great Schism, 1378–1417*. State College, PA: Pennsylvania State University Press, 2006.
Boué, Pilar Andrade. "Quelques aspect de la Merencolie de Charles d'Orléans." *Thélème: Revista complutense de estudios franceses* 15 (2000): 167–77.
Castarède, Jean. *Histoire de la Guyenne et de la Gascogne*. Paris: France-Empire, 1997.
Cecchetto, Céline. "Charles d'Orléans et Joachim Du Bellay." In *Écritures de l'exil*, edited by Danièle Sabbah, 103–17. Pessac: Presses Universitaires de Bordeaux, 2009.
Champion, Pierre. *Vie de Charles d'Orléans (1394–1465)*. Paris: Honoré Champion, 2010.
Charles d'Orléans. *Ballades et rondeaux*. Edited and translated by Jean Claude Mühlethaler. Paris: Librairie Générale française, 1992.
Chronique du Religieux de Saint Denis. Vol. 5. Edited and translated by M. L. Bellaguet. Paris: Éditions du comité de travaux historiques et scientifiques, 1994.
Clauzel, Denis, Charles Giry-Deloison, and Christophe Leduc, eds. *Arras et la diplomatie européenne, XVe–XVIe siècles*. Arras: Artois presses université, 1999.
Colas, Émile. *Valentine Visconti duchesse d'Orléans*. Paris: Plon, 1911.
Deschamps, Eustache. *Oeuvres complètes*. Vol. 8. Edited by Gaston Raynaud. Paris: Firmin Didot, 1893.

Edkins, Jenny. *Trauma and the Memory of Politics*. Cambridge: Cambridge University Press, 2003.
Fox, John, and Mary-Jo Arn, eds. and trans. *Poetry of Charles d'Orléans and His Circle: A Critical Edition of BnF MS. fr. 25458, Charles d'Orléans's Personal Manuscript*. Tempe, AZ: ACMRS, 2010.
Guenée, Bernard. *Un meurtre, une société: L'assassinat du duc d'Orléans, 23 novembre 1407*. Paris: Gallimard, 1992.
Journal d'un bourgeois de Paris de 1405 à 1449. Edited by Colette Beaune. Paris: Librairie générale de France, 1990.
Klosowska, Anna. "Tearsong: Valentine Visconti's Inverted Stoicism." In "On the Love of Commentary," ed. N. Masciandio and Scott Wilson. Special issue, *Glossator* 5 (2011): 173–98.
McLeod, Enid. *Charles of Orléans, Prince and Poet*. New York: Viking Press, 1969.
Monstrelet, Enguerrand de. *Chroniques d'Enguerrand de Monstrelet*. Edited by J. A. C. Buchon. Paris: Desrez, 1836.
Morand-Métivier, Charles-Louis. "Creation and Union through Death and Massacre: The Crusade of Nicopolis and Philippe de Mézières' *Epistre lamentable et consolatoire*." In Turner and Lee, *Trauma in Medieval Society*, 298–319.
Morawski, Joseph. *Proverbes français antérieurs au XVe siècle*. Paris: Champion, 1925.
Mühlethaler, Jean-Claude. *Charles d'Orléans: Un lyrisme entre Moyen-âge et modernité*. Paris: Classique Garnier, 2010.
Pizan, Christine de. *The Book of the City of Ladies*. Translated by Earl Jeffrey Richards. New York: Persea Books, 1998.
Poirion, Daniel. *Le lexique de Charles d'Orléans dans les ballades*. Geneva: Droz, 1952.
Summers, Joanna. *Late Medieval Prison Writing and the Politics of Autobiography*. Oxford: Clarendon Press, 2004.
Turner, Wendy J., and Christina Lee, eds. *Trauma in Medieval Society*. Turnhout: Brill, 2018.
Varaut, Jean-Marc. *Poètes en prison, de Charles d'Orléans à Jean Genet*. Paris: Perrin, 1989.

NOTES

1. Currently known as Nikopol in Bulgaria. Aziz Atiya, *The Crusade of Nicopolis* (London: Methuen, 1934).

2. Renate Blumenfeld-Kosinski, *Poets, Saints, and Visionaries of the Great Schism, 1378–1417* (University Park: Pennsylvania State University Press, 2006).

3. Bernard Guenée, *Un meurtre, une société: L'assassinat du duc d'Orléans, 23 novembre 1407* (Paris: Gallimard, 1992). John the Fearless would himself be assassinated on September 10, 1419, in Montereau during a tense meeting with the Dauphin.

4. Enid McLeod, *Charles of Orléans, Prince and Poet* (New York: Viking Press, 1969). McLeod notably explains how Charles was captured at the end of the battle,

completely unwounded: "Charles of Orléans . . . had been discovered, as had many others, under one of the piles of corpses" (69).

5. The conditions of his detention were fairly loose. Indeed, he was not locked in a cell. During these twenty-five years, he was held in different places: in the Tower of London, and in Pontefract Castle.

6. She is notably known for adopting, in widowhood, a new emblem of a fountain or tearsong, to which she inscribed a new devise: "Rien ne m'est plus, plus ne m'est rien" (literally, "Nothing is ever anything for me anymore"). Anna Klosowska, "Tearsong: Valentine Visconti's Inverted Stoicism," in "On the Love of Commentary," ed. N. Masciandio and Scott Wilson, special issue, *Glossator* 5 (2011): 173–98.

7. McLeod explains, "Louis' enemies began to attribute Valentina's ability to soothe the patient to some kind of witchcraft, designed to get him in her power in order to further her husband's ambitions." *Charles of Orléans*, 16.

8. McLeod explains that, in spite of her unpopularity, Valentina could still count on the support of political and literary figures like Honoré Bovet and Eustache Deschamps. *Charles of Orleans*, 17. Likewise, Christine de Pizan, in the *Book of the City of Ladies* (1405), includes her in her eulogy of glorious women: "What could I say about Valentina Visconti, the Duchess of Orléans. Wife of Duke Louis, son of Charles, the wise king of France, and daughter of the duke of Milan? What more could be said about such a prudent lady? A lady who is strong and constant in heart, filled with devotion to her lord and good teaching for her children, well-informed in government, just toward all, sensible in her conduct, and virtuous in all things—and all of this is well known." Christine de Pizan, *The Book of the City of Ladies*, trans. Earl Jeffrey Richards (New York: Persea Books, 1998). Emile Colas, in *Valentine Visconti duchesse d'Orléans* (Paris: Plon, 1911), provides the most in-depth analysis and biography on Valentina.

9. When John the Fearless died in 1419, Charles, who had been imprisoned for four years, did not celebrate; he was instead mortified by the potentially disastrous consequences the death could have for the Dauphin and the kingdom. McLeod, "December 1415–August 1422," in *Charles of Orléans*, 134–58.

10. The *Retenue d'Amours* was allegedly written in 1415.

11. Joanna Summers, *Late Medieval Prison Writing and the Politics of Autobiography* (Oxford: Clarendon Press, 2004), 3.

12. Jean-Marc Varaut, *Poètes en prison, de Charles d'Orléans à Jean Genet* (Paris: Perrin, 1989), 11. Unless stated otherwise, all the translations in this chapter are mine.

13. Of the many authors addressing the subject, Eustache Deschamps specifically stands out with two poems written in 1396 that focus on the reaction to Nicopolis: ballad MCCCXVI and ballad MCCCCXVII, "Faicte pour ceuls de France quant ils furent en Hongrie." The refrain of the latter is particularly emotional: "Je ne voy que tristesce et plour / Et obseques soir et matin" (I see only sadness and weeping / And funerals night and day). Eustache Deschamps, *Oeuvres completes*, vol. 8 (Paris: Firmin Didot, 1893), 84–85. Unless stated otherwise, all translations are mine.

14. *Chronique du Religieux de Saint Denis*, vol. 5, ed. and trans. M. L. Bellaguet (Paris: Éditions du comité de travaux historiques et scientifiques, 1994), specifically chapters 7–12.

15. *Journal d'un bourgeois de Paris de 1405 à 1449*, ed. Colette Beaune (Paris: Librairie générale de France, 1990), 88.

16. Enguerrand de Monstrelet, *Chroniques d'Enguerrand de Monstrelet*, ed. J. A. C. Buchon (Paris: Desrez, 1836), 377.

17. Monstrelet, 380. For the list, see chapter 155, "Comment plusieurs princes et autres notables séigneurs de divers pays furent morts à cette piteuse besogne, et aussi les aucuns faits prisonniers," 377–80.

18. Wendy J. Turner and Christina Lee, eds., *Trauma in Medieval Society* (Turnhout: Brill, 2018).

19. Jenny Edkins, *Trauma and the Memory of Politics* (Cambridge: Cambridge University Press, 2003).

20. From the Greek τραύμα, meaning "wound," "damage."

21. Charles-Louis Morand-Métivier, "Creation and Union through Death and Massacre: The Crusade of Nicopolis and Philippe de Mézières' *Epistre lamentable et consolatoire*," in Turner and Lee, *Trauma in Medieval Society*, 298–319.

22. Jeffrey C. Alexander, *Trauma: A Social Theory* (Cambridge: Polity Press, 2012), 6.

23. Alexander, *Trauma*, 8.

24. Varaut, *Poètes en prison*, 26.

25. Catherine Atwood, "Prison d'amour, prison de guerre: Service ou servage? L'exemple de Charles d'Orléans," in *Être poète au temps de Charles d'Orléans (XVe siècle)*, ed. Hélène Basso and Michèle Gally (Avignon: Éditions universitaires d'Avignon, 2012), 210–22.

26. Jean-Claude Mühlethaler, *Charles d'Orléans: Un lyrisme entre Moyen-âge et modernité* (Paris: Classique Garnier, 2010), 196.

27. Céline Cecchetto, "Charles d'Orléans et Joachim Du Bellay," in *Écritures de l'exil*, ed. Danièle Sabbah (Pessac: Presses Universitaires de Bordeaux, 2009), 103–17.

28. For the text in French and its translation, see John Fox and Mary-Jo Arn, eds. and trans., *Poetry of Charles d'Orléans and His Circle: A Critical Edition of BnF MS. fr. 25458, Charles d'Orléans's Personal Manuscript* (Tempe, AZ: ACMRS, 2010), 8, line 114. The edition of his works by Jean Claude Mühlethaler was also used in this paper (Paris: Librairie Générale française, 1992).

29. "Ce jeune filz qui en moy a fiance / Qui est sailly de la maison de France, / Creu ou jardin semé de fleurs de lis" (This young man who trusts in me / Who sprang from the House of France / Grew up in the garden planted with the lily flower). Fox and Arn, *Poetry of Charles d'Orléans*, 10, lines 165–67.

30. Pilar Andrade Boué, "Quelques aspect de la Merencolie de Charles d'Orléans," *Thélème: Revista complutense de estudios franceses* 15 (2000): 169.

31. See Mary-Jo Arn, "Manuscrit français, manuscrit anglais: De la ductilité du propos poétique," in *Lectures de Charles d'Orléans: Les ballades*, ed. Denis Hüe (Rennes: Presses universitaires de Rennes, 2010), 19–42.

32. A search of the word "France" returned only fourteen occurrences (based on the glossary in Mühlethaler's edition).

33. Fox and Arn, *Poetry of Charles d'Orléans*, 258, lines 1–7. Italics mine.

34. Fox and Arn, *Poetry of Charles d'Orléans*, 259, lines 1–7. Italics mine.

35. Pierre Champion, *Vie de Charles d'Orléans (1394–1465)* (Paris: Honoré Champion, 2010), particularly chapter 8, "La 'prison' anglaise," 155–208.
36. The coast of France can be seen from Dover, and vice versa.
37. Fox and Arn, *Poetry of Charles d'Orléans*, 258–59, line 1.
38. Fox and Arn, *Poetry of Charles d'Orléans*, 260–61, line 44. Translation modified.
39. Fox and Arn, *Poetry of Charles d'Orléans*, 260–61, line 47. Translation modified.
40. Carole Bauguion, "Charles d'Orléans: La plume et l'épée; Étude des métaphores toponymiques rimées par le prisonnier d'Azincourt en exil à Albion," *Dalhousie French Studies* 104 (Winter 2014): 45–60.
41. Fox and Arn, *Poetry of Charles d'Orléans*, 272–73, lines 1–2, 8–9. Translation modified. The last sentence is a famous medieval proverb, "Qu'encore est vive la souris." Daniel Poirion, *Le lexique de Charles d'Orléans dans les ballades* (Geneva: Droz, 1952), 126. Both Poirion and Fox and Arn note that this proverb is present in Joseph Morawski, *Proverbes français antérieurs au XVe siècle* (Paris: Champion, 1925), under the form "encore est vive la soris" (23).
42. Fox and Arn, *Poetry of Charles d'Orléans*, 272–73, lines 3–4, 5–8]
43. Fox and Arn, *Poetry of Charles d'Orléans*, 272–73, lines 10–11.
44. Fox and Arn, *Poetry of Charles d'Orléans*, 272–73, lines 19–21.
45. Fox and Arn, *Poetry of Charles d'Orléans*, 276–77, lines 25–28.
46. For an in-depth analysis of the origins and consequences of the treaty, see Denis Clauzel, Charles Giry-Deloison, and Christophe Leduc, eds., *Arras et la diplomatie européenne, XVe–XVIe siècles* (Arras: Artois presses université, 1999).
47. Pierre Champion, "La Délivrance," in *Vie de Charles d'Orléans (1394–1465)*, 272–312.
48. Fox and Arn, *Poetry of Charles d'Orléans*, 280–81, line 3.
49. Fox and Arn, *Poetry of Charles d'Orléans*, 286–87, line 3.
50. Fox and Arn, *Poetry of Charles d'Orléans*, 280–81, line 2.
51. Fox and Arn, *Poetry of Charles d'Orléans*, 282–83, lines 10–11.
52. Fox and Arn, *Poetry of Charles d'Orléans*, 284–85, lines 23–26.
53. Fox and Arn, *Poetry of Charles d'Orléans*, 284–85, lines 38–39.
54. Philip II was a member of the regency council during the infamous "Gouvernement des oncles" (government of the uncles) under Charles VI. The council greatly angered Louis d'Orléans (Charles's father), who did not see their actions as positive for the kingdom. When he died, his son, John the Fearless (the nickname refers to his prowess and courage at the Battle of Nicopolis in 1396) replaced him. John's much harsher politics ended with the assassination of Louis d'Orléans, which started the civil war.
55. Fox and Arn, *Poetry of Charles d'Orléans*, 280–83, lines 3–7. The ballad is number 128.
56. Fox and Arn, *Poetry of Charles d'Orléans*, 284–85, lines 10–13.
57. Fox and Arn, *Poetry of Charles d'Orléans*, 286–87, lines 28–31.
58. Fox and Arn, *Poetry of Charles d'Orléans*, 294–95, lines 21–23.
59. Fox and Arn, *Poetry of Charles d'Orléans*, 294–95, line 2.

60. Fox and Arn, *Poetry of Charles d'Orléans*, 294–95, lines 2, 9–10.
61. Fox and Arn, *Poetry of Charles d'Orléans*, 284–85, lines 10–13.
62. Fox and Arn, *Poetry of Charles d'Orléans*, 294–95, lines 4, 7–8, 11, 18–19, 21–22.
63. Fox and Arn, *Poetry of Charles d'Orléans*, 296–97, lines 41–45.
64. Fox and Arn, *Poetry of Charles d'Orléans*, 188–89, lines 4, 19–20, 23.
65. For the history of the province before and after its return to France, see Jean Castarède, *Histoire de la Guyenne et de la Gascogne* (Paris: France-Empire, 1997).
66. Fox and Arn, *Poetry of Charles d'Orléans*, 188–89, lines 3, 14–15, 16, 2.

Chapter Three

Bringing up the Dead

The Grotesque in Literature after the French Wars of Religion

Kathleen Long

LOSS AND SILENCE

The eight Wars of Religion in France (1562–1629)[1] inflicted widespread damage upon almost every region of the country, leaving between two and four million people dead from war, massacre, famine, and disease.[2] The unprecedented scale of these wars defied representation, posing the question of how to evoke such a loss, a difficulty further compounded by the absence of witnesses in many cases, as whole families and even villages "disappeared." This problem of representation was compounded by the policy of *oubliance*, a policy of deliberate forgetting of events that took place during the wars.[3] The injunction that such events should remain dead and buried is first stated in the Edict of Amboise of 1563:

> Avons ordonné et ordonnons, entendons, voulons et nous plait, que toutes injures et offenses que l'iniquité du temps, et les occasions qui en sont survenues, ont pu faire naître entre nosdits sujets, et toutes autres choses passées et causées de ces présents tumultes, demeureront éteintes, comme mortes, ensevelies et non advenues.[4]

> We have ordered and order, intend, wish, and it pleases us, that all injuries and offenses that the iniquity of the times, and the events which have occurred, could have given rise to among our said subjects, and all other things that have

happened and were caused by the present disorders, remain extinguished, as if dead, buried, and never having happened.

This injunction is repeated in the Edict of Saint-Germain (1570) and in the Edicts of Boulogne (1573), Beaulieu (1576), and Bergerac (1577), as well as the Edict of Nantes in 1598. These edicts disturbingly gesture toward the deaths they wish to "bury" ("demeureront éteintes, comme mortes, ensevelies"), thus evoking the very events they seek to silence.

An exception to this silencing was that for "cas exécrables" (atrocious cases), violent crimes committed during the wars by individuals on their own private initiative rather than in the course of battle or on the orders of a superior.[5] For Protestant authors such as Théodore Agrippa d'Aubigné (1552–1630), author of the epic poem *Les Tragiques* (1616), this exception allows him to defy the injunction against resuscitating past events, as he makes abundantly clear:

> On dit qu'il faut couler les execrables choses
> Dans le puits de l'oubly et au sepulchre encloses,
> Et que par les escrits le mal resuscité
> Infectera les moeurs de la posterité:
> Mais le vice n'a point pour mere la science,
> Et la vertu n'est pas fille de l'ignorance;
> Elle est le chaud fumier sous qui les ords pechez
> S'engraissent en croissant s'ilz ne sont arrachez . . .[6]

> Some claim that detestable things should be poured
> To the bottom of the well of oblivion sealed in tombs
> And that resurrecting evil in writings
> Will harm the morals of posterity:
> But knowledge is not the mother of vice,
> And virtue is not the daughter of ignorance;
> Ignorance is warm compost in which the shameful sins
> Grow and mature apace unless they are plucked out . . .[7]

Agrippa d'Aubigné suggests that sins merely multiply under the compost (or dung heap, "fumier") of ignorance. He alludes to the imposition of silence by means of the edicts in his choice of terms: "oubly" and "sepulchre" evoking both the policy of *oubliance* and the image of burying the past deployed in these royal orders. The threat of this violence proliferating precisely because of such silencing was an accurate assessment of the effect of these edicts, which seemed to lead perpetually to yet more wars.

PROLIFERATION AND REPRESENTATIONAL EXCESS

In fact, during and after these protracted wars, hyperviolent genres of writing were born and multiplied. In addition to new forms of martyrology and various historical accounts of the wars,[8] the new and extremely popular genre of *histoires tragiques* (tragic tales) flourished, with its bloody punishments meted out to evildoers. Classical tragedy was reborn in France in this period, often based on Seneca's violent plays.[9] Epics such as *Les Tragiques* and lyric poetry written in the late sixteenth century evoked the horror of the wars, directly or indirectly. Violent imagery or even just violent metaphors make their appearance in satirical works (novels, poetry, travel narratives), subtly inflecting works that do not seem to take on the subject of civil war directly.[10] Thus, representations were either relatively direct or displaced onto other times or places, in both cases giving voice to that which was not supposed to be said.

Within this proliferation of genres and works, excessive modes of representation evoked the overwhelming nature of events with an accumulation of images, often monstrous in their hybridity or disorienting in their complexity. Even in the more direct representations of the wars, there is a strange doubling effect as absent bodies are replaced by other bodies from other times

Figure 3.1 Hans Vredeman de Vries, *Caryatidum . . . sive Athlantidum multiformium*, plate 7, ca. 1565. Etching, 161 x 237 mm, Elisha Whittelsey Collection, Metropolitan Museum of Art, New York, accession number 66.545.4 (1–17). Source: Image © by courtesy Metropolitan Museum of Art, New York.

(as in the case of classical tragedy) or re-created in imaginative and often troubling ways. The bodies in these literary works often call into question distinctions between the living and the dead, the human and the mechanical, the human and the animal, or the human and the vegetal (Fig. 3.1).

Artistic images of the grotesque from this period, which were widely circulated as prints, offer a window into the complex aesthetics of French literary works produced in the wake of civil war. In some cases, these texts seem to directly evoke artistic styles and compositions, even particular works. This chapter will consider the use of the grotesque in literature as a strategy for representing horrific violence and loss. Whereas grotesque forms had been previously used in art to offer a monstrous or disorderly foil to the more classical and orderly elements within the frame, they became central to representations of France's civil conflicts, disturbing any possibility of a comfortable viewing or reading experience.

Examining the grotesque as the element that frames a central image or remains outside of the frame as a foil to that image, this essay will trace how these initially marginal or ornamental forms became central to the representation of religious violence in works that memorialized those wars. As the deaths caused by the conflicts were pushed out of the central focus in royal edicts, the grotesque became one means of returning those deaths to the center in much of the literature of late sixteenth- and early seventeenth-century France. This analysis will focus on Théodore Agrippa d'Aubigné's epic about the wars, *Les Tragiques* (composed over the course of several decades during the Wars of Religion and published in 1616), and on a satirical novel about the French court, *L'Isle des hermaphrodites* (*The Island of Hermaphrodites*, published in 1605) as examples of the use of the grotesque in representations of the wars, even while royal edicts promulgated over the course of this period forbade such representations.

THE GROTESQUE IN ART: VISUALIZING THE PROBLEM OF REPRESENTATION

The grotesque ornamental style developed in the wake of the discovery of Nero's Domus Aurea in Rome, built sometime after 64 CE and discovered underground in the late fifteenth century. Because of its location, this palace was thought to be a sort of massive grotto. The detailed and often delicate decorations with their fantastical creatures and hybrid forms, which covered much of the walls and ceilings in this palace, were immediately popular and frequently imitated over the course of the sixteenth century, first in Italy and then throughout Europe. Grotesque ornament became popular in France in the wake of the construction and decoration of the Gallery of François I in Fontainebleau, and the production and dissemination of prints representing works in this gallery and other subjects by artists known collectively as the "School of Fontainebleau."[11] Used to frame mythological or classical scenes in the gallery, grotesque ornaments were circulated as works in their own right in many of these prints, often as frames surrounding an empty space, known as a cartouche.

Maria Fabricius Hansen, in *The Art of Transformation*, places the reign of grotesques within a short temporal range: "My point of departure is thus the observation that, in terms of decorative fresco painting, grotesques were particularly in vogue during a quite starkly delimited period within the history of art, from the late 1400s to around 1600."[12] Hansen is defining grotesques in a very specific way: "As decorative art, they were linked with a wide range of framing, marginal strategies, in contrast to grander, figurative compositions with mythological, religious, or historical content."[13] But the characteristics she observes as typical of the grotesque appear even outside the narrow domain of this decorative practice. Most frequent are representations that blur boundaries between different states of being, between the natural and the monstrous, the natural and the artificial, the living and the inanimate, the human and the vegetal, or the human and the nonhuman animal. Different forms are entangled, or caught in the process of transformation between states, evoking movement or activity. They seem to develop in a temporal sequence and require that the spectator move through the space of the room to view the images, thus making movement a crucial part of perception, and implicating the observer in the work.[14] The grotesque "diverges from naturalistic rationality through the inventive juxtaposition of motifs observed from nature (such as flowers, animals, and landscapes) with bizarre motifs and fantastic, even monstrous creatures."[15] They seem to be set in motion, and often even have mechanical devices as part of the composition. Hansen also sees the grotesques as "metamorphic," with a "transition between forms" that "results in visual ambiguity." These mutable forms[16] that seem to elicit the physical engagement of the viewer (and not just the sense of sight used passively) appear both to demand and defy interpretation.[17]

The grotesque, in its complexity, mobility, and disruption of classical forms, becomes a means of signaling the inherent difficulty of representing overwhelming events and the mass trauma of the wars. The ways in which grotesque forms function as undecipherable signs resonate with discussions of the problematic nature of the sign in Pyrrhonian skepticism (particularly the works of Sextus Empiricus), thus offering an understanding that the instability of representation in the context of trauma is linked to the problematic nature of representation more generally. The sign is never sufficient to represent that which is signified, according to Pyrrhonian skeptics; either the thing signified is evident in itself, and therefore the sign is not necessary, or the sign which indicates it relates to it only by the association we have chosen to impose, making the relationship between that sign and the thing it signifies unstable. That association must always be further explained (by use of yet more signs), thus creating a regress ad infinitum.[18] In this case, meaning is always deferred to some future point at which we never arrive; in the meantime, a proliferation of signs both evokes what is to be represented and blocks our access to full understanding of it. This approach to the problematic nature of representation resonates with descriptions of the complex relationship between trauma and knowledge, in which trauma can be seen as "a crisis that is marked, not by a simple knowledge, but by the ways it simultaneously defies and demands our witness."[19] This demand to seek knowledge even as it defies our claims on it resonates with Michel de Montaigne's (1533–1592) assertion that Pyrrhonian skeptics reject the dogmatic claim of having found the truth even as they continue their continual quest for the truth. Montaigne's essays were foundational for discussions of representation in French philosophy, as he transmitted many of the concepts of Pyrrhonian skepticism to a wider audience, particularly in his "Apology for Raymond Sebond."[20]

Aphasia is the opposite extreme of Pyrrhonian thought from the regress ad infinitum; faced with the undecidability of observed phenomena and the impossibility of coming to a fixed or dogmatic conclusion, skeptical philosophers can choose not to pronounce a judgment.[21] Both regress ad infinitum and non-assertion or aphasia lead to the suspension of judgment, holding two contradictory perspectives or ideas in the mind at the same time, without resolving those perspectives into one synthesized whole. Suspension of judgment is the goal of all of the modes of thinking described as part of skeptical philosophy.[22] The goal of the suspension of judgment is quietude or tranquility of mind; one can easily imagine why this nondogmatic philosophy might have been enticing to intellectuals in a period of religious wars.[23] These two skeptical strategies, along with the regress ad infinitum, suggest three approaches to the representation of the unrepresentable: silence in literature (aphasia) or the empty space (the void) in art; suspension of judgment, often made visible as some sort of hybridity, joining different forms, perspectives, or concepts together without resolution; and infinite regress, in which a proliferation of forms both evokes and masks that which is to be represented.

The overt denial of voice to those wishing to represent the trauma of the Wars of Religion renders explicit the problems of representation associated with trauma. The rhetorical aspects of Pyrrhonian skepticism offer models for representing both the problem of representation and the trauma itself. The grotesque as it is used in the late sixteenth century seems to offer a visual vocabulary for these skeptical concepts of representation. What arises in much of the artwork and in the literary works that echo artistic forms is the interplay between absence or void and proliferation of forms, between aphasia and infinite regress. The infinite regress is also evoked by odd or impossibly distant perspectives within a work, suggesting a continual deferral of the object the eye is seeking out (the vanishing point or a center to the work). The hybridity of grotesque forms echoes the cognitive dissonance of the suspension of judgment, causing the viewer to hesitate between two forms that contradict each other (in any one of a range of ways: life/death, human/mechanical, human/animal, human/vegetal). The effect of the grotesque in these works is one of instability and movement, creating a restless effect or discomfort with the unfamiliar and that which cannot be processed according to the schemas we have developed for understanding the world. In short, the grotesque is the ideal form for representing the impossibility of understanding, for accessing in some manner that which we cannot process intellectually. Grotesque aesthetics become crucial for the representation of the unrepresentable.

THE GROTESQUE IN LITERATURE

The unstable role of the grotesque, making apparent the play between subject and framing, object and ornament, absence and presence, enters late sixteenth-century literature by means of Montaigne, who famously presents his essays, in "De l'Amitié" ("Of Friendship"), as the grotesques that provide a frame around the absent work of his deceased friend Etienne de la Boétie:

> Considérant la conduite de la besongne d'un peintre que j'ay, il m'a pris envie de l'ensuivre. Il choisit le plus bel endroit et milieu de chaque paroy, pour y loger un tableau élabouré de toute sa suffisance; et, le vuide tout au tour, il le remplit de crotesques, qui sont peintures fantasques, n'ayant grace qu'en la varieté et estrangeté. Que sont-ce icy aussi, à la verité, que crotesques et corps monstrueux, rappiecez de divers membres, sans certaine figure, n'ayants ordre, suite ny proportion que fortuite?
>
> . . .
>
> Je vay bien jusques à ce second point avec mon peintre, mais je demeure court en l'autre et meilleure partie: car ma suffisance ne va pas si avant que d'oser entreprendre un tableau riche, poly et formé selon l'art. Je me suis advisé d'en emprunter un d'Estienne de la Boitie, qui honorera tout le reste de cette besongne. C'est un discours auquel il donna nom La Servitude Volontaire; mais ceux qui l'ont ignoré, l'ont bien proprement dépuis rebaptisé Le Contre Un.[24]

As I was considering the way a painter I employ went about his work, I had a mind to imitate him. He chooses the best spot, the middle of each wall, to put a picture labored over with all his skill, and the empty space all around it he fills with grotesques, which are fantastic paintings whose only charm lies in their variety and strangeness. And what are these things of mine, in truth, but grotesques and monstrous bodies, pieced together of divers members, without definite shape, having no order, sequence, or proportion other than accidental?

. . .

I do indeed go along with my painter in this second point, but I fall short in the first and better part; for my ability does not go far enough for me to dare to undertake a rich, polished picture, formed according to art. It occurred to me to borrow one from Etienne de la Boétie, which will do honor to all the rest of this work. It is a discourse to which he gave the name *La Servitude Volontaire*; but those who did not know this have since very fitly rebaptized it *Le Contre Un*.[25]

Montaigne presents his essays as a cartouche in which the grotesque frame surrounds a blank space—where the work of his friend, itself standing in for the lost friend, should be. Much has been made of this passage in the scholarship on Montaigne, from Jean Starobinski, who sees the hole at the center of the essayist's work as the sign of his inadequacy,[26] to Brad Epps, who notes that this inadequacy leads to "a proliferation of signs and images."[27] Montaigne's literary gesture calls into question the distinction between a work and its ornamental frame, and his grotesques take on their own monstrous life. This interplay between silence or aphasia and a glut of monstrous forms echoes both the skeptical discussions of representation and the effects of trauma brought on by loss (Fig. 3.2).

These ideas offer context to the notion of the grotesque as a means of framing loss and of framing the impossibility of representing that loss in literature produced in the wake of the French Wars of Religion. The particular excess of signs and forms (or forms as signs) in the grotesque renders evident the problematic dual aspect of representation as both marking and covering over losses inflicted over the course of the wars. At the same time, these signs highlight their own problematic nature as well as the contradictions that form the very basis of representation as the substitution of one thing (the sign) for the other (the thing represented).

Théodore Agrippa d'Aubigné, known for his militant Protestantism and defiance of royal censorship, wrestled throughout his literary career with the problems posed by any representation of the massive violence unleashed by the Wars of Religion. He composed his epic, *Les Tragiques*, both in the course and in the wake of those wars. As a soldier fighting for the Protestant cause, he was a direct witness of many battles and of the numerous power

Figure 3.2 After Hans Vredeman de Vries, *Diamond-shaped cartouche*, ca. 1547–1605. Engraving, 215 x 170 mm, bequest of Herbert Mitchell, Metropolitan Museum of Art, New York, inv. no. 2018.839.15. Source: Image © by courtesy Metropolitan Museum of Art, New York.

struggles at court. He was also a historian of events, authorized at the 1603 Synod of Gap to collect documents concerning the persecution of Protestants in France and to write a history of the period of the wars from the Protestant perspective. Virtually all of his writing is intertwined with this history.[28] He published *Les Tragiques* in 1616, well after the 1598 Edict of Nantes and more than a decade before the final siege of La Rochelle (1627–1628). The result is a mixture of vivid but confusing scenes that focus more on the affect of events, that is, how such events might have felt to those in the middle of them, than on the usual chronological narrative.

In the second book, "Princes," the poet describes Catherine de' Medici's (1519–1589) project to build the Tuileries Palace as inspired by Satan:

> Ce que premier il trouve à son advenement
> Fut le preparatif du brave bastiment
> Que desseignoit pour lors la peste florentine:
> De dix mille maisons il voüa la ruine
> Pour estoffe au dessein: le serpent captieux
> Entra dans cette royne et pour y entrer mieux
> Fit un corps aeré de colomnes parfaictes,
> De pavillons hautains, de folles giroüettes
> De domes accomplis, d'escaliers sans noyaux,
> Fenestrages dorez, pilastres, et portaux,
> Des salles, cabinets, des chambres, galeries,
> En fin d'un tel project que sont les Thuileries:
> Comme idee il gaigna l'imagination,
> Du chef de Jesabel il prit possession,
> L'ardent desir logé avorte d'autres vices,
> Car ce qui peut troubler ces desseins d'edifices
> Est condamné à mort par ces volans desirs.[29]

> What he first finds on his arrival
> Were the foundations of the fine building
> Then being planned by the Florentine plague
> Ten thousand houses he pledged to demolish
> To furnish the plan. The wily snake
> Penetrated this queen, and to penetrate better
> Made an airy body with perfect columns,
> Lofty pavilions, wild weather vanes [spirals],
> Perfect domes, spiral staircases,
> Gilded window frames, pillars, and portals,
> Rooms, antechambers, chambers, galleries,
> In short of such a kind as are the Tuileries:
> In the guise of an idea, he took over the imagination;

Of Jezebel's head he took possession:
This ardent desire lodged there gives monstrous birth to other vices,
For anything that might disturb these plans for building
Is condemned to death by these flighty desires.[30]

This passage echoes contemporary accounts accusing Catherine de' Medici of massacring thousands of Protestants to clear the neighborhood on which the Tuileries Palace was constructed. What is presented to the mind's eye in this passage is Catherine's body becoming one with the palace itself, as Satan possesses her by means of the promise of this project. The description oscillates between hinting at actual sexual and corporeal possession and the competing notion that Satan takes control of the imagination of his followers.[31] Catherine's body, or her imagination, is presented as an empty vessel filled with elements of the palace to be built. This emptiness also evokes the neighborhood that was razed to the ground and emptied of people in preparation for the project. In turn, the palace becomes a body ("un corps aeré"), dynamic, filled with air and light, but with an abundance of detail that overwhelms the reader.[32] And while the architectural features are in themselves lovely, when joined with the queen they become ghastly, engendering monstrous births that kill anyone standing in the way of the project. And so, human and architectural, animate and inanimate, life and death are joined in disturbing fashion.

This association between the void and literary/conceptual/imagistic productivity or proliferation touches upon Jacques Derrida's description of the parergon, the decorative element that frames a work and functions as an embellishment or supplement to that work. From the very beginning of his seminar on the subject, Derrida evokes satire, which he links to the concept of *satis* (enough), but which can also be linked to the overfull plate (the *satura*) and the excess of marginalized forms. He links satire with the *abîme*, with the abyss or void: "it's enough to say: abyss and satire of the abyss."[33] He balances these two seemingly opposing concepts of excess and lack in complex ways, never resolving their differences into a harmonious whole, in imitation of the suspension of judgment so favored by Pyrrhonian skepticism.[34] Rebecca Zorach's explanation of what Derrida is doing with this association is particularly helpful:

What constitutes the parergon, Derrida writes, "is not simply [its] exteriority as surplus, it is the internal structural link which rivets [it] to the lack in the interior of the ergon." Derrida is not specifically addressing the empty frame, but rather the framed or otherwise ornamented image. The question of lack can be understood in a purely semiotic sense: if the framed image is a representational one, its lack is its failure to render its "subject" fully present. Its character as a sign, however, depends upon this very lack—because if it would be "successful" in rendering present, it would no longer be a sign but the thing itself . . . this lack is both highlighted and supplemented by the frame.[35]

The parergon both marks the lack inherent in that which it frames and serves as an attempt to supplement that lack. In the case of Catherine's possession, this dual role sutures the Tuileries Palace, with its excessive ornamentation, to the eradication of the Protestant neighborhood on whose ruins the palace was built. This grotesque piece of architecture thus becomes a memorial for the Protestant dead Catherine sought to efface, even as it signals the impossibility of adequately representing that lack.

The Tuileries Palace stood both as a sign of sovereign power and a masking of and evidence for the cruelty that was foundational to that power. This covering over of the many dead is reversed at the end of the epic:

> La terre ouvre son sein, du ventre des tombeaux
> Naissent des enterrez les visages nouveaux:
> Du pré, du bois, du champ, presque de toutes places,
> Sortent les corps nouveaux, et les nouvelles faces:
> Icy les fondements des chasteaux rehaussez
> Par les ressuscitans promptement sont percez:
> Icy un arbre sent des bras de sa racine
> Grouiller un chef vivant, sortir une poictrine:
> Là l'eau trouble bouillonne, et puis s'esparpillant
> Sent en soy des cheveux, et un chef s'esveillant:
> Comme un nageur venant du profond de son plonge:
> Tous sortent de la mort, comme l'on sort d'un songe.[36]

> Earth opens her bosom, from the sepulchral womb
> Are born the new faces of those who lie buried;
> From meadows, woods, fields, and almost everywhere,
> There emerge new bodies and new features.
> Here the foundations of lofty castles
> Are quickly breached by the resurrected:
> Here, in the arms of its roots, a tree senses
> A living head quiver, a chest come forth;
> There the murky waters churn and then part
> As they sense hairs and a head awaken:
> Like a diver who emerges from the depths,
> All leave death as one leaves a dream.[37]

These buried bodies seem to have become one with nature, returning at the end of time to accuse their persecutors and seek both their place as the divinely chosen and vengeance. We see them at the moment when they are suspended between the natural forms of plants, water, or earth and their human form. While there is an Ovidian flavor to much of this passage, the proliferation of forms that hover between two states of being is reminiscent of grotesque forms in disturbing ways. A previous scene referencing Ezekiel 37:7–8 (popularly known as the Valley of the Dry Bones; *Les Tragiques*, lines 600–620), where bones are resurrected as human bodies without human souls, warns us that the resurrected may or may not be human. And in fact, the resurrected have to shed their humanity, or at least the conventional signs of it such as language and reason, in order to achieve salvation.

And so this reversal is not a resolution of the loss. The meaning of all this is constantly deferred to the end of time as depicted at the end of the epic:

> Chetif je ne puis plus approcher de mon oeil
> L'oeil du ciel, je ne puis supporter le soleil,
> Encor tout esblouy en raisons je me fonde
> Pour de mon ame voir la grand'ame du monde,
> Sçavoir ce qu'on ne sçait, et qu'on ne peut sçavoir,
> Ce que n'a ouy l'oreille, et que l'oeil n'a peû voir:
> Mes sens n'ont plus de sens, l'esprit de moy s'envolle,
> Le coeur ravy se taist, ma bouche est sans parole:
> Tout meurt, l'ame s'enfuit, et reprenant son lieu
> Extaticque se pasme au giron de son Dieu.[38]

> I tremble, and cannot look more closely
> At the eye of heaven, I cannot gaze upon the sun,
> Still dazzled, I look to the mind
> That my soul may see the great soul of the world,
> That it may know the unknown and the unknowable,
> That which no ear heard, no eye seen;
> My senses can no longer feel, my spirit departs from me,
> My heart is overwhelmed and falls silent, my mouth is wordless;
> Everything dies, the soul flees, and regaining its rightful place
> In ecstasy swoons in the bosom of its God.[39]

As in the cartouche discussed by Derrida, the parergon (here as grotesque forms) surrounds a vanishing point that leads to meaning without representation or expression; meaning which cannot enter into human experience. That which has been lost cannot be regained in the realm of human experience but can only be found in the erasure of the human (which raises the question of whether we can find it at all). Once again, the grotesque forms signal both the necessity and the impossibility of representing loss or lack, of gaining access to the knowledge that resolves all human events and the horror they elicit. Knowledge occupies a space and time beyond representation; this proliferation of disturbingly hybrid forms around the void left by this continual deferral or absence echoes the empty cartouche surrounded by grotesques. Or, it evokes the absent meaning of the ergon framed by the insufficient supplement of the parergon, continually adding signs meant to give us access to the truth, but in reality distancing us from it or even covering it over.

GROTESQUE AESTHETICS AND VIOLENCE: *L'ISLE DES HERMAPHRODITES* (*THE ISLAND OF HERMAPHRODITES*)

Use of the grotesque to represent the problematic nature of the sign and of knowledge in the context of traumatic events achieves complex, metatextual levels of expression in a satirical novel about the French court, *L'Isle des hermaphrodites*, published anonymously in 1605.[40] The action of this novel consists entirely of a narrator recounting what he saw as he walked through a palace supposedly located on an exotic island ruled by people he describes as "hermaphrodites," but who in modern terms are more genderqueer (in that their gender identities can change on a daily basis). The proliferation of ornamentation in the palace is echoed by descriptions of the inhabitants as ornamental figures whose appearances are highly manipulated for aesthetic reasons, rendering them not only indeterminate in terms of binary gender, but also hybrids of human and artificial forms or of human and animal forms.

The narrator is a nonviolent man who is forced into exile by the Wars of Religion. He is shipwrecked on his way back to France, having decided to return because of news of Henri IV's enlightened reign (1589–1610). Washed up on an island, he spends his time there walking endlessly through an elaborate palace, returning again and again to the same room, which seems quite different each time he sees it. The palace, constructed of gold, expensive stones, and enamels, is characterized as a "masterpiece of nature," thus calling into question from the beginning of the narrative the distinction between natural and artificial:

> Et tandis nous nous mismes à contempler un edifice assez proche de nous, la beauté duquel ravit tellement nos esprits, que nous avions plustost opinion que ce fust une illusion qu'une chose veritable. Le marbre, le Jaspe, le Porphire, l'or, et la diversité des émaux estoit ce qu'il y avait du moindre; car l'architecture, la sculpture, et l'ordre que l'on y voyait compassé en toutes ses parties, attiroit tellement l'esprit en admiration, que l'œil, qui peut voir tant de choses en un instant, n'estoit pas assez suffisant pour comprendre le contenu de ce beau palais. Et comme la beauté est une chose qui attire ordinairement à soy ce qui en est, ce semble, le plus esloigné, oubliant nos lassitudes et les travaux que

nous avions si longuement soufferts, nous fusmes tentez ou plustost forcez par la curiosité, de voir plus particulierement ce rare chef-d'oeuvre de la nature.⁴¹

In the meantime, we went to contemplate a building that was fairly close to us, the beauty of which so ravished our spirits that we were of the opinion that it was an illusion rather than a real thing. Marble, jasper, porphyry, gold, and a variety of enamels were the least of it, for the architecture, the sculpture, and the order we saw there encompassed in all its parts so drew the spirit into admiration that the eye, which can see so many things in one instant, was not sufficient to take in all that this beautiful palace contained. And as beauty is a thing, which ordinarily draws to itself that which is (it seems) the most distant from it, forgetting our exhaustion and the trials which we had so long endured, we were tempted, or rather forced by curiosity, to see more particularly this rare masterpiece of nature.

The narrator is perturbed at first, because he has not yet seen any living human; the ornamentation of the palace, which includes statues representing humanlike forms, seems to stand in the place of its inhabitants. It also

Figure 3.3 Johannes or Lucas van Doetecum after Hans Vredeman de Vries, *Scenographiae sive perspectivae*, plate 16, 1563. Engraving, 209 x 256 mm, Rijksmuseum, Amsterdam, inv. no. BI-1897-A-972-18. Source: Image © by courtesy Rijksmuseum, Amsterdam.

seems far more compelling, both beautiful and violent, as the novel uses the word "ravis" ("ravished") to describe the effect of this place on the shipwrecked men.

In the courtyard of the palace, the narrator sees human forms carved into architectural features made of stone. Some of these forms are caryatids, humanlike load-bearing columns that are sometimes human-animal, human-vegetal, or human-mechanical hybrids (Fig. 3.3, 3.1). Another form is the statue of an ambiguously gendered person rising half out of the ocean. None of these figures represents a complete or completely human body. This proliferation of partial humans supplements and signals the absence of humans, creating a disturbing scene:

> Nous deux vers ce riche palais où nous arrivasmes en peu de temps, et trouvasmes de premier abord un long Peristyle ou rang de colonnes Caryatides, lesquelles avoient pour chapiteau la teste d'une femme . . . au dessus de l'architrave duquel se voyoit une statue d'albastre, sortant le corps à demy hors d'une mer, qui estoit assez bien representée par diverses sortes de marbres et de porphires. Ceste statuë estoit autant bien proportionnee qu'il se pouvoit, laquelle tenoit en l'une de ses mains un rouleau où estoit escrit ce mot *Planiandrion*. A peine osions nous sortir de ce lieu, tant nous estions pleins de merveille d'y voir une si grande solitude, que nous n'avions encore rencontré personne depuis que nos estions entrez.[42]

> And we two [went] toward this rich palace, where we arrived in a little while, and found a long Peristyle or row of Caryatid columns, which had as their capitol the head of a woman; from there we entered into a great courtyard in which the pavement was so lustrous and slippery that we could barely keep on our feet there. Nonetheless the desire to continue made us stumble toward the great staircase, in front of which there was another staircase from the courtyard, surrounded by twelve columns, accompanied by such a superbly ornamented formal entry that it was impossible to contemplate it without being dazzled. Above its architrave an alabaster statue was visible, with the body half-rising from the sea, which was quite well depicted by various sorts of marble and porphyry. This statue was as well-proportioned as could be and held in one of its hands a scroll upon which was written the word *Planiandrion* [a woman's diadem on the head of a man].

While the narrator eventually encounters a "great multitude" of actual living people moving around outside of the palace and within it,[43] his first encounter is with these works of art that evoke the human without fully representing it.

This proliferation of truncated bodies is reminiscent of the work of Hans Vredeman de Vries (1526–1609), possibly "the most prolific Netherlandish print designer of the sixteenth century"⁴⁴ and an influential figure in set design, landscape design, and urban design. He "wrote and illustrated one of the strangest, most influential, and most misunderstood tracts on art ever published," his work on perspective.⁴⁵ He composed a series of allegorical prints and collections of grotesque images,⁴⁶ as well as of cartouches with strapwork and grotesques.⁴⁷ Many of these works were produced in multiple languages and distributed throughout Europe, and so it seems likely that the author of *L'Isle des hermaphrodites* was familiar with them, as he appears to have been conversant in the visual arts, given the extensive descriptions of such works in the novel.

One of the more influential works Vredeman de Vries produced was his *Scenographiae, sive Perspectivae*,⁴⁸ a series of architectural scenes empty of representations of living human beings, but which are littered with humanoid statues, often mutilated or grotesque. Christopher Heuer notes the scholarly response to Vredeman de Vries's work as "surreal" and "grotesque." Also particularly unsettling is the exaggerated use of perspective, which forces the reader's gaze toward a distant point that is never actually seen (see Fig.

Figure 3.4 Johannes or Lucas van Doetecum after Hans Vredeman de Vries, *Scenographiae sive perspectivae*, **plate 18, 1563. Engraving, 211 x 260 mm, Rijksmuseum, Amsterdam, inv. no. BI-1897-A-972-20. Source: Image © by courtesy Rijksmuseum, Amsterdam.**

3.4).⁴⁹ Heuer also discusses the allegorical function of "empty architecture," pointing to the emphasis on decay and loss in many of the architectural works of Hieronymus Cock and Vredeman de Vries.⁵⁰ The latter artist's engravings in particular are "exaggeratedly imaginary,"⁵¹ thus calling for interpretation while remaining opaque to any definitive meaning.

One fairly typical example of the use of the grotesque as both frame and focus of a mysterious scene featuring a space devoid of human occupants is the eighteenth architectural engraving in the *Scenographiae*, which depicts an interior where the vanishing point is perpetually deferred (Fig. 3.4). A long hallway leads outside to the entrance of yet another building in the distance, presumably with its own long hall leading to yet another building, a visual representation of the deferral of knowledge evoked by Agrippa d'Aubigné at the end of *Les Tragiques*. This void is surrounded by grotesque forms, some of which seem to be crawling out of their space and moving. Along with the more conventional grotesque hybrid forms, humanlike forms, seemingly trapped in the strapwork, appear to gesture for help. The bas-relief on the upper right represents the sacrifice of Isaac, with Abraham's sword, lifted to kill his son, stopped only by the angel. This mysterious interior, in which the grotesque frame becomes the focus, is largely indecipherable. The parergon, taking the place of the central work or object that it is usually meant to frame, foregrounds the ever-elusive nature of meaning within the realm of representation.

The elusive nature of meaning is also underscored when the narrator of *L'Isle des hermaphrodites* enters the palace, encounters living human beings who are the inhabitants of the island, and finds himself confused about what is human and what is not, what is animate and what is inanimate, and what is natural and what is artificial. It seems as if confusion is an integral element of the narrative; for example, the narrator does not make any progress in the palace once he has entered, moving instead in circles and constantly returning to the same bedroom, in which much of the action of the novel takes place. This bedroom somehow always seems different, as the narrator notices new elements, such as flowers strewn on the floor and tapestries on the wall. He never fully understands what he sees, as he keeps thinking that what is presented to him are instances of the violence he had sought to escape. When he sees the inhabitants of this island getting their hair curled, he thinks they are being tortured with *tenailles*, pincers used to increase the pain in torture or during execution. He nearly screams in horror at what he thinks is a scene of torment, only to realize that the "victims" are merely having their hair done.⁵² And when he returns to the bedroom of the first inhabitant he encountered at the end of the novel, he thinks he sees decapitated heads, only to be told that what is actually in front of him are wigs.⁵³ In the recursive narrative of the novel, the narrator processes repetitive traumatic memories, never arriving at a resolution but continually moving on to another encounter.

After a long scene of body modification, in which makeup, curling irons, tight clothing and ruffs, and tiny shoes are used to transform the living human inhabitants of the island into works of art, at the same time compensating for their diseased and nonnormative bodies,[54] the narrator finds himself incapable of believing that the humans he sees before him are truly human:

> Au milieu du lict on voyoit une statue d'un homme à demy hors du lict. . . . Le visage estoit si blanc, si luysant, et d'un rouge si esclatant, qu'on voyoit bien qu'il y avoit plus d'artifice que de nature; ce qui me faisoit aisément croire que ce n'estoit que peinture.[55]
>
> In the middle of the bed, one could see a statue of a man half out of the bed. . . . His face was so white, so shiny, and of a red so striking, that one could well see that there was more artifice than nature involved, which led me easily to believe that this was only a painting.

Not only can a work of art be substituted for a human being in this setting, but the human itself is reduced to a construction, easily manipulable into different forms, and thus also easily replaced by works of art.

In this novel, the grotesque, with its fanciful combinations of forms and its transgressions of all the boundaries that are created to define our humanity, serves as the aesthetic support for a skeptical understanding of the violence and loss inflicted by the Wars of Religion. The first inhabitant the narrator observes closely is in bed, fully dressed in nightclothes and a bed jacket, with gloves on their hands and both a mask and a veil on their face. At no point in the novel does the narrator see unmediated bodies or body parts, suggesting the absent presence of the island's inhabitants, who are constructed by the clothing and makeup that they wear. These constructed bodies are neither male nor female, but a constantly fluid combination of both gender roles. Nor are they human or animal; these modified bodies are compared to monstrous animal forms like the griffin. Material objects and artistic forms proliferate in the palace, surrounding and signaling the void of meaning at its center.

This aspect of the so-called "hermaphrodites" could be seen as comical or satirical, but for the hints of violence in the scenes that frame various points of the narrative. The narrator leaves France because he does not want to soak his hands in the blood of his fellow men.[56] Yet everything he sees on this island seems to recall a past trauma, which is then dispelled by the benign nature of the scene before him. At first, his past trauma seems to prevent his understanding, and he sees everything and everyone as bizarre. But the grotesque nature of the island's inhabitants does not threaten him, offering the possibility of a more healing strangeness, an acceptance of not knowing combined with the embrace of seeking to know these strangers. By the end of the novel, our narrator has returned to France, where he tells the story of this strange land repeatedly to his compatriots, with the promise of perpetual continuation of the narrative, seducing them into embracing the strangeness of the grotesque and the pleasures not of knowing, but of seeking to know.[57]

CONCLUSION

In the grotesque version of demonic possession portrayed in the epic *Les Tragiques*, Catherine's body and mind are inhabited by the decorative elements of the Tuileries Palace, which overwhelm any image of the queen that might remain in the reader's mind, thus dehumanizing her as she has dehumanized her Protestant subjects by massacring them simply for the pleasure of building yet another palace. The meaning of this cruelty is deferred to somewhere and sometime beyond both the text of the epic and human time; the proliferation of grotesque forms throughout the epic points to the absence of meaning, perhaps the impossibility of meaning in the context of human catastrophe.

The work of Vredeman de Vries offers an aesthetic with similar elements, as architectural structures and other elements of design surround empty spaces with a proliferation of grotesque forms, hybrid human/animal or human/vegetal forms that hint at violence with their truncated or twisted bodies. Extreme perspective forces the viewer's gaze into the distance, never to arrive at a resting point, with a point of focus and the meaning of the work always deferred to some distant point.

L'Isle des hermaphrodites takes on these questions of humanity in a more satirical manner, as it replaces human bodies and lives with artificial constructions. The grotesque statue, both ornamental and disturbing, enters the bedroom and takes the place of the living human being (or so it seems), confounding the distinction between humanity and its simulacra. The constantly changing nature of the characters in this novel is evoked as they reshape their bodies and their identities by means of clothing. The narrator remarks that "they never cease to change like this in this country, day or night" ("ils ne laissent pas de changer ainsi en ce pays-là de jour et de nuict").[58] This proliferation of forms offers a supplement to the absent bodies that the narrator seems to see in traumatic flashbacks. But they also create the lack they reflect, as the narrator says that he cannot see the faces or hands of these individuals, and so dehumanizes them in a tangled formulation that confuses "what" and "who": "Je n'avoir encore veu ce que c'estoit qui estoit dans ce lict" (I couldn't yet see what it was that—or who—was in this bed).[59]

This dehumanization is only overcome in a text that hovers outside of the frame of the narration, a treatise of political philosophy that counters an argument justifying violence in the name of sovereignty offered in a previous treatise:

> Je sçay que je suis né parmy les hommes, en un certain païs, et sous un estat, c'est à dire sous certaines loix. Pourquoy trouvez vous mauvais si, voyant ces hommes affligez, le pays ruiné, et les loix renversées, je discours, je me plains, et je medite sur les moyens du restablissement. Ne sçay je pas que je suis lié avec eux? Que ce perdant je me perds, que ce bouleversement m'acableroit sous leur ruine?[60]

> I know that I was born among men, in a certain country, and in a state, that is to say, under certain laws. Why do you find it bad if, when I see these suffering men, the country ruined, and the laws overturned, I speak of it, I complain, and I meditate on the means to rebuild (reestablish) it? Do I not know that I am bound together with them? That in losing this I lose myself, that this upheaval would overwhelm me under their ruin?

The anonymous author of this fictional treatise, strangely resembling Montaigne in their writing style, sees themselves as bound to their fellow men, doomed to the same fate as they face. This potentially grotesque image of conjoined humanity, evoking Montaigne's monstrous child in the essay of the same title and evoked throughout the novel, becomes the solution for the problem of meaning: acceptance of the other as oneself, engaging in an ethical relationship with others, and rebuilding the world on this basis without searching for one all-encompassing truth (a search or claim that was, after all, the basis for sixty years of religious war in France).

Both the epic poem *Les Tragiques* and the novel *L'Isle des hermaphrodites* evoke the grotesque aesthetics of designs such as those of Vredeman de Vries to convey the horror not only of the French Wars of Religion but also of the projects designed to both cover over them and justify them. They use a proliferation of images and signs to frame the loss or absence of humanity and to underscore the impossibility of representing or ascribing meaning to this absence. They also convey the uncertainty caused by this loss and this impossibility, rejecting the imposed meanings of religious dogmatism and monarchical sovereignty that claimed to offer order in the chaos of civil conflict, but that in fact fueled the catastrophic violence of the wars. In doing all this, they use the grotesque as a critique of the illusion of order and sense imposed by silencing survivors of this conflict, an illusion that covers over the loss of meaning caused by devastating violence and trauma.

But *L'Isle des hermaphrodites* also turns the grotesque—with its hybridity, its proliferation of images without fixed meaning, and its refusal to pronounce judgment—toward an ethics of care and an acceptance of differences. If knowledge can never be stable and assured, it should not be enforced by violent means, but sought after endlessly and in dialogue with others. The grotesque suggests our connection to others, even to the others we do not understand or accept, in an environment that we do not control. It shows us the dystopian world we create when we seek to destroy others, but it also shows us the possibilities of other, better worlds that could appear when we stop seeing ourselves as separate and distinct from those around us.

WORKS CITED

Anderson, Lisa. "Masquing/(Un)Masking: Animation and the Restless Ornament of Fontainebleau." In *Ornament and Monstrosity in Early Modern Art*, ed. Chris Askholt Hammeken and Maria Fabricius Hansen, 179–87. Amsterdam: Amsterdam University Press, 2019.

Aubigné, Théodore Agrippa d.' *Histoire universelle*. Edited by André Thierry. Geneva: Droz, 1981–2000. First published 1616–1620 by Jean Moussat (Maillé).

———. *Les Tragiques*. Edited by Jean-Raymond Fanlo. Paris: Champion, 2006.

———. *Les Tragiques*. Translated by Valerie Worth-Stylianou. Tempe: Arizona Center for Medieval and Renaissance Studies, 2020.

Biet, Christian, ed. *Théâtre de la cruauté et récits sanglants en France (XVIe–XVIIe siècle)*. Paris: R. Laffont, 2006.

Brahami, Frédéric. *Le Scepticisme de Montaigne*. Paris: Presses universitaires de France, 1997.

Broedel, Hans. "Fifteenth Century Witch Beliefs." In *The Oxford Handbook of Witchcraft in Early Modern Europe and Colonial America*, 1–20. Oxford Handbooks Online. Oxford: Oxford University Press.

Caruth, Cathy. *Unclaimed Experience: Trauma, Narrative, and History*. Baltimore: Johns Hopkins University Press, 1996.

Cook, Kelly Dianne. "Power Play: Grotesque Ornament and the Art of Political Persuasion in Early Modern France." PhD diss., Cornell University, 2012.

Crespin, Jean, and Simon Goulart. *Histoires des martyrs persecutez et mis à mort pour la verite de l'Evangile depuis le temps des Apostres jusques à present*. Geneva: Pierre Aubert, 1619.

Derrida, Jacques. *The Truth in Painting*. Translated by Geoff Bennington and Ian McLeod. Chicago: University of Chicago Press, 1987.

Epps, Brad. "Grotesque Identities: Writing, Death, and the Space of the Subject (Between Michel de Montaigne and Reinaldo Arenas)." *Journal of the Midwest Modern Language Association* 28, no. 1 (1995): 38–55.

Frisch, Andrea. *Forgetting Differences: Tragedy, Historiography, and the French Wars of Religion*. Edinburgh: Edinburgh University Press, 2015.

Goulart, Simon. *Mémoires de la Ligue sous Henri III & Henri IV*. S.l.: s.n., 1602.

Hamilton, Tom. "Adjudicating the Troubles: Violence, Memory and Criminal Justice at the End of the Wars of Religion." *French History* 34, no. 4 (2020): 417–34.

Hammeken, Chris Askholt, and Maria Fabricius Hansen. Introduction to *Ornament and Monstrosity in Early Modern Art*, ed. Chris Askholt Hammeken and Maria Fabricius Hansen, 13–41. Amsterdam: Amsterdam University Press, 2019.

Hansen, Maria Fabricius. *The Art of Transformation: Grotesques in Sixteenth-Century Italy*. Rome: Edizioni Quasar, 2018.

Heuer, Christopher P. *The City Rehearsed: Object, Architecture, and Print in the Worlds of Hans Vredeman de Vries*. London: Routledge, 2009.

Hollstein's Dutch & Flemish Etchings, Engravings and Woodcuts, 1450–1700, Volume 47: Vredeman de Vries, Part 1. Compiled by Peter Fuhring. Rotterdam: Sound & Vision Interactive, 1997.

Hollstein's Dutch & Flemish Etchings, Engravings and Woodcuts, 1450–1700, Volume 48: Vredeman de Vries, Part 2. Compiled by Peter Fuhring. Rotterdam: Sound & Vision Interactive, 1997.

Holt, Mack. *The French Wars of Religion, 1562–1629*. Cambridge: Cambridge University Press, 2005.

L'Isle des hermaphrodites. Edited by Claude-Gilbert Dubois. Geneva: Droz, 1996.

Kendrick, Jeff, and Katherine S. Maynard, eds. *Polemic and Literature Surrounding the French Wars of Religion*. Boston: De Gruyter, 2019.

Knecht, R. J. *The French Religious Wars, 1562–1598*. Oxford: Osprey, 2002.

Kommerell, Victor. *Metamorphosed Margins: The Case for a Visual Rhetoric of the Renaissance Grottesche under the Influence of Ovid's "Metamorphoses."* Hildesheim: Georg Olms Verlag, 2008.

Long, Kathleen P. "Improper Perspective: Anamorphosis in the Works of Theodore Agrippa d'Aubigné." In "Figuring Protest and Lament," edited by Dora Polachek. Special issue, *Medievalia* 22 (1999): 103–26.

———. "Shaping Bodies, Reimagining the World: Sartorial Prosthesis in *L'Isle des hermaphrodites* (1605)." In "Disability's Worldmaking," edited by Tammy Berberi and Jennifer Row. Special issue, *L'Esprit créateur* 61, no. 4 (2021): 127–39.

———. "Théodore Agrippa d'Aubigné." In *Dictionary of Literary Biography*, ed. Megan Conway, 9–23. Farmington Hills, MI: Thomson Gale, 2006.

Montaigne, Michel de. *Les Essais de Montaigne*, ed. Pierre Villey. Paris: Presses universitaires de France, 1978.

———. *The Complete Essays of Montaigne*. Translated by Donald Frame. Stanford, CA: Stanford University Press, 1965.

Popkin, Richard H. *The History of Scepticism from Savonarola to Bayle*. Oxford: Oxford University Press, 2003.

Sedley, David. *Sublimity and Skepticism in Montaigne and Milton*. Ann Arbor: University of Michigan Press, 2005.

Sextus Empiricus. *Outlines of Pyrrhonism*. Translated by R. G. Bury. Loeb Classical Library. Cambridge, MA: Harvard University Press, 1933.

Starobinski, Jean. *Montaigne in Motion*. Translated by Arthur Goldhammer. Chicago: University of Chicago Press, 1985.

Stegmann, André, ed. *Édits des guerres de religion*. Paris: J. Vrin, 1979.

Vincent, Hubert. *Vérité du scepticisme chez Montaigne*. Paris: Harmattan, 1998.
Vredeman de Vries, Hans. *Architectura*. Anvers: Gerard Smits, 1577.
———. *Coenotaphiorum*. S.l.: Hieronymus Cock, 1563.
———. *Differents Pourtraicts de menuiserie*. S.l.: Philippe Galle, s.d.
———. *Grottesco*. Antwerp: Gerard de Jode, 1565–71. Republished by Karel van Mallery, 1612.
———. *Hortorum*. S.l.: Philippe Galle, 1583.
———. *Perspective, id est celeberrima ars inspicientis aut transpicientis oculorum aciei, in pariete, tabula aut tele depicta*. Leiden: Henricus Hondius, 1604.
———. *Scenographiae, sive Perspectivae*. Anvers: Hieronymus Cock, 1560. Reprinted in 1604.
———. *Variae Architecturae Formae*. Antwerp: Theodoor Galle, 1601.
Zalloua, Zahi. *Montaigne and the Ethics of Skepticism*. Charlottesville, VA: Rookwood Press, 2005.
Zerner, Henri. *The School of Fontainebleau: Etchings and Engravings*. New York: Abrams, 1969.
Zorach, Rebecca. *Blood, Milk, Ink, Gold: Abundance and Excess in the French Renaissance*. Chicago: University of Chicago Press, 2005.

NOTES

1. Mack Holt, introduction and "Epilogue: The Last War of Religion, 1610–1629," in *The French Wars of Religion, 1562–1629* (Cambridge: University of Cambridge Press, 2005), 3–4, 178–94.

2. R. J. Knecht, *The French Religious Wars, 1562–1598* (Oxford: Osprey, 2002), 91. Holt traces the economic consequences of the wars briefly in the conclusion to *French Wars of Religion*, 195–222, in particular 203–4, where he examines the impact of extensive mortality among the peasants on agricultural production.

3. Andrea Frisch, "Learning to Forget," in *Forgetting Differences: Tragedy, Historiography, and the French Wars of Religion* (Edinburgh: Edinburgh University Press, 2015), 1–25.

4. André Stegmann, ed., *Édits des guerres de religion* (Paris: J. Vrin, 1979), 35–36. All translations by the author unless otherwise indicated.

5. Tom Hamilton, "Adjudicating the Troubles: Violence, Memory and Criminal Justice at the End of the Wars of Religion," *French History* 34, no. 4 (2020): 417–34.

6. Théodore Agrippa d'Aubigné, "Princes," in *Les Tragiques*, ed. Jean-Raymond Fanlo (Paris: Champion, 2006), lines 1083–90, 408.

7. Théodore Agrippa d'Aubigné, *Les Tragiques*, trans. Valerie Worth-Stylianou (Tempe: Arizona Center for Medieval and Renaissance Studies, 2020), 168.

8. For example, for the martyrology, see Jean Crespin's *Histoires des martyrs persecutez et mis à mort pour la verite de l'Evangile depuis le temps des Apostres jusques à present*, continued by Simon Goulart (Geneva: Pierre Aubert, 1619). For the history, see Simon Goulart, *Mémoires de la Ligue sous Henri III & Henri IV* (s.l.: s.n., 1602);

and Théodore Agrippa d'Aubigné's own *Histoire universelle* (Maillé: Jean Moussat, 1616–1620; Geneva: Droz, 1981–2000).

9. For some examples of these literary forms, see Christian Biet, ed., *Théâtre de la cruauté et récits sanglants en France (XVIe–XVIIe siècle)* (Paris: R. Laffont, 2006).

10. For an overview of literary and polemic representations of the Wars of Religion, see Jeff Kendrick and Katherine S. Maynard, eds., *Polemic and Literature Surrounding the French Wars of Religion* (Boston: De Gruyter, 2019).

11. For the early history of grotesque ornament in France, see Kelly Dianne Cook, "Meanings and Manifestations," in "Power Play: Grotesque Ornament and the Art of Political Persuasion in Early Modern France" (PhD diss., Cornell University, 2012), 74–134, in particular 84: "It was at Fontainebleau that the use of the grotesque motif became fundamental to the making of art in France during the sixteenth century." For more on the School of Fontainebleau, see Henri Zerner, *The School of Fontainebleau: Etchings and Engravings* (New York: Abrams, 1969). See also Lisa Anderson, "Masquing/(Un)Masking: Animation and the Restless Ornament of Fontainebleau," in *Ornament and Monstrosity in Early Modern Art*, ed. Chris Askholt Hammeken and Maria Fabricius Hansen (Amsterdam: Amsterdam University Press, 2019), 82: "Primarily through the technology of print (both engraving and etching), the ornamental frames were separated from the central frescoes and circulated either as vacant cartouches or as frames for a wide variety of new content. In this intermedial process, ornament also moved from periphery to centre."

12. Maria Fabricius Hansen, *The Art of Transformation: Grotesques in Sixteenth-Century Italy* (Rome: Edizioni Quasar, 2018), 15.

13. Hansen, *Art of Transformation*, 15.

14. Hansen, *Art of Transformation*, 22: "Moreover, grotesques' compositional principles imbue them with temporality: They involve a sequentiality, implying the passage of time as one figure gradually develops into another in the beholder's perception. They cannot be grasped in a glance since they typically cover the walls and ceiling of a certain room, making the spectator's movement in space—and thus in time—implicit in the mode of perception."

15. Hansen, *Art of Transformation*, 16.

16. For the metamorphic nature of the grotesque, see Victor Kommerell, "How Ovid's *Metamorphoses* Intertwined with the Domus Aurea Grottesche," in *Metamorphosed Margins: The Case for a Visual Rhetoric of the Renaissance Grottesche under the Influence of Ovid's "Metamorphoses"* (Hildesheim: Georg Olms Verlag, 2008), 81–116.

17. Chris Askholt Hammeken and Maria Fabricius Hansen, introduction to *Ornament and Monstrosity*, 13. According to Hammeken and Hansen, the grotesque expresses "an interest in strange exaggeration and curious artifice while engaging in constant interaction between centre and periphery, content and ornament, or *ergon* and *parergon*, to employ a Kantian vocabulary. A parergon is a framework in the broadest sense and appears as that which surround or supports the ergon, which is the centrepiece, in terms of form, content, or argument. The *parergon* is not, however, a superfluous or superficial addition to the work, but is a precondition for the *ergon*."

18. Sextus Empiricus, "Concerning Sign," in *Outlines of Pyrrhonism*, trans. R. G. Bury, Loeb Classical Library (Cambridge, MA: Harvard University Press, 1933), 212–37.

19. Cathy Caruth, *Unclaimed Experience: Trauma, Narrative, and History* (Baltimore: Johns Hopkins University Press, 1996), 5.

20. Michel de Montaigne, "Apologie de Raymond Sebond," in *Les Essais de Montaigne*, ed. Pierre Villey (Paris: Presses universitaires de France, 1978), 502: "Pyrrho et autres Skeptiques ou Epechistes . . . disent qu'ils sont encore en cherche de la verité. Ceux-cy jugent que ceux qui pensent l'avoir trouvée, se trompent infiniment: et qu'il y a encore de la vanité trop hardie en ce second degré qui asseure que les forces humaines ne sont pas capables d'y atteindre." For the English, see "Apology for Raymond Sebond," in *The Complete Essays of Montaigne*, trans. Donald Frame (Stanford, CA: Stanford University Press, 1965), 371: "Pyrrho and other Skeptics or Epechists . . . say that they are still in search of the truth. These men judge that those who think they have found it are infinitely mistaken; and that there is an overbold vanity in that second class that assures us that human powers are not capable of attaining it." On Montaigne's skepticism, see, among others, Frédéric Brahami, *Le Scepticisme de Montaigne* (Paris: Presses universitaires de France, 1997); Hubert Vincent, *Vérité du scepticisme chez Montaigne* (Paris: Harmattan, 1998); Zahi Zalloua, *Montaigne and the Ethics of Skepticism* (Charlottesville, VA: Rookwood Press, 2005); David Sedley, *Sublimity and Skepticism in Montaigne and Milton* (Ann Arbor: University of Michigan Press, 2005).

21. Sextus Empiricus, "Of 'Aphasia' or Non-assertion," in *Outlines of Pyrrhonism*, 110–13.

22. Sextus Empiricus, "What Is the End of Scepticism?," in *Outlines of Pyrrhonism*, 18–21.

23. For the foundational work on the importance of skepticism for early modern thought, see Richard H. Popkin, *The History of Scepticism from Savonarola to Bayle* (Oxford: Oxford University Press, 2003).

24. Montaigne, *Essais*, 183.

25. Montaigne, *Complete Essays*, 135.

26. Jean Starobinski, *Montaigne in Motion*, trans. Arthur Goldhammer (Chicago: University of Chicago Press, 1985), 232.

27. Brad Epps, "Grotesque Identities: Writing, Death, and the Space of the Subject (Between Michel de Montaigne and Reinaldo Arenas)," *Journal of the Midwest Modern Language Association* 28, no. 1 (1995): 40. I am also indebted for any special insight I have into this passage to the as-yet-unpublished essay by my colleague Chad Cordóva, "Life in the Grotto: Montaigne and the Meaning of Posthumanism," presented at Emory University on March 1, 2021.

28. Kathleen P. Long, "Théodore Agrippa d'Aubigné," in *Dictionary of Literary Biography*, ed. Megan Conway (Farmington Hills, MI: Thomson Gale, 2006), 9–23.

29. Théodore Agrippa d'Aubigné, "Les Fers," in *Les Tragiques*, ed. Fanlo, lines 193–209, 582–84.

30. Aubigné, *Les Tragiques*, trans. Worth-Stylianou, 277. I have substituted my own translation for line 207, as it is closer to a common use of the verb "avorter" in

the period (when an "avorton" can be a monstrous birth). Dictionnaires d'autrefois, ARTFL Project (website), https://artflsrv03.uchicago.edu/philologic4/publicdicos/query?report=bibliography&head=avorton.

31. For the debate over whether demonic possession was a physiological event or merely took place in the imagination, see Hans Broedel, "Fifteenth Century Witch Beliefs," in *The Oxford Handbook of Witchcraft in Early Modern Europe and Colonial America*, Oxford Handbooks Online (Oxford: Oxford University Press), 11–14.

32. For a different perspective on the aesthetics of this passage, see Kathleen P. Long, "Improper Perspective: Anamorphosis in the Works of Theodore Agrippa d'Aubigné," in "Figuring Protest and Lament," ed. Dora Polachek, special issue, *Medievalia* 22 (1999): 103–26.

33. Jacques Derrida, *The Truth in Painting*, trans. Geoff Bennington and Ian McLeod (Chicago: University of Chicago Press, 1987), 17.

34. For the suspension of judgment, see Sextus Empiricus, *Outlines of Pyrrhonism*, book 1, chapter 12, 18–21.

35. Rebecca Zorach, *Blood, Milk, Ink, Gold: Abundance and Excess in the French Renaissance* (Chicago: University of Chicago Press, 2005), 151.

36. Aubigné, "Jugement," in *Les Tragiques*, ed. Fanlo, lines 665–76, 769–70.

37. Aubigné, "Jugement," in *Les Tragiques*, trans. Worth-Stylianou, lines 665–76, 391.

38. Aubigné, "Jugement," ed. Fanlo, lines 1209–18, 800–801.

39. Aubigné, "Jugement," trans. Worth-Stylianou, lines 1209–18, 407.

40. The most likely author is Arthus Thomas, a little-known figure who published a number of works, including a commentary for Blaise de Vigenère's translation of Philostratus's *Life of Apollonius* (1611), and a continuation of de Vigenère's *History of the Decline of the Greek Empire*, which was published in 1650 under the title *Continuation of the History of the Turks*. He added epigrams to the translation of *Images or Paintings of the Two Philostrates, Greek Sophists, and Statues of Callistrates* (1614), in a style reminiscent of the beginning of *The Island of Hermaphrodites*. Probably from the circle of de Vigenère, he demonstrates a manifest interest in classical Greek and in the more recent history of the Near East, as well as the relationship between power and decadence. He also produced a work predicting the ruin of the Ottoman Empire, works on Catholic doctrine, and, according to Ilana Zinguer, pamphlets against calumny and concerning the punishment of virtue, as well as a protofeminist work, *That It Is Proper That Women Be Knowledgeable* (1600).

41. *L'Isle des hermaphrodites*, ed. Claude-Gilbert Dubois (Geneva: Droz, 1996), 57. All references to this novel are to this edition; all translations are my own.

42. *L'Isle des hermaphrodites*, 58.

43. *L'Isle des hermaphrodites*, 59.

44. Christopher P. Heuer, introduction to *The City Rehearsed: Object, Architecture, and Print in the Worlds of Hans Vredeman de Vries* (London: Routledge, 2009), 1. For a brief biography of Vredeman de Vries, see pp. 6–7.

45. Heuer, *The City Rehearsed*, 2. The Latin edition of this work is *Perspective, id est celeberrima ars inspicientis aut transpicientis oculorum aciei, in pariete, tabula aut tele depicta* (Leiden: Henricus Hondius, 1604). Vredeman de Vries also

composed designs for formal gardens: *Hortorum* (s.l.: Philippe Galle, 1583); see *Hollstein's Dutch & Flemish Etchings, Engravings and Woodcuts, 1450–1700, Volume 48: Vredeman de Vries, Part 2*, compiled by Peter Fuhring (Rotterdam: Sound & Vision Interactive, 1997), 122–36. He produced designs for tombs: *Coenotaphiorum* (s.l.: Hieronymus Cock, 1563); see *Hollstein's Dutch & Flemish Etchings, Engravings and Woodcuts, 1450–1700, Volume 47: Vredeman de Vries, Part 1*, compiled by Peter Fuhring (Rotterdam: Sound & Vision Interactive, 1997), 129–50. He published furniture designs: *Differents Pourtraicts de menuiserie* (s.l.: Philippe Galle, s.d.); see *Hollstein's*, 48: 137–55. And he produced a number of works on architecture, including *Architectura* (Antwerp: Gerard Smits, 1577), *Hollstein's*, 48: 56–85; and *Variae Architecturae Formae* (Antwerp: Theodoor Galle, 1601), *Hollstein's*, 47: 69–108.

46. Hans Vredeman de Vries, *Grottesco* (Gerard de Jode, 1565–71; Karel van Mallery, 1612). The reference is from *Hollstein's*, 47: 215–31.

47. *Hollstein's*, 47: 109–28.

48. Hans Vredeman de Vries, *Scenographiae, sive Perspectivae* (Antwerp: Hieronymus Cock, 1560; repr., 1604); *Hollstein's*, 47: 52–68.

49. Heuer, *The City Rehearsed*, 6.

50. Heuer, *The City Rehearsed*, 8–10.

51. Heuer, *The City Rehearsed*, 10.

52. *L'Isle des hermaphrodites*, 61.

53. *L'Isle des hermaphrodites*, 152.

54. For more on this, see Kathleen Long, "Shaping Bodies, Reimagining the World: Sartorial Prosthesis in *L'Isle des hermaphrodites* (1605)," in "Disability's Worldmaking," ed. Tammy Berberi and Jennifer Row, special issue, *L'Esprit créateur* (December 2021), 127–39.

55. *L'Isle des hermaphrodites*, 70–71.

56. *L'Isle des hermaphrodites*, 54.

57. *L'Isle des hermaphrodites*, 187.

58. *L'Isle des hermaphrodites*, 64.

59. *L'Isle des hermaphrodites*, 60.

60. *L'Isle des hermaphrodites*, 180.

PART TWO
The Hispanic World

Chapter Four

Desire, Trauma, and Warfare in Fernando de Rojas's *Celestina*

Nicholas Ealy

At the close of Fernando de Rojas's fifteenth-century Spanish masterwork *Celestina*, Pleberio, the patriarchal figure whose presence looms large in the text, witnesses the unexpected suicide of his daughter Melibea, who, bereft over the death of her lover Calisto, throws herself from a tower to the ground below. In a subsequent interrogation of his inability to accept this loss, Pleberio gives a speech portraying the human experience, with its endless suffering, longing, and desperation, as a lifelong—and ultimately losing—battle with *amor* (desire).[1] Encapsulating a larger narrative shaped by the violence of desire, Pleberio's speech positions *Celestina* at a crossroads. At once steeped in the familiar medieval traditions of erotic love and passion, it simultaneously aligns itself with a burgeoning early modern sensibility of an illogical universe where hopelessness and alienation inform terrestrial existence.[2] Such hopelessness, stemming in part from the interreligious strife and civil unrest of the era, comes to be reflected in the bellicose landscape of *Celestina*, which similarly structures its plot within a world of characters who traffic in deception, strife, and bloodshed. In this context, it is not surprising that the theme of war, which shapes *Celestina*'s prologue and informs its characters' actions toward one another and themselves, finds such a prominent focus in the work.

The violence caused by war, in this sense, comes to mirror the violence caused by desire, which, as we see in Melibea's suicide, results in dismembered bodies and death. Exploring this nexus of desire and war—of desire *as* war—this chapter examines the ways various characters (primarily Calisto and Pleberio, and to some extent Melibea) struggle with their unforeseen yearnings, not simply in ways that embody the chaos of war, but in how they bear the psycho-physiological markings of war injuries—of wounds—upon their bodies. It is this emphasis upon the wound, I argue, that serves as a permanent reminder of the war waged by desire (many times personified as Cupid) upon these desiring subjects, exposing their vulnerabilities and eroding their integrity in ways that doom them to a seemingly endless repetition of unfulfilled longing, solitude, and annihilation. Contemporary thought on trauma, as a theory of the wound, will prove important to my analysis; these injuries, as a result of desire's attacks, disturb once-familiar notions of temporality and language that work, ultimately, to alienate these characters from their own longings and their sense of self and place in the world.

In this exploration of the wounded human condition, Rojas's work, which first appeared in Burgos, Spain, around 1499 as the *Comedia de Calisto y Melibea*, traces the story of Calisto, who hires Celestina, the work's titular character (a "puta vieja" [old whore]), as a matchmaker to help him procure Pleberio's daughter, Melibea.[3] As the Spanish literary text that has probably garnered the most critical attention after *Don Quixote*, *Celestina* underwent various iterations, with what many critics consider the definitive version published in 1502. This edition, rebranded a tragicomedy, contains a prose prologue where Rojas assails his critics, who earlier had taken issue with the work's dark content, by introducing the theme of war in a move that frames *Celestina*'s exploration of desire—in a stark parallel to Pleberio's speech—within the context of bellicosity.[4] Citing Heraclitus from Petrarch's *De remediis utriusque fortunae*, which examines the fickle nature of fortune, Rojas opens the prologue declaring: "Todas las cosas ser criadas a manera de contienda o batalla dice aquel gran sabio Heráclito en este modo: 'Omnia secundum litem fiunt,' sentencia a mi ver digna de perpetua y recordable memoria" (That great and wise philosopher Heraclitus states that all things are created as a struggle or battle: 'All things come into being through strife,' a saying, in my opinion, worthy of perpetual remembrance).[5] With strife and battle as the prologue's central tenet, Rojas, now directly citing Petrarch, continues, positing that "sin lid y ofensión ninguna cosa engendró la natura, madre de todo" (nature, the mother of all, brings forth nothing without battle and contention).[6] Arming himself with this dual textual authority, he emphasizes that conflict is the normal state of affairs, as all of nature, divided from within, is in a battle with itself; opposing elements (such as earth/water and air/fire) consistently break out in fights ("rompen pelea"), the winds are at perpetual war ("perpetua guerra") with themselves, overly hot summers and bitterly cold winters are akin to war ("no es sino guerra"), and every species of the animal kingdom, a world of carnage and consumption, has its own wars ("ningún género carece de guerra").[7] In this ferocious landscape, however, no figure embodies a propensity for war more than humans—a lifelong savagery Rojas recognizes as both innate and undeniable: "¿Quién explanará sus guerras, sus enemistades, sus envidias, sus aceleramientos y movimientos y descontentamientos? . . . aun la mesma vida de los hombres, si bien lo miramos, desde la primera edad hasta que blanquean las canas, es batalla" (Who will explain their wars, their feuds, their envy, their haste and movements and discontentments? . . . for even the very life of men, if we consider it carefully, from their earliest years until their hair turns gray, is a battle).[8]

Much of the savagery that attacks humanity, as evident within *Celestina*, is present in the figure of Cupid, whose name appears numerous times throughout the work. Understood since the late classical era as the son of Venus (the goddess of love) and Mars (the god of war), Cupid, the god of desire, allegorizes the inextricable link between passion and bellicosity so central to Rojas's text.[9] According to the *Picatrix*, an important and influential text on astrology translated from Arabic into both Spanish and Latin in the thirteenth century, Mars—as the embodiment of war—traffics in "oppressiones, dolores, hominum discordias, terrores, . . . anxietates sive miserias, penas, vulneraciones" (oppressions, pains, human strife, terrors, . . . anxieties or miseries, punishments, wounds).[10] Stripped of any sense of honor or glory in its destruction of all "veritate et legalitate" (truth and lawfulness), war, as presented here, overwhelms the individual in a barrage of psycho-physiological injuries that, as I explore, situate the wounded body as both the aim and end result of such violent forces.[11]

Such a confluence of wounding and war in *Celestina* finds a theoretical parallel in contemporary approaches to the study of trauma, first arising in the twentieth century as a means of explaining the "nervous disorders," similar to the anxiety and terror of the *Picatrix*, experienced by soldiers after the horrors of battle.[12] Trauma, from the Greek words for wound ($\tau\rho\alpha\tilde{\upsilon}\mu\alpha$, *trauma*) and piercing ($\tau\iota\tau\rho\pi\sigma\chi\omega$, *titrpscho*), has nevertheless been used to indicate, ever since the classical period, "an injury where the skin is broken as a consequence of external violence, and the effects of such an injury upon the organism as a whole."[13] Modern theoretical (as well as clinical) conceptions, which expand this definition to include mental scarring that nonetheless acts as if it were a physical wound, can be equally located in and applied to medieval society. As Wendy J. Turner and Christina Lee have argued, individual and societal traumas are prominent in medieval literature and legal records, as well as forensic evidence.[14] This connection between physical and mental scarring as a model of trauma, I argue, is present in Calisto's (and later Melibea's and Pleberio's) experience with Cupid's arrow, where a weapon pierces the body's flesh and causes a wound that, in turn, reveals psychic tumult. Although not damaged in physical battle by an opposing army, these wounded bodies nonetheless manifest this ethos of war as traumatic injury, as desire, in its unrelenting assault, comes to mirror the bellicose discord outlined in *Celestina*'s prologue.

Bookending the entire work, such an acute sense of conflict reflects the historical context surrounding the publication of *Celestina*, itself the product of a world very much at war.[15] The date of its first publication (1499), for instance, comes a mere seven years after the Granada War, the Christian "reconquest" of the Iberian Peninsula that, in 1492, ended the last Islamic stronghold in Spain. Along with this victory, that same year saw the forced expulsion of Jews who refused to accept Catholicism from the kingdom's newly Christianized realms. This purge, the culmination of increasing segregation, discrimination, and violence directed at Spanish Jews over the latter half of the fifteenth century, indicated not simply the official end of the religion in Spain, but also opened the opportunity for atrocities committed against the recent converts (conversos), believed by some still to be Jews but in disguise, at the hands of Inquisitorial and political powers. Such horrors manifested themselves, in numerous cases, as outright warfare involving armies and battles between the so-called "old Christians" (those from non-convert families) and the conversos.[16]

Violence and Christianity in the Iberian Peninsula were therefore not at odds. Indeed, the notion of a holy war, a precedent already set by the Crusades, was the driving force behind much of this interreligious strife.[17] As various scholars suggest, Rojas, himself a descendent of conversos, most likely thus saw Petrarch's *De remediis*, a work exploring the capricious nature of fortune, as a mirror reflecting the tumult of his environment.[18] Beginning with references from a text concerning mistrust in fortune, *Celestina*, in other words, speaks to a pervasive culture of skepticism in fifteenth-century Spain. Informed by societal unrest, Rojas saw God as an entity removed from a world now ruled by the disorder caused by humanity's more destructive and baser instincts.[19] As such, Rojas, completely rejecting any remedy for this disorganization, overlooks (and indeed reverses) the second half of Petrarch's message: that harmony can come from reason and God's benediction. Instead, we find the divine, and the solace it might bring, completely absent from his work.[20]

This lack of a godly presence in *Celestina*, which would otherwise serve to stabilize the human experience, manifests itself not simply as the image of a world unconvinced by reason and justice, but also undoes, in quite radical ways, the supposed "ethical aspects" of a certain understanding of desire popular in the High and Late Middle Ages. Referred to as *fin'amor* by the troubadour poets ("courtly love" in English), this mode of love tended to dominate narratives (such as those of chivalric romances) where a male character pursues a woman as his beloved object, with the pretense that his desire for her will lead to spiritual and/or moral betterment.[21]

While the characters in *Celestina* do express their desires, with some claiming to fall in love in ways that parallel the structure of *fin'amor*, their yearnings are instead based upon transient corporeal and psycho-physiological needs (e.g., sex, wealth, prestige, etc.) that typically end in violent acts of destruction. For instance, Calisto's servants Sempronio and Pármeno, wanting a larger share of the payment given to Celestina, murder her and consequently receive the death penalty. In addition, Calisto, after meeting Melibea in the garden of her parents' home for one final amorous encounter, falls to his death while climbing down the ladder set up for him against the garden's walls; distraught, Melibea in turn commits suicide. Completely upending the ethos of *fin'amor*, *Celestina* thereby strips human longing of any redemptive qualities, revealing it instead as a chaotic force that seeks both to harm and eliminate the desiring subject.

This overturning of *fin'amor* becomes apparent in the text's opening scene where, chasing his falcon while out hunting, Calisto sees Melibea in the garden of her father's house, the symbolic space for the destructive love of the story (this is the garden, for instance, where both Calisto and Melibea will die). The first words he speaks to the maiden, in which he compares her beauty to divine glory ("En esto veo, Melibea, la grandeza de Dios" [In this I see, Melibea, the greatness of God]), seem to uphold the transcendental aspects of *fin'amor*; her immediate rejection of him (because she also plays the "game of love" as the attractive yet elusive object of desire) foretells the carnality to come.[22] For, although Calisto falls into the role of the suffering lover of medieval erotic literature upon returning home (he experiences melancholic longing, professes his devotion to Melibea's image, composes song lyrics, etc.), he nonetheless decides to hire Celestina as a mediator in the hope of trapping Melibea, despite the old bawd's widely known reputation for deception.[23] The struggles and pursuits of the animal world, used metaphorically in the work's prologue to signify the bellicose nature of the cosmic order, therefore come to be reflected in Calisto's own actions. Instead of any motivation for a sense of divine or moral betterment as the courtly knight or forlorn poet he might appear to emulate, he maintains a steadfast determination to trap and conquer Melibea. The falcon, a bird of prey serving as the symbol for this "hunt of love" and a motif *Celestina* borrows directly from earlier medieval sources, implies accordingly both violent attack and possession, with death and consumption as its end game.[24] Calisto and the falcon, mirroring one another in rapacious domination, thus work together—the bird searching for prey brings him into the space where he, with Celestina's help, will work to ensnare the young maiden.

The longing Calisto experiences, however, does not simply emanate from within him as desiring subject, toward Melibea as his intended object, but rather remains a mystery to him as he suffers its merciless attacks. In this sense, Calisto, first portrayed as the hunting subject, is in truth the hunted object, pursued by a longing that traps him in a constant state of dissatisfaction. His servant Pármeno, tracing his master's suffering to the text's opening scene, astutely recognizes its potential effects when he declares that: "porque perderse el otro día el neblí fue causa de tu entrada en la huerta de Melibea a le buscar; la entrada causa de la veer y hablar; la habla engendró amor; el amor parió tu pena; la pena causará perder tu cuerpo y alma y hacienda" (because the loss of your falcon the other day caused you to enter Melibea's garden looking for it; your entry caused you to see and speak to her. Talking brought about love, love brought about your pain, and the pain will cause you to lose your body, soul, and estate).[25] Calisto's pain, though, is not something that exists simply in the abstract, but rather is a phenomenon that starts with his sight as it negotiates between the outside visual world and an interior realm of imagery and emotions. Addressing this, Calisto describes his initial encounter with Melibea, who eventually succumbs to her own desires for him, as an attack upon his sight and, subsequently, his heart: "O mis ojos, acordaos cómo fuistes causa y puerta por donde fue mi corazón llagado" (O my eyes, remember how you were the cause and the door through which my heart was wounded).[26] The process of love here, in other words, is that of the human body under assault, as Calisto experiences desire as physical violence resulting in an "ardiente llaga" (fiery wound) caused by "la cruel frecha de Cupido" (Cupid's cruel arrow).[27]

Calisto's words open a discourse on desire, not simply as a violent act where Cupid's weapon pierces his heart, but also as an overwhelming force that wounds.[28] While suffering the effects of his unfulfilled longing, Calisto, for instance, references this connection between love and war when he, arriving at Melibea's home and wanting to be with her, finds himself unable to enter her house. Speaking through closed doors, he explains how his desire has set his heart on fire ("encendieron mi corazón") and then, addressing the doors, declares his wish that the longing "waging war" ("como a mí da guerra") against him would also set them ablaze.[29] The desire he visually projected onto Melibea has thus returned to him, not as a harmonious reciprocation but as a fiery attack symbolically paralleling Cupid's arrow, which has struck his eye and lacerated his heart.[30] In this sense, the weapon, having permanently sundered his body, acts like the first shot of a war, the domain Cupid inherits from his father Mars. Trapped within a cruel battle that consumes his bruised heart, Calisto thereby remains captivated and captured by desire for Melibea, whose beautiful attributes, he laments, mortally wound and destroy him in their ferocity; for these are "sus armas; con éstas mata y vence" (her weapons; with these she kills and conquers).[31]

Such a battle, however, can be traced back to Calisto's initial encounter with Melibea in the garden. After she first rejects him, for instance, he returns home complaining of a "llaga interior" (interior wound) and, mentioning the human body, speaks of it as a site barraged by disharmony, where opposing forces battle for dominance: "¿Cómo sentirá el armonía aquel que consigo está tan discorde, aquel en quien la voluntad a la razón no obedece, quien tiene dentro del pecho aguijones, paz, guerra, tregua, amor, enemistad, injurias, pecados, sospechas, toda a una causa?" (How would someone who is so out of tune know harmony, someone whose will does not obey reason, who has within their chest thorns, peace, war, truce, love, enmity, injuries, offenses, suspicions, all due to one cause?).[32] Calisto's statement here, which references *Eunuchus* by the Latin playwright Terence, squarely places desire (*amor*) as the origin of such an internalized background. When put in context with their classical source, therefore, Calisto's words demonstrate how desire works in an oppositional manner (holding out the promise of love and peace while trafficking in violence) that exposes how it has ensnared him: "In amore haec omnia insunt uitia: iniuriae, suspiciones, inimicitiae, indutiae, bellum, pax rursum" (In desire all these vices are found: injuries, suspicions, enmity, truce, war, and even peace).[33] In this manner, desire, consistently operating on such contraries, divides itself as a force arising from within while also attacking from without in the symbolic form of Cupid's arrow; possessing a longing that simultaneously possesses him, he is left, as a result, irrevocably alienated from his own desires. Exposing the vulnerability of his corporeal and mental state to a yearning that—now weaponized—has forcibly invaded him, Calisto's wound, a passageway to the interior, allows for his pain and frustration to spill outwards in his longing for a healing that will forever be denied. In this breakdown of oppositions, trauma—as a theory of the wound—can thus be understood in *Celestina*, at least initially, as a wound that permeates and destabilizes the distinction between antitheses such as to possess/to be possessed and longing/satisfaction in a manner that psychically overwhelms and disturbs the desiring subject. As such, the wound—the trauma—becomes, as Roger Luckhurst posits, the "breach of a border" that, once thought to protect, now "puts inside and outside into a strange communication . . . open[ing] passageways between systems that were once discrete, making unforeseen connections that distress or confound."[34] For, if Calisto's wound teaches him that he cannot possess his desires, cannot possess *his own self*, he finds himself not simply in a crisis over his longing, but in a crisis over his very subjectivity.

This crisis has a further manifestation in how trauma also alters Calisto's understanding of temporality, disturbing his interaction with the past, present, and future in a manner that underscores the wound's hold on him. As various scholars have pointed out, the characters in *Celestina* deal with time in an obsessive manner, frequently mentioning its passing as well as referencing specific times of day marked by the clock.[35] Consolación Baranda equates this emphasis to their impatience in seeking to satisfy their desires, an insight

I find important, especially when examining how precise moments in time intersect with Calisto's hurriedness throughout the text when he endeavors to fulfill his longing.[36] One such attempt, for example, occurs when Calisto meets Melibea at her house with the doors closed. Beforehand, much is made of the fact that they are meeting at twelve midnight, a time Celestina tells Calisto that she has arranged for the encounter: "Nunca el corazón lastimado de deseo toma la buena nueva por cierta ni la mala por dudosa. . . . verlo has yendo esta noche . . . a su casa, en dando el reloj doce, a la hablar por entre las puertas; de cuya boca sabrás más por entero . . . su deseo, y el amor que te tiene" (The heart wounded by desire never takes good news for truth nor bad news as doubtful. . . . You will see her tonight . . . at her house, when the clock strikes twelve, and will talk to her through the doors; from her mouth you will entirely know her desire and the love she has for you).[37] Calisto, eager for this hour to arrive, is already worried at ten o'clock, imagining that, had he fallen asleep, he might have missed the rendezvous: "Saliera Melibea, yo no fuera ido, tornárase; de manera que ni mi mal hobiera fin ni mi deseo ejecución" (Melibea would have come out, I would not have gone, and she would have turned back, in such a way that my illness would have no end nor my desire fulfillment).[38] The clock, in this context, seems to have the capacity to indicate a precise moment for his long-awaited wish to meet with Melibea and experience his longing reciprocated back to him from her. Such a meeting, in other words, would undo the moment in the garden when Cupid's arrow first struck him, Melibea rejected him, and his melancholic yearning began.

His anxiety over missing this meeting at twelve o'clock nonetheless embodies a specific temporal crisis located in this opening scene where, believing himself to be the hunter and not the hunted, Calisto finds himself completely unprepared for desire's brutal onslaught. His wounding, in other words, happens too soon, an unpreparedness symbolized by the radiance of Melibea's countenance which, striking his eyes, connotes a moment of blindness, a "missed event," incomprehensible to him as it occurs. This is why, as Cathy Caruth holds, the traumatic moment is never found in what might be perceived as the "original event" (here in Pleberio's garden, for example), but instead embodies a certain "unassimilated nature" existing outside of a comprehensible temporal structure. As such, the moment of trauma, not grasped in its first occurrence, "returns to haunt [the wounded subject] later on."[39] The encounter with Melibea at midnight, in other words, is an attempt to "recapture" and undo the unassimilated moment of his *innamoramento* (falling in love) and, by strictly adhering here to a specific time on the clock, he hopes to understand the desire that possesses him, heal his wound, and free himself from suffering. At twelve o'clock, however, Calisto, separated from Melibea through the closed doors, remains unable to see or touch her and, as the two decide to meet at another time, he leaves with his satisfaction delayed once again.

This continuously postponed arrival at fulfillment is perhaps most evident after Calisto sleeps with Melibea and he—achieving what he thought he wanted—instead finds himself dejected, devoid of sustained happiness. The ever-present wound, he discovers, strangely reflects an absence of the satisfaction he sought: "esta herida es la que siento, agora que se ha resfriado" (this wound, which now has cooled, is what I feel).[40] The clock, failing to guarantee any recapturing of his *innamoramento*, also marks his having missed the moment of dissatisfaction that, to his surprise, is just as troubling as the wounding itself: "agora que está helada la sangre que ayer hervía. . . . ¿Qué hice? ¿En qué me detuve?" (now the blood that boiled yesterday is frozen. . . . What did I do? Where did I fail?).[41] Determined to repeat a moment that might bring satisfaction, he nonetheless finds himself torn between anticipating such an appointed hour and realizing that further attempts may result in yet another missed opportunity to achieve this goal, thereby simply reinscribing the wound and reaffirming his alienation. Each present disappointment fails to undo the previous trauma of Cupid's arrow and instead projects him toward hope for fulfillment at a specific time in the future, a moment that can never arrive.[42] Calisto, in other words, is always met with delay—he can only ever be too late—and the moment of satisfaction, once missed, is perpetually deferred, with every attempt to assimilate his desire in time revealed as an iteration of his inability to control its capricious nature: "¡Oh espacioso reloj, aún te vea yo arder en vivo huego de amor! . . . ¿Qué me aprovecha a mí que dé doce horas el reloj de hierro si no las ha dado el del cielo? Pues por mucho que madrugue, no amanece más aína" (Oh slow clock, I still might see you while I am ablaze with love's fire! . . . What does it benefit me that the mechanical clock strikes twelve if that in the heavens has not struck twelve? For however early I get up, dawn does not come any sooner).[43]

As Calisto subsequently discovers, time has exposed a fundamental lack within him, an absence he attempted to overcome at a specific hour that now appears strangely and irrevocably out of reach. He finds that his desire, removed from a comprehensible temporal structure, resists all understanding, with the clock never coinciding with a prescribed moment that might heal his wound. Failing to distinguish an orderly chronology to daily existence, time accordingly collapses; reflecting now the chaos of a bellicose world, it merely increases the unknowable nature of his trauma and the unfulfillable lack that has come to define him. And just as time consistently reinforces the trauma of his desire, it foretells his eventual death, which can strike, like Cupid's arrow, at any moment. Time, in other words, may never release Calisto from his suffering, but it does mark his death, mark him as the living dead: "¡Oh mísera suavidad desta brevísima vida! . . . Mayormente que no hay hora cierta ni limitada, ni aun un solo momento: deudores somos sin tiempo; contino estamos obligados a pagar luego. . . . ¡Oh breve deleite mundano, cómo duran poco y cuestan mucho tus dulzores! . . . ¡Oh triste yo!" (Oh miserable gentleness of this brief life! . . . Principally because there is no certain or prescribed hour, not even a single moment: we are all debtors without time, always obliged to pay later. . . . Oh brief worldly pleasure, how your sweetness lasts little and costs much! . . . Oh sad me!).[44] As such, Calisto's very sense of self, in this confluence of desire and death, propels an undoing of his belief to be "self-possessed and self-possessing," resulting in a trauma defined, according to Andrew Barnaby, as a crisis of self sparked by the "sudden, shocking discovery that the consciousness by which we think, engage the world, and even know ourselves is an illusion, or worse, a lie."[45] And, as Rachel Scott has posited, such a crisis of the desiring subject as displaced within an alienated world is due precisely to the brutal environment in which these characters find themselves, where the strife and battle of *Celestina*'s prologue "depict a world in which individuals struggle to define themselves and their place in society."[46] In such a context, trauma in Rojas's text, with its emphasis upon bellicosity and chaos, thereby creates a disillusioned and wounded self at war with itself and its sense of self, with its self *as* self, adrift in the chaos of a violent and godless world that, through repeated assaults, keeps the traumatic wound persistently open with reminders of incomprehensible loss, lack, and unfulfilled desires.

The exploration of this disillusioned self, undone by trauma in a collapsing world, reaches its height with the concluding soliloquy Pleberio gives after witnessing his daughter, made distraught by Calisto's death after their final encounter, throw herself from a tower in the garden. Before jumping, however, Melibea confesses her affair with Calisto, whose passing has given her "una mortal llaga en medio del corazón que no me consiente hablar" (a mortal wound in the midst of my heart that does not allow me to speak).[47] Her suicide, which she believes will heal the wound by reuniting her with Calisto, stuns Pleberio so much that, upon seeing his daughter "hecha pedazos" (in pieces) on the ground, his cries awaken his wife Alisa, who emerges exclaiming: "oyendo tus gemidos, tus voces tan altas . . . en tal manera penetraron mis entrañas, en tal manera traspasaron mi corazón, así avivaron mis turbados sentidos, que el ya recebido pesar alancé de mí. Un dolor sacó otro, un sentimiento otro" (hearing your sobs, your loud voice . . . they penetrated me to the core and ran through my heart, thus reviving my distraught senses in a way that the previously heard sorrow shot through me. One pain brought forth another, one feeling another).[48] Alisa's words here, expected given the circumstances, nonetheless reveal Pleberio's outcry as having the ability to strike her body (her heart, the core of her being) in ways eerily similar to Cupid's assault on Calisto and Melibea. Pleberio's lament, in other words, pierces her body in a way that infiltrates her psyche, even before she knows what has happened, to become her pain as well—as she then falls, as if dead, upon her daughter's corpse.

Melibea's death, therefore, does not negate her trauma or close her wound so much as repeat and extend its violent effects upon others, who are then joined to it, continuing to bear the wound. Her frustrated desire and her fractured body, which at this point in the narrative is simply the latest in a line of mutilated corpses, will now, to paraphrase her mother's words, *sacar otro*, bring forth another, in an iterative process of traumatic wounding. And it appears that not simply Melibea and her parents fall victim here; for, as she states before jumping, the city—and all of society—has broken out in a discordant cacophony due to Calisto's funeral: "Bien ves y oyes este triste y doloroso sentimiento que toda la ciudad hace. Bien oyes este clamor de campanas, este alarido de gentes, este aullido de canes, este estrépito de armas. De todo esto fui yo causa" (You clearly see and hear this sad and painful sentiment that the entire city expresses. You clearly hear these bells ringing, these people yelling, these dogs barking, these loud weapons. I was the cause of all this).[49] In the midst of this chaos, the result of Cupid's war upon humanity, Pleberio experiences an irreversible isolation within the garden's walls, realizing that his sense of self is, like Calisto's and Melibea's before him, in *pedazos* (pieces), devoid of agency and alienated from others as well as from his own self. As such, his speech explores the injurious consequences of traumatic desire as it converges with death in a final battle where, he learns, Cupid vanquishes all: "¡Oh amor, amor, que no pensé que tenías fuerza ni poder de matar a tus sujetos! Herida fue de ti mi juventud; por medio de tus brasas pasé. ¿Cómo me soltaste para me dar la paga de la huida en mi vejez? Bien pensé que de tus lazos me había librado" (Oh love, love, I did not think you had the strength or power to kill your subjects! My youth was wounded by you; through your embers I crossed. How did you release me only to make me pay for my flight from you in my old age? I truly thought I had freed myself from your traps.)[50]

Desperate for relief from his painful solitude, Pleberio seeks consolation from Cupid's war by curiously turning to war. Looking to the examples of six historical figures who, having also lost children, embody an ethos of bellicosity, a preparedness for battle, and a seeming ability to navigate and make sense of the onslaughts of life's tragedies, he attempts to locate some meaning that might stabilize the unbearable chaos of his present situation. The first three, Paulo Emilio (Lucius Aemilius Paullus), the Roman senator who victoriously led his army into Macedonia; Xenophon, the Athenian military leader who almost captured Babylon; and Pericles, the Greek general who fought in the Peloponnesian War, ultimately reflect, to Pleberio's disappointment, a stoic and emotionless masculinity that he finds off-putting. Asking for patience like that of Paulo Emilio who lost two sons in seven days, he remains unsatisfied. Furthermore, Xenophon, who maintained his serenity upon hearing news of his son's death, and Pericles, who refused to grieve, affirming that he "no sentía pesar" (felt no pain), offer Pleberio nothing.[51] He then conjures the Greek philosopher Anaxagoras who, upon learning that his son had died in war, reacted in a cold, albeit logical, manner, declaring that because he knew himself to be mortal, he knew his offspring was as well. Finally, Pleberio finds no relief in the story of the king and prophet David, who found it useless to mourn his infant son, dead from divine retribution, after he had Uriah the Hittite killed in battle, or in that of Lamba Doria (Lambas de Auria), who threw his mortally wounded son, shot through with an arrow during a naval battle they were both fighting, into the raging waves of the sea.

In the end, each of these men fails to offer Pleberio guidance as he finds in his loss only a haunting meaninglessness. When comparing Melibea's demise to that of Anaxagoras's son, for instance, he blames her death on "la gran fatiga de amor que le aquejaba" (the immense fatigue of a troubling love) while the young man met his end "en muy lícita batalla" (in a very licit battle), that is, in a manner sanctioned as legal (*lícito> licitum*, Latin for "lawful"), as an acceptable way to die.[52] The implication, of course, is that Cupid's assault on his daughter is illicit, against the law, in a world where the law—along with everything else—has ceased to signify anything meaningful. As such, Pleberio's quest for a stabilizing force in war fails, as he rejects everything these men and their stories represent—family, masculine ideals, fame and glory, political power, military might, philosophical and legal reasoning, religious tradition, divine intervention, and history. The battle with Love in which he finds himself, where there is no honor in death, is simply about injury and elimination. All the paragons of masculine power stand demolished, and Pleberio, understanding himself as a powerless victim of Cupid's assaults, can look to no sociocultural institution or tradition that might offer escape from his desperation. The universe of the prologue, as a place of disorder and chaos, thus comes to be reflected at its conclusion, where Pleberio, struggling to define himself, finds that he has—ultimately—no place in society.[53]

It is in such a tumultuous environment that Pleberio, staring into the unknown, has therefore been tasked with testifying to this struggle, to his alienation in an unwelcoming world, to Cupid's prolonged assault on him. Melibea, for instance, understanding hopelessness all too well, recognizes her father as someone capable of witnessing her wounded subjectivity when, before killing herself, she says to him: "Tu, Señor, que de mi habla eres testigo, ves mi poco poder, ves cuán cativa tengo mi libertad, cuán presos mis sentidos de tan poderoso amor del muerto caballero" (You, sir, who are witness to my words, see how little power I have, see how my liberty is captive, how my feelings are imprisoned from so strong a love for this dead gentleman).[54] Attempting to testify, however, Pleberio has asked his collapsed wife to share in his grief, called upon his friends to feel his pain, and sought consolation from great men in history—none of whom come to his aid. While it is true, as Shoshana Felman posits, that testimony is a solitary experience, as no one can testify in place of the witness, it simultaneously has a collective aim, directed to others as the "vehicle for an occurrence, a reality, a stance or a dimension *beyond* [the witness]."[55] In this dual aspect of testimony, at once individualistic and communal, Pleberio thus finds himself in a precarious situation; bereft of any historical or contemporary companions, he speaks into the void with nobody to hear his plaint or the devastating effects of desire's wounding.

Pleberio's speech is consequently rendered mute, a silence repeating Melibea's trauma that, as she says, does not allow her to speak ("no me consiente hablar").[56] The questions concluding his plaint, addressed first to desire (*amor*) and then his daughter in the face of overwhelming grief and powerlessness, all go without reply: "¿Quién te dio tanto poder? . . . ¿Por qué te riges sin orden ni concierto?" (Who gave you so much power? . . . Why do you rule without order or harmony?); "¿Por qué me dejaste cuando yo te había de dejar? ¿Por qué me dejaste penado? ¿Por qué me dejaste triste y solo *in hac lachrimarum valle*?" (Why did you leave me when I should have left you? Why did you leave me in grief? Why did you leave me sad and alone in this vale of tears?).[57] Stemming from his frustration with desire's omnipotence, temporality's whims, and fortune's capriciousness, these questions remain unanswered, not simply because there is nobody present who might respond, but because they are all, fundamentally, unanswerable. The traumas of this war upon humanity, from which Pleberio thought himself exempt, resist answers because, as he learns, they are unsayable, unknowable; that to live means to be already destroyed by desire, *to be already destroyed*. As with all stories of trauma, *Celestina* therefore carries within it what Felman would call a resistance to its own telling, a *"negative story element, an anti-story."*[58] As such, Pleberio discovers that his language, which contained the power to strike down his wife, has now turned and struck him down as well. Like Calisto's search for relief through temporal structures, Pleberio finds that language, the only thing that might allow him to question and seek answers, similarly reiterates and reinscribes his wound in the repetition of each failed response to his questions. A hope for answers, mirroring Calisto's hope that the clock could remedy his wound, reveals such answers as unlocatable, outside of language and time; they are, in other words, nowhere. Attempting, therefore, to reverse this irreversible narrative, Pleberio thus postulates near the end of his soliloquy an alternate scenario, the story retold as if he were never born: "Del mundo me quejo porque en sí me crió, porque, no me dando vida, no engendrara en él a Melibea; no nacida, no amara; no amando, cesara mi quejosa y desconsolada postremería" (I complain about the world because I grew up in it, because, not giving me life, I would not have brought Melibea forth into it; not born, she would not have loved; had she not loved, my plaintive and disconsolate old age would have run its course).[59] Such a history, however, is impossible. To wish never to be born, never to have lived; to say, in essence, that he is born dead, shot down by Cupid in the moment of his birth—these are thoughts that cannot be maintained because their implications are too horrific, evaporating as soon as he utters them, with nobody there present capable of hearing or remembering them.

Pleberio's final speech, nonetheless, turns ever more jarring when considered through the lens of where *Celestina* begins. For here, in a poem preceding the prologue, it would appear that the text curiously attempts to undo the impossible nature of its storytelling, this silencing of love's traumatizing power, by establishing itself as a cautionary tale to its audience:

> Oh damas, matronas, mancebos, casados.
> Notad bien la vida que aquestos hicieron,
> Tened por espejo su fin cual hobieron,
> A otro que amores dad vuestros cuidados,
> Limpiad ya los ojos, los ciegos errados,
> Virtudes sembrando con casto vivir,
> A todo correr debéis de huir,
> No os lance Cupido sus tiros dorados.[60]

O ladies, mothers, young men, married men, / Note well the life these characters had, / Hold up the end they had as a mirror, / Give your attention to something other than love, / Clean your eyes you who are waywardly blind, / Live while sowing virtue with purity, / You must flee at full speed, / So Cupid does not shoot his golden arrows at you.

By focusing on Pleberio's isolation, the text's ending therefore appears to be missing final instructions on how to avoid the dangers of love. His plaint, in other words, does not reflect the tenor of its beginning, something that, as Scott points out, is surprising, given that "*Celestina* was apparently composed in reprehension of *loco amor*" and, as such, "does not return to these specific problems."[61] In having what appears to be a consolatory message regarding love at its start and then failing to present one at its end, where desire's unavoidably destructive nature confronts Pleberio, *Celestina* consequently seems to operate according to a type of premeditated forgetting. This prefatory poem informs readers that its tragic elements can instead be instructive, as a mirror where its readers might see a reflection of their supposed moral superiority over these "misguided" characters. In the tradition of *fin'amor*, however, one's image—*the* image—always ensnares the onlooker, a trap Celestina references when recounting to Melibea the tale of Narcissus, the adolescent boy from Ovid's *Metamorphoses* who, upon seeing his reflection, was fatally besieged by impossible desires.[62] As the poem instructs readers to avoid Cupid's arrows, we are seduced by its reassuring message into a world where characters, oblivious to the power of his weapons, become unavoidably alienated by desires and ensnared by death; characters who, in turn, reflect our own wounding in the face of overwhelming longing and the enigma of mortality. And, as we learn in the text's prologue, this is inevitable, the natural state of things. We find no consolatory message at the end of Pleberio's lament because, as he realizes, no consolation is possible, and his speech, now weaponized, strikes down not only his wife and then himself but us as well. Ultimately, *Celestina* reveals a humanity created in and defined by the war that desire unleashes upon us, a war without which we could not exist, nor could we imagine our existence.

BIBLIOGRAPHY

Agamben, Giorgio. *Stanzas: Word and Phantasm in Western Culture*. Translated by Ronald L. Martinez. Minneapolis: University of Minnesota Press, 1993.

Aronson-Friedman, Amy. "Identifying the Converso Voice in Rojas' *La Celestina*." *Mediterranean Studies* 13 (2004): 77–105.

Asensio, Manuel J. "El tiempo en *La Celestina*." *Hispanic Review* 20, no. 1 (1952): 28–43.

Baranda, Consolación. *"La Celestina" y el mundo como conflicto*. Salamanca: Universidad de Salamanca, 2004.

Barnaby, Andrew. "The Psychoanalytic Origins of Literary Trauma Studies." In *Trauma and Literature*, edited by J. Roger Kurtz, 21–35. Cambridge: Cambridge University Press, 2018.

Bond, Lucy, and Stef Craps. *Trauma*. New York: Routledge, 2020.

Camille, Michael. *The Art of Medieval Love: Objects and Subjects of Desire*. New York: Harry N. Abrams, 1998.

Caruth, Cathy. *Unclaimed Experience: Trauma, Narrative, and History*. Baltimore: Johns Hopkins University Press, 1996.

Castells, Ricardo. "Lovesickness and the Problematical Text of *Celestina*, Act I." In *A Companion to "Celestina,"* edited by Enrique Fernandez, 225–41. Boston: Brill, 2017.

Deyermond, A. D. *The Petrarchan Sources of "La Celestina."* London: Oxford University Press, 1961.

Ealy, Nicholas. "Calisto's Narcissistic Visions: A Reexamination of Melibea's '*Ojos Verdes*' in *Celestina*." *eHumanista: Journal of Iberian Studies* 12 (2012): 390–409.

Felman, Shoshana. *The Juridical Unconscious: Trials and Traumas of the Twentieth Century*. Cambridge, MA: Harvard University Press, 2002.

———. "Education in Crisis, or the Vicissitudes of Teaching." In *Testimony: Crises of Witnessing in Literature, Psychoanalysis, and History*, by Shoshana Felman and Dori Laub, 1–56. New York: Routledge, 1992.

Fernández Rivera, Enrique. "El reloj, la hora y la economía del tiempo en *La Celestina*." *Celestinesca* 34 (2010): 31–40.

Gerli, E. Michael. *"Celestina" and the Ends of Desire*. Toronto: University of Toronto Press, 2011.

Labbie, Erin Felicia. *Lacan's Medievalism*. Minneapolis: University of Minnesota Press, 2006.

LaPlanche, Jean, and Jean-Bertrand Pontalis. *The Language of Psychoanalysis*. Translated by Donald Nicholson-Smith. New York: W. W. Norton, 1973.

Lazar, Moshe. "Fin'amor." In *A Handbook of the Troubadours*, edited by F. R. P. Akehurst and Judith M. Davis, 61–100. Berkeley: University of California Press, 1995.

Luckhurst, Roger. *The Trauma Question*. London: Routledge, 2008.

Márquez Villanueva, Francisco. "'Nascer e morir como bestias' (Criptojudaísmo y Criptoaverroísmo)." In *Los judaizantes en Europa y la literatura castellana del Siglo de Oro*, edited by Fernando Díaz Esteban, 273–93. Madrid: Letrúmero, 1994.

Nicholson, Helen. *Medieval Warfare*. New York: Palgrave Macmillan, 2004.

Pérez-Romero, Antonio. "Modernity and *Celestina*: The Future of Our Past and of Our Present." In *A Companion to "Celestina,"* edited by Enrique Fernandez, 275–91. Boston: Brill, 2017.

Picatrix: The Latin Version of the "Ghāyat Al-Hakīm." Edited by David Pingree. London: University of London, 1986.

Rojas, Fernando de. *La Celestina*. Edited by Francisco J. Lobera et al. Madrid: Real Academia Española, 2011.

Roth, Norman. *Conversos, Inquisition, and the Expulsion of the Jews from Spain*. Madison: University of Wisconsin Press, 1995.

Scott, Rachel. *"Celestina" and the Human Condition in Early Modern Spain and Italy*. Woodbridge: Tamesis, 2017.

Sevilla Arroyo, Florencia. "Amor, magia y tiempo en *La Celestina*." *Celestinesca* 33 (2009): 173–214.

Sutherland, Madeline. "Mimetic Desire, Violence and Sacrifice in the *Celestina*." *Hispania* 86, no. 2 (2003): 181–90.

Terence. *Eunuchus*. In *The Comedies of Terrence*, edited by Sidney G. Ashmore, 100–150. New York: Oxford University Press, 1910.

Turner, Wendy J., and Christina Lee. "Conceptualizing Trauma for the Middle Ages." In *Trauma in Medieval Society*, edited by Wendy J. Turner and Christina Lee, 3–12. Leiden: Brill, 2018.

NOTES

1. E. Michael Gerli posits that Pleberio's use of *amor* is, in fact, desire. *"Celestina" and the Ends of Desire* (Toronto: University of Toronto Press, 2011), 213. Though separate concepts, desire (that longing for fulfillment) and love (the state in which desiring subjects find themselves when expecting fulfillment) share a theoretical relationship. For this reason, authors may tend to use the term "love" for both, especially given that *amor* in Latin signifies "love" and "desire," with *Amor* personified as Cupid. For more, see Erin Felicia Labbie, *Lacan's Medievalism* (Minneapolis: University of Minnesota Press, 2006), 107–45.

2. For a discussion of *Celestina*'s modernity, see Antonio Pérez-Romero, "Modernity and *Celestina*: The Future of Our Past and of Our Present," in *A Companion to "Celestina,"* ed. Enrique Fernández (Boston: Brill, 2017), 275–91.

3. Fernando de Rojas, *La Celestina*, ed. Francisco J. Lobera et al. (Madrid: Real Academia Española, 2011), 53. All translations are by the author unless otherwise indicated.

4. The earliest edition of *Celestina* had the title *Comedia de Calisto y Melibea* (*Comedy of Calisto and Melibea*), with *Tragicomedia de Calisto y Melibea* appearing in 1502.

5. Rojas, *Celestina*, 15. For more on Petrarch's influence in *Celestina*, see A. D. Deyermond, *The Petrarchan Sources of "La Celestina"* (London: Oxford University Press, 1961).

6. Rojas, *Celestina*, 15.

7. Rojas, *Celestina*, 16.

8. Rojas, *Celestina*, 19.

9. Melibea mentions Cupid's parentage while referencing Venus's affair with Mars: "Venus madre de Eneas y de Cupido, el dios de amor, que, siendo casada, corrumpió la prometida fe marital" (Venus, mother of Eneas and Cupid, the god of love, who, being married, corrupted her promise of her marital vow). Rojas, *Celestina*, 297.

10. *Picatrix: The Latin Version of the "Ghāyat Al-Hakīm,"* ed. David Pingree (London: University of London, 1986), 115.

11. *Picatrix*, 115.

12. For a discussion on war and trauma, see Lucy Bond and Stef Craps, *Trauma* (New York: Routledge, 2020), 28–33.

13. Jean LaPlanche and Jean-Bertrand Pontalis, *The Language of Psychoanalysis*, trans. Donald Nicholson-Smith (New York: W. W. Norton, 1973), 456.

14. Roger Luckhurst, *The Trauma Question* (London: Routledge, 2008), 3; Wendy J. Turner and Christina Lee, "Conceptualizing Trauma for the Middle Ages," in *Trauma in Medieval Society*, ed. Wendy J. Turner and Christina Lee (Leiden: Brill, 2018), 8.

15. Although physical war does not form part of *Celestina*, Areúsa, one of Celestina's protégées, states that her lover Centurio has left for a war, suggesting that ongoing battle is not far off and that it serves as the backdrop to these characters' lives in ways that parallel the strife and debauchery of their daily existence. Rojas, *Celestina*, 286.

16. For more on these conflicts, see Norman Roth, *Conversos, Inquisition, and the Expulsion of the Jews from Spain* (Madison: University of Wisconsin Press, 1995).

17. Helen Nicholson, *Medieval Warfare* (New York: Palgrave Macmillan, 2004), 2.

18. For more on Rojas's *converso* status, see Amy Aronson-Friedman, "Identifying the Converso Voice in Rojas' *La Celestina*," *Mediterranean Studies* 13 (2004): 77–105.

19. Francisco Márquez Villanueva, "'Nasçer e morir como bestias' (Criptojudaísmo y Criptoaverroísmo)," in *Los judaizantes en Europa y la literatura castellana del Siglo de Oro*, ed. Fernando Díaz Esteban (Madrid: Letrúmero, 1994), 284.

20. Consolación Baranda, *"La Celestina" y el mundo como conflicto* (Salamanca: Universidad de Salamanca, 2004), 29–30.

21. For a discussion of *fin'amor*, see Moshe Lazar, "*Fin'amor*," in *A Handbook of the Troubadours*, ed. F. R. P. Akehurst and Judith M. Davis (Berkeley: University of California Press, 1995), 61–100. For a discussion of *fin'amor* in *Celestina*, see Ricardo Castells, "Lovesickness and the Problematical Text of *Celestina*, Act I," in *A Companion to "Celestina,"* ed. Enrique Fernandez (Boston: Brill, 2017), 225–41.

22. Rojas, *Celestina*, 27.

23. For more on melancholic lovesickness, see Giorgio Agamben, *Stanzas: Word and Phantasm in Western Culture*, trans. Robert L. Martinez (Minneapolis: University of Minnesota Press, 1993), 11–18.

24. For a discussion of falconry in *Celestina*, see Gerli, *Ends of Desire*, 64–97.

25. Rojas, *Celestina*, 89.

26. Rojas, *Celestina*, 157.

27. Rojas, *Celestina*, 90.

28. In much of medieval literary and visual culture, the heart is believed to be the organ that retains images and memory. Michael Camille, *The Art of Medieval Love: Objects and Subjects of Desire* (New York: Harry N. Abrams, 1998), 111–19.

29. Rojas, Celestina, 245–46.

30. At various points, Calisto makes the connection that vision is the cause of his wounded heart, thereby likening the image of Melibea that strikes his eye to Cupid's arrow.

31. Rojas, *Celestina*, 161.

32. Rojas, *Celestina*, 32–33. Although Calisto speaks here about Sempronio's body, the internalized conflict is also, I posit, a self-reference.

33. Terence, *Eunuchus*, in *The Comedies of Terence*, ed. Sidney G. Ashmore (New York: Oxford University Press, 1910), 104.

34. Luckhurst, *Trauma*, 3.

35. Manuel J. Asensio, "El tiempo en *La Celestina*," *Hispanic Review* 20, no. 1 (1952): 28–43; Florencia Sevilla Arroyo, "Amor, magia y tiempo en *La Celestina*," *Celestinesca* 33 (2009): 173–214.

36. Baranda, *"La Celestina,"* 157–58.

37. Rojas, *Celestina*, 234.

38. Rojas, *Celestina*, 240.

39. Cathy Caruth, *Unclaimed Experience: Trauma, Narrative, and History* (Baltimore: Johns Hopkins University Press, 1996), 4.

40. Rojas, *Celestina*, 277.
41. Rojas, *Celestina*, 277–78. Calisto's monologue here is influenced by his surprise that sex with Melibea has not brought him a sustainable fulfillment as well as by the recent death of his servants, Sempronio and Pármeno.
42. For a discussion of Calisto's dissatisfaction in the context of *fin'amor*, see Nicholas Ealy, "Calisto's Narcissistic Visions: A Reexamination of Melibea's '*Ojos Verdes*' in *Celestina*," *eHumanista: Journal of Iberian Studies* 12 (2012): 390–409.
43. Rojas, *Celestina*, 282. As Enrique Fernández Rivera observes, this reference underscores the imprecise nature of mechanical clocks, which could be discordant with astronomical time. "El reloj, la hora y la economía del tiempo en *La Celestina*," *Celestinesca* 34 (2010): 34.
44. Rojas, *Celestina*, 278. I borrow this notion of trauma as an event that happens both "too soon" and "too late" from Caruth. *Unclaimed*, 62–65.
45. Andrew Barnaby, "The Psychoanalytic Origins of Literary Trauma Studies," in *Trauma and Literature*, ed. J. Roger Kurtz (Cambridge: Cambridge University Press, 2018), 22.
46. Rachel Scott, *"Celestina" and the Human Condition in Early Modern Spain and Italy* (Woodbridge: Tamesis, 2017), 106.
47. Rojas, *Celestina*, 328.
48. Rojas, *Celestina*, 338, 337.
49. Rojas, *Celestina*, 332.
50. Rojas, *Celestina*, 343–44.
51. Rojas, *Celestina*, 342.
52. Rojas, *Celestina*, 342.
53. Framed within a historical context, Pleberio's isolation in an indifferent world may relate, as scholars have argued, to Spain's bellicose and tumultuous environment. Amy Aronson-Friedman, for instance, sees Pleberio as a "Jewish/converso archetype" with Rojas "projecting his voice" through his work's patriarchal figure, "mourn[ing] his plight as a converso [while] also represent[ing] the sentiments felt by other members of the converso caste of fifteenth-century Spain." Aronson-Friedman, "Identifying," 84, 88. Echoing such sentiments, Madeline Sutherland similarly posits that the desperation at *Celestina*'s conclusion has links to Rojas's converso status, as this era constituted "an often terrifying period as loss of difference or, perhaps we should more accurately say the willful and often violent destruction of religious difference, became official policy." Madeline Sutherland, "Mimetic Desire, Violence and Sacrifice in the *Celestina*," *Hispania* 86, no. 2 (2003): 188.
54. Rojas, *Celestina*, 331.
55. Shoshana Felman, "Education in Crisis, or the Vicissitudes of Teaching," in *Testimony: Crises of Witnessing in Literature, Psychoanalysis, and History*, by Shoshana Felman and Dori Laub (New York: Routledge, 1992), 3.
56. Rojas, *Celestina*, 328.
57. Rojas, *Celestina*, 344–47.
58. Shoshana Felman, *The Juridical Unconscious: Trials and Traumas of the Twentieth Century* (Cambridge, MA: Harvard University Press, 2002), 204. Italics are original to Felman's work.

59. Rojas, *Celestina*, 346.
60. Rojas, *Celestina*, 14.
61. Scott, *Human Condition*, 49.
62. "Gentil Narciso que se enamoró de su propria figura cuando se vido en las aguas de la fuente" (courteous Narcissus who fell in love with his own image when he looked into the waters of the fountain). Rojas, *Celestina*, 133.

Chapter Five

Violence in the Making

Remembering the Viceroy's Assassination during the Catalan Revolt of 1640

Ivan Gracia-Arnau

At dusk on June 7, 1640, Corpus Christi Day, the viceroy of Catalonia was found dead just outside Barcelona. Shaken by the news, the local authorities ordered that the body be brought into the city in order to protect it from the crowd. That morning, hundreds of peasants—*segadors* (reapers), to be more precise—had taken up arms against the ministers of King Philip IV and had made the viceroy, Dalmau de Queralt, the main target of their protest. The houses of ministers were raided and some of these representatives of royal power were murdered: they were held responsible for the abuses committed against the population by the Spanish *tercios*, troops who had been stationed in Catalan territory since 1635 with the aim of fighting Louis XIII of France.
That same summer, the Spanish court decreed the dispatch of a new army to Barcelona to restore royal authority and also to prevent the French monarchy from capitalizing on the power vacuum in Catalonia and intervening in the peninsula. In early 1641, however, a few days after the arrival of Spanish troops in Barcelona, the Catalan leaders swore allegiance to Louis XIII. On January 26, 1641, Philips IV's *tercios* were defeated by a Franco-Catalan army. The Catalan revolt, at least for the moment, continued.[1]
Dozens of sources that narrate the events of June 7, 1640, have been preserved.[2] Some accounts, like that of Inquisitor Juan Adam de la Parra, reported that the viceroy of Catalonia, trying to escape from the crowd, was surrounded by a group of *segadors* who stabbed him five times in the chest, mortally wounding him.[3] Others, however, like that of the Augustinian

Gaspar Sala, claimed that the stab wounds received were carried out postmortem. According to this second testimony, the viceroy fainted and died from a blow to the head as he fell to the ground.[4] Both documents were written at the beginning of the war that broke out in autumn 1640, known as the War of the Reapers (1640–1652). This conflict was accompanied by a print war that, among other things, aspired to establish a hegemonic narrative of the events and to convince their readers of the "true" causes of the war, either through scholarly writings destined for high dignitaries or through *relaciones* of the events[5] and other types of popular literature that were more accessible to broad sectors of the population.[6]

This chapter sets out to analyze the texts written to reconstruct the popular insurrection that took place in Barcelona on June 7, 1640, paying special attention to the representations of the violence carried out by the armed crowd. The main aim is to identify what was hidden, what was exaggerated, and what was manipulated in the narratives written during the Catalan revolt. That is, to study how, following Pierre Nora, the viceroy's assassination was delivered to the "dialectic of memory and amnesia, unaware of its later deformations, vulnerable to all kinds of uses and manipulations,"[7] between 1640 and 1652—the year in which Barcelona surrendered to the troops of Philip IV and Catalonia was restored to the House of Habsburg.

In recent decades, scholars including Enzo Traverso have reflected on the nature and characteristics of collective memory and its complex relationship with history in modern societies. For Traverso, memory is a construction that is always produced in the present: it is the present, conditioned by its political and cultural context, that selects the events that are to be kept in the memory and that governs their interpretation.[8] Thus memory can be an object of study of history. The 1640 insurrection of Corpus Christi is a clear example of this trend. Rescued from oblivion by both Romanticism and Catalan nationalism of the late nineteenth century, the event went on to become a key nationalist myth in the shaping of Catalan historical memory and collective identity. In fact, the national anthem of Catalonia today bears the name "Els Segadors" (The Reapers)—a popular song from the seventeenth century that commemorates the armed popular uprising.[9]

Recent studies have shown that collective memory is not only an issue for modern societies, and that early modern societies also had rich and complex ways of relating to their past. These forms of memory transcended the scholarly circles of the elites and permeated the consciousness of the population at large.[10]

The field of revolts and revolutions has been an especially fertile ground for memory studies, since, as recent research has shown, during the early modern era the memory of revolts was often evoked, either by protest movements or political dissidents to legitimize their resistance, or by the authorities in order to control and repress the population. So whether it was used to encourage or justify protest,[11] or to subsume and consign it to oblivion,[12] the memory of ancien régime societies was a powerful tool in revolts and revolutions. The sixteenth, seventeenth, and eighteenth centuries therefore saw "the construction of a public space for discussion, in which critical discourses on power alternated with the use of episodes of political disorder as an antidote to the spread of new revolts."[13] This chapter explores this dialectic in depth and examines how the Corpus Christi Day revolt was remembered through the writings produced by both the rebels, who supported an alliance between Catalonia and the House of Bourbon, and the royalists, who defended the continuation of the principality's allegiance to the House of Habsburg.

The following pages center on political writings promoted by various institutions in conflict: the Spanish court of the Habsburgs, on the one hand, and the Diputació del General of Catalonia[14] and the Consell de Cent of Barcelona,[15] on the other.[16] I also consider other documentary evidence that, though not written under the auspices of particular institutions, also helped to consolidate the accounts of the events, either consciously or unconsciously, through *relaciones*, chronicles and stories, or diaries and personal testimonies that recorded not just family and private matters but also aspects of the public life of the city of Barcelona. In short, the essay focuses on narrative sources that, as well as providing information about the events themselves, can also be studied as evidence of a struggle to order and control the memory of that immediate past—a struggle for an interpretation of events that, in the words of Francesco Benigno, is "a constitutive part—rather than an ancillary one— of the competition for hegemony."[17]

THE CATALAN REVOLT

Henry Ettinghausen has listed more than three hundred print documents from the Iberian Peninsula during the Catalan revolt that gave accounts of various aspects of the war. These documents are mostly in the form of *relaciones*, which were mainly intended for popular consumption.[18] Political writings were also widely disseminated; these are longer, more erudite texts addressed to the king, the court, or the European chancelleries. Xavier Torres Sans has identified as many as forty-two political tracts financed by institutions on both sides that defended the competing political positions based on historical and legal precepts: the right of the Catalans to resist tyranny and the duty of the Crown to put down a rebellion against the king.[19]

The effort invested in this rhetorical battle was not the same for both sides. The Catalan institutions had the harder task: to explain to Christendom why they were taking up arms against their lord and allying themselves with a foreign prince, which of course represented the most heinous crime that a people could commit against its king. One of the arguments they employed was the billeting of the *tercios* in Catalan towns, an act that the king's ministers had imposed. Since the outbreak of the war with France in 1635 against the background of the Thirty Years' War, the arrival of the *tercios* in the principality had created a climate of serious discontent among the rural population, a situation that was in fact responsible for the 1640 uprising as well as the Corpus Christi Day assassination.[20] In addition to this grievance, the Catalan institutions—above all the Diputació del General in Catalonia and the Consell de Cent in Barcelona—offered others to justify their rebellion: the repeated violation of the Catalan constitutions by the king's ministers, along with recent tax increases and the creation of entirely new taxes.[21]

However, the argument most frequently put forward by rebel propaganda against the ministers of Philip IV was religious in nature—especially, as Torres Sans points out, "when it came to reinforcing the notion of just war or propagating the image of a common enemy."[22] Just as the propaganda of the Spanish Crown presented the House of Habsburg as the sword of the Catholic Church against heresy, the Catalan rebels dressed their political revolt against the Spanish Crown in the robes of providence.

In early May 1640, as conflict raged between the royal soldiers and the Catalan population, Leonardo Moles's *tercio* looted and burned the church of Riudarenes. The town's residents had hidden food and belongings in the church; these were destroyed by the soldiers as a punishment. News of the event spread rapidly through the *relaciones*, which emphasized the sacrilegious nature of the violence perpetrated by the soldiers. The *relaciones* highlighted the burning of the monstrance bearing the consecrated host, an act that outraged a large part of the population.[23] The *tercio* responsible was excommunicated by the Bishop of Girona, a step that contributed to mobilizing the population against the soldiers.[24] The month of May was, without a doubt, a turning point in the crisis between the Catalan institutions and the Crown.[25]

When the war broke out in autumn of that year, the sacrilege committed by the soldiers in Riudarenes became a key argument in Catalan rebel propaganda, which presented the revolt to the world as an uprising of good Catholics—that is, as an act in defense of the faith against the heretical soldiers of Philip IV.[26] Indeed, the death of the viceroy would be interpreted as a divine response to those grave sacrileges. Needless to say, this version of events was rejected out of hand by the Spanish court, whose accounts painted a very different picture.

A PROVIDENTIAL DEATH

The vast majority of the writings disseminated by the Catalan rebels claimed that the viceroy of Catalonia had died because of an accident. They alleged that he had collapsed after trying to run away from his pursuers and had hit his head on the rocks of Montjuïc, a small hill near the city. The crowd had then proceeded to stab his lifeless body.[27] But the argument went further: his death had not been a mishap but the result of divine punishment. For Gaspar Sala, writing in 1644 under the pseudonym of Francesc Vopis, it was the "revenge of the Eucharist."[28]

The coincidence of the popular insurrection with the celebration of the religious festival of Corpus Christi was one of the factors that encouraged the providential reading of the viceroy's death. In Counter-Reformation Europe, the Blessed Sacrament had become the centerpiece of the liturgical and devotional practices of Catholics. Among the Catalan population, Corpus Christi was a deeply rooted religious celebration in which the sacramental body of Christ was exalted—that very body that the king's soldiers had burned in Riudarenes the previous month. This point was made by Sala, who was a fervent supporter of the alliance with France and had been commissioned by the Consell de Cent of Barcelona to write the *Proclamación Católica*, one of the most widely disseminated Catalan works in early modern Europe: "To avenge these affected omissions, particularly to punish the affronts to the Blessed Sacrament, the Lord waited for his most solemn day, which is Corpus Christi: through the *segadors*, divine justice thus held the agents of human justice to account."[29] Human justice had been unable to protect the Blessed Sacrament but now, on the sacred day of Corpus Christi, which was devoted to the celebration of the sacramental body of Christ, divine justice had been meted out by the *segadors*.[30]

Dedicated to King Philip IV, upon whom it called to stop the invasion of the principality and to depose the Count Duke of Olivares, the *Proclamación Católica* was published four times between 1640 and 1641 in eight thousand printed copies. During the following years, translations were printed in Lisbon, Rouen, and Amsterdam.[31] This work established the account that would be expanded upon by other authors, such as the jurist Francesc Martí Viladamor, a prolific writer and the main supporter of Louis XIII in the principality, and the Augustinian Antoni Marquès, author of a panegyric on the virtues of the Catalans published in 1641.

Both these authors saw the designs of God in the deaths of the king's ministers. On June 7, the priest Gabriel Berart, judge of the royal council in Catalonia, was also assassinated. In the opinion of Martí Viladamor and Marquès, the fact that Berart was both a judge and a priest demonstrated the providential nature of the popular violence. The argument went as follows: of all the ministers responsible for judging heretical soldiers, those who were clerics bore the greatest guilt, since they had a greater obligation to redress the offences to the Blessed Sacrament. That is why both Berart and, a few months later, Jeroni Grau, another minister who was also a priest, were assassinated. The evidence of the hand of God in the murder of the two judges did not end there; the fact that both were killed near or inside churches was taken to indicate God's displeasure with their actions. According to the rebels' interpretation of events, the churches where the judges sought refuge were the stage on which the punishment of those who had offended the Blessed Sacrament was administered.[32]

The rebel propaganda thus saw the revolt as an act of providence, and many descriptions of the populace's violence were colored by a component of justice and purification. One of the most frequently repeated tropes is the idea that morality guided the violence during the assaults on the houses of the king's ministers: the attacks were not the work of vandals or thieves seeking personal profit but were acts underpinned by solid ethical principles.

Martí Viladamor, in another of his works, stated that when the *segadors* broke into the houses, they threw all the objects they found into the street to set them on fire, but did not steal anything.[33] Josep Sarroca, author of a libel against Olivares, repeated this argument, claiming that the *segadors*' violence was "disinterested"—that is, not motivated by a desire for personal or material gain. The *segadors* were the means through which God exacted his vengeance; for Sarroca, the proof of this was their lack of interest in gold, silver, coins, or other luxury objects belonging to the royal ministers that were also thrown into the fire.[34]

Charles Sorel, a writer and chronicler of France between 1635 and 1663, expressed similar ideas in *La Deffence des Catalans*, published in 1642, a work in which he called for Catalonia to become part of the kingdom of France.[35] Sorel stated that the *segadors* burned the furniture of the king's ministers as if in "atonement for the offences committed against the Holy Sacrament," coinciding with the celebration of the Blessed Sacrament itself on Corpus Christi Day. The *segadors* burned those objects in order to demonstrate "that they did not want to make any profit as brigands, but to carry out an act of justice, and to make themselves the executors of divine vengeance."[36] The behavior of the crowd transcended human greed precisely because it was guided by divine will.

Without a doubt, the most comprehensive portrayal of the violence of the *segadors* from this standpoint was provided by Miquel Parets, a tanner from Barcelona and an enthusiastic defender of the Catalan revolt who authored a chronicle that was never printed.[37] Steeped in the propaganda of the moment, the work of this artisan faithfully reflects some of the recurrent representations of the violence in the literature of the rebels. In his account of the events, Parets claimed that, during the assaults on the houses of the ministers, "God inspired [i.e., opened their eyes to] the treasons that were being carried out in this principality."[38] That is, God inspired them to combat traitors to the faith and to the homeland. Faced with such a maelstrom of violence, the tanner explained, friars and clergy marched in procession bearing sacred images to try to stop the *segadors*. But their efforts came to nothing because, according to Parets, the rebels were convinced that they were defending the Catholic faith: "Since [the ministers] did not want to punish those who burned the churches, they [the *segadors*] wanted to burn them [the ministers] and they [did so] for the Holy Faith and for their Homeland."[39]

The testimony of Parets is particularly interesting because of his meticulous description of the violent treatment of the royal ministers' possessions. First, he presents a list of the misdeeds of each minister in question, and then describes the assault. He repeats this sequence throughout his chronicle. According to Parets, after storming a minister's house, the crowd threw all his possessions into the street and burned them in large pyres, shouting "death to traitors." Among these belongings were gold and silver objects, tapestries, and silk fabrics—luxury goods that, as they burned in the fire, were watched over by groups of guards formed by the *segadors* themselves to ensure that nothing was stolen.[40]

A CRUEL ASSASSINATION

This representation of popular violence, however, was not the norm either during the Catalan revolt or in the early modern period as a whole. Members of the mob—protagonists of so many riots and revolts all over Europe in the seventeenth century—were often victims of a series of negative tropes that condemned their irrational and destructive behavior. Christian Jouhaud has discussed the image of the people offered, for example, by Pierre Charron in *De la sagesse* (1601): "A strange, wild, many-headed beast, dominated by envy, malicious, the enemy of the upstanding members of society, of peace, of honesty, of the public good and, on the contrary, the friend of novelties, their own interests, and sedition."[41] The depiction in royal propaganda of the *segadors*' insurrection capitalized on many of these stereotypes in an attempt to counteract rebel propaganda.

In response to the rebels' reading of the viceroy's death as an act of providence, the writers of the court and others loyal to Philip IV (among them, many Catalans) lamented the fact that, on June 7, 1640, the viceroy had been the victim of a cruel murder—a murder that marked the beginning of a path of sedition that would culminate in the oath of allegiance to Louis XIII and that, according to a print published in mid-1641, should be regarded as an act of religious insubordination. Subjects owed strict obedience to their monarchs, who were vicars of Christ on Earth: killing the viceroy, "the living representation of the King's person," was comparable to the crime of idolatry.[42]

In autumn 1640, at the start of the war, the *Súplica de la Muy Noble y Muy Leal Ciudad de Tortosa* was published anonymously, although it has been attributed to Inquisitor Juan Adam de la Parra.[43] The *Súplica* was one of the many responses made by the royalist side to try to counteract the effects of the *Proclamación Católica*. This response contained a new version of the narrative the June 7, 1640, events that aimed to show that the death of the viceroy had in no way been inspired by providence, as Sala had claimed, but was instead the result of the superstitious action of the mob and of their darkest instincts and intentions.

The *Súplica* paid particular attention to the acts of violence carried out by the crowd during the attacks on the ministers' houses. According to Adam de la Parra, the claims of authors such as Martí Viladamor and Sorel (that is, that the violence of the *segadors* was not motivated by a desire for personal gain) were false. The mob had only pretended to burn the ministers' possessions in the street pyres; this act of simulation had enabled them to loot and steal the objects of value with total abandon, "stealing as much as possible of the contents of the houses, although in appearance they implied that they burned them."[44] For Adam de la Parra, the *segadors*' rituals of purification were a hoax with which the rebel writers had covered up the malicious and dishonest intentions of the mob.

Alonso Guillén de la Carrera, commissioned by the Count Duke of Olivares to write the *Iustificació Real*,[45] also underlined the role of robbery in the attacks. In this text, Guillén de la Carrera lamented that on Corpus Christi Day the *segadors* had "killed the judges of the royal council, burned and plundered the houses of the King's ministers."[46] The trope reappeared frequently, and historians including Luca Assarino, Italian author of a history that was profoundly hostile to the Catalan rebels, reiterated that: "They threw all the possessions into the square, and after stealing the best ones, they set fire to the rest."[47] The violence, in this account too, was motivated by a desire for personal gain.

In addition to emphasizing this aspect of the rebellion, royalist propaganda appealed to superstition in an attempt to delegitimize the providential interpretation of the viceroy's death. Adam de la Parra explained that during Corpus Christi Day the rumor spread that at the house of one of the ministers were hidden "four thousand large blades with which the throats of the residents of Barcelona were to be cut. That Your Majesty's militia were to enter [the city] through a tunnel, which, they [the *segadors*] claimed, passed under the walls of the city. . . . This was so firmly believed, that the city councillors called on masons to investigate, who with pickaxes and tools examined the floors and walls."[48] Apparently, the *segadors* were convinced that the king's ministers were planning a massacre of the people of Barcelona. This was something that "was believed more firmly than the Gospel,"[49] according to Ramon Rubí de Marimon, one of the judges of the royal council who managed to escape Barcelona and wrote an account of the event in 1642. In line with this strategy, Francesc Pasqual de Panno, a Catalan nobleman exiled to Madrid in 1643 for refusing to swear allegiance to Louis XIII, explained in his *Motines de Cataluña des de el año 1622* that in the house of one of the ministers, the *segadors* found some stamps that they thought, "absurdly," were going to be used to identify the king's supporters, and would be worn by the ministers to save themselves from harm when the king's soldiers arrived in Barcelona to carry out the slaughter.[50]

In fact, the royalist narratives insisted so much on this strategy that even the viceroy's murder was presented as a result of the mob's superstition. According to Adam de la Parra, on Corpus Christi Day 1640, the *segadors* acted under the guidance not of God but of a fortuneteller who had spread the rumor that the king's representative was destined to die soon. The fortuneteller was a nun who claimed to be the voice of God but in fact was nothing more than a charlatan who invented fantastical notions to stir up the crowd. According to the inquisitor, it was this false premonition of the viceroy's death that had spurred on the *segadors* to try to assassinate him.[51]

The mob was therefore ignorant and superstitious—but also sacrilegious. In the same way that the rebel propaganda created a heretical image of the royal soldiers, the royalist writings emphasized the sacrilegious nature of the violence carried out by the *segadors*. According to the royalist tracts, the mob stormed the houses of the ministers "firing arquebuses, and throwing stones at the images, altarpieces, and the monstrance of the Blessed Sacrament."[52] Many ministers took refuge in churches and convents; the mob had no compunction in following them there, thus "violating the sanctuaries and temples."[53] Francisco de Rioja, the king's librarian and scribe in the service of Olivares, expressed himself in similar terms, lamenting the murder of ministers and soldiers "whose hiding in the temples, altars and tombs served no purpose."[54] The murder of Berart inside a church ceased to be the unequivocal sign that the Lord was denying protection to priest-judges, as the rebel propaganda had claimed; rather, his death was here regarded as the sacrilegious murder of a Christian and the desecration of a Catholic church at the hands of an unruly mob.

The violence was portrayed as an impious act of desecration, and the forms that it took as particularly revolting: cannibalism, the murder of innocents, and pleasure derived from the suffering of others. Evidently, this was a far cry from the rebels' depiction of the events. The text by the royalist Alexandre

Ros published in 1641, for example, narrates the events that occurred on the days prior to Corpus Christi, when the *segadors* "carried out acts of unbelievable cruelty, killing the soldiers, cutting off their heads, ripping open their breasts, and stabbing them in the heart with their daggers."[55] The atrocities, Ros continued, came to a head in Barcelona on June 7 with the murder of the viceroy. On that day, the *segadors* turned into monsters "thirsty for human blood," beasts whose ferocity "exceeded that of the Caribs" of America.[56] Ros not only referred to cannibalism to demonstrate the barbarity of the Catalans but also explicitly compared them to the Caribs who, according to Columbus, were extremely violent and consumed human flesh.[57] Francisco de Rioja offers a similar account, explaining that, during the holy day of Corpus Christi, the *segadors* "took out the hearts of many dead soldiers and ate them, and the Catalan women trampled over the faces of the dead out of indignation and a thirst for revenge, and . . . none of the soldiers who died of disease were given the sacraments."[58] Stereotypes about the peoples of America that served to justify the conquest of the New World were projected onto the Catalan rebels by the royalist propaganda.[59]

Ros and Rioja barbarized the Catalans by attributing to them acts of atrocious violence;[60] their aim was to counter the Catalan institutions' attempts to present the rebellion as both an act of providence and an act of justice. Royalists compared the rebels' conduct with savage practices that colonial narratives attributed to non-Christian peoples and that Catholics regarded as wholly barbaric. It was, in short, a narrative strategy based on equating the Catalans with the inhabitants of the New World—two territories that had to be conquered by the evangelizing weapons of the monarchy.

CONCLUSION

During the Catalan revolt of 1640, the assassination of the viceroy of Catalonia at the hands of the populace inspired a great many written accounts. The events of the Day of Corpus Christi were subjected to a dialectic between two interpretations that strove to appropriate the memory of the event. These two versions aspired to control what should be remembered about the insurrection—and how it should be remembered—in order to justify the immediate political and military goals of each side. The present comparative analysis reveals the multiple tensions that emerged in the reporting of the event. Very few elements were left to chance or improvisation. On the contrary: most accounts relayed stories that, in continual construction and with more or less explicit political intentions, organized reality in the way that best suited their patrons and authors.

On the one hand, we have a providential account of the viceroy's death that depicted the event as an act in defense of the Catholic faith and against the heresy represented by the king's soldiers. The assassination's coincidence with Corpus Christi Day, the fact that some ministers killed were both judges and priests, the sacred character of the sites of the murders, and the portrayal of the violence as acts of justice motivated not by a desire for material gain provided the basis for this interpretation, which was supported by authors on the rebel side. On the other hand, the royalist side promoted—either through officially commissioned works or by reports written more or less spontaneously—a vision of the uprising that sought to combat the providential reading put forward in the rebel propaganda and thus establish a counter-narrative of the events. The royalist account spoke of sacrilegious acts, the desecration of holy places, superstition, robbery, looting, and atrocities against innocents and cannibalism—an atrocious story of terror and violence that was intended to combat and discredit the rhetoric of the Catalan rebels.

After the fall of Barcelona in 1652 and the reincorporation of Catalonia into the House of Habsburg, the Catalan revolt was largely silenced. Over the next forty years, the printing presses of the Iberian Peninsula said nothing of the events of 1640. This silence was accompanied by the prosecution and destruction by the royal censors of all the seditious papers that, during the previous years, had called for the integration of Catalonia into France.[61] On the few occasions that the events were remembered, it was through an institutional discourse that silenced and intimidated dissident movements such as the revolt of the Barretines, also in Catalonia (1687–1689).[62] It would not be until the outbreak of the War of the Spanish Succession (1701–1714) that the memory of the revolt of the Day of Corpus Christi would be recovered by the Catalans, in a new confrontation with the Spanish monarchy.

WORKS CITED

[Adam de la Parra, Juan]. *Súplica de la Muy Noble y Muy Leal Ciudad de Tortosa.* Tortosa: Pedro Martorell, 1640.
Arens, William. *El mito del canibalismo: antropología y antropofagia.* Mexico City: Siglo XXI, 1981.
Arredondo, María Soledad. *Literatura y propaganda en tiempo de Quevedo: Guerras y plumas contra Francia, Cataluña y Portugal.* Madrid: Vervuert, 2011.
———. "Noticia de la *Súplica de Tortosa* (1640), atribuida al Inquisidor Juan Adam de la Parra." *Cuadernos de Historia Moderna*, 22 (1999): 139–46.
Assarino, Luca. *Delle Rivolutioni di Catalogna.* Genoa: Giovanni Maria Farroni, 1644.
Aznar, Daniel. "Cataluña y el rey: Representaciones y prácticas de la Majestad durante el cambio de soberanía (1640–1655)." PhD thesis, University of Barcelona, 2016.

Beik, William. *Urban Protest in Seventeenth-Century France*. Cambridge: Cambridge University Press, 1997.
Benigno, Francesco. *Specchi della rivoluzione: Conflitto e identità politica nell'Europa moderna*. Rome: Donzelli editore, 1999.
Benigno, Francesco, Laurent Bourquin, and Alain Hugon, eds. *Violences en révolte: Une histoire culturelle européenne (XIVe–XVIIIe siècle)*. Rennes: Presses Universitaires de Rennes, 2019.
Burke, Peter. "The Virgin of the Carmine and the Revolt of Masaniello." *Past & Present* 99 (1983): 3–21.
Busquets, Joan. "Revolta popular i religiositat barroca: L'excomunió de l'exèrcit espanyol a la catedral de Girona en 1640." In *Treballs d'història: Estudis de demografia, economia i societat a les comarques gironines*, by Ramon Alberch et al., 63–87. Girona: Patronat Eiximenis de l'Excma. Diputacio Provincial de Girona, 1976.
Cattini, Giovanni C. "Myths and Symbols in the Political Culture of Catalan Nationalism (1880–1914)." *Nations & Nationalism* 21, no. 3 (July 2015): 445–60.
Crouzet, Denis. *Les Guerriers de Dieu: La violence au temps des troubles de religion (vers 1525–vers 1610)*. Seyssel: Champ Vallon, 1990.
Davis, Natalie Z. "The Rites of Violence: Religious Riot in Sixteenth-Century France." *Past & Present* 59 (1973): 51–91.
Elliott, John H. *The Revolt of the Catalans: A Study in the Decline of Spain (1598–1640)*. Cambridge: Cambridge University Press, 1963.
Ettinghausen, Henry. *La Guerra dels Segadors a través de la premsa de l'època*. Barcelona: Curial, 1993.
Friedrichs, Christopher R. "House-Destruction as a Ritual of Punishment in Early Modern Europe." *European History Quarterly* 50, no. 4 (2020): 599–624.
Gracia-Arnau, Ivan. "Els usos polítics de la Revolta dels Segadors: L'estratègia narrativa de Gaspar Sala a la *Proclamación Católica*." In *Actes del VIIIè Congrés d'Història Moderna de Catalunya "Catalunya i el Mediterrani,"* coordinated by Jaume Dantí, Xavier Gil, Diego Sola, and Ida Mauro, 90–112. Barcelona: Edicions de la Universitat de Barcelona, 2019.
[Guillén de la Carrera, Alonso]. *La Iustificació Real*. S.l.: s.n., [1640].
Guillorel, Éva. "La mémoire comme moteur de la révolte: Réflexions autour du rôle subversif des traditions orales dans l'Europe moderne." In Merle, Jettot, and Herrero, *La mémoire des révoltes en Europe*, 251–67.
Hermant, Héloïse. "Les mises en récit du soulèvement des Barretines (1687–1690): Construction politique, construction culturelle, construction mémorielle." *Cahiers du CRHQ* 4 (2013): 1–30.
Hugon, Alain, and Mathias Ledroit. "La bataille de l'imprimé en Catalogne à l'époque de la Guerre de Séparation (1640–1652)." *Histoire et civilisation du livre* 12 (December 2016): 361–76.
Kuijpers, Erika, Judith Pollmann, Johannes Müller, and Jasper van der Steen, eds. *Memory before Modernity: Practices of Memory in Early Modern Europe*. Leiden: Brill, 2013.

Marquès, Antoni. *Cataluña Defendida de sus Émulos, Illustrada con sus Hechos, Fidelidad y Servicio a sus Reyes.* Lleida: Enrique Castañ, 1641.
[Martí Viladamor, Francesc]. *Apoyos a la Verdad Catalana, Opugnada por un Papel que Comiença: Justificación Real.* S.l.: s.n., [1640].
———. *Noticia Universal de Cataluña.* S.l.: s.n., [1640].
Merle, Alexandra, Stéphane Jettot, and Manuel Herraro, eds. *La mémoire des révoltes en Europe à l'époque moderne.* Paris: Classiques Garnier, 2018.
Murdock, Graeme, Penny Roberts, and Andrew Spicer, eds. "Ritual and Violence." Special issue, *Past & Present* 214, no. 7 (2012).
Neumann, Karsten. "La justificación 'ante el mundo': Difusión y recepción de la propaganda catalana en Europa en 1640." *Pedralbes: Revista d'Història Moderna* 18 (1998): 373–81.
Nora, Pierre. "Entre histoire et mémoire: La problématique des lieux." In *Les lieux de mémoire.* Vol. 1, *La république*, edited by Pierre Nora, xvii–xlii. Paris: Gallimard, 1984.
Palos, Joan Lluís. *Els juristes i la defensa de les Constitucions: Joan Pere Fontanella (1575–1649).* Vic: Eumo, 1997.
Panno, Francesc Pasqual de. *Motines de Cataluña.* Edited by Isabel Juncosa and Jordi Vidal. Barcelona: Curial, 1993.
Parets, Miquel. *Crònica.* Edited by M. Rosa Margalef. 3 vols. Barcelona: Barcino, 2011–2020.
Peña Díaz, Manuel. "La Inquisición y la memoria histórica de la revuelta catalana de 1640." *Bulletin of Hispanic Studies: Hispanic Studies and Researches on Spain, Portugal and Latin America* 92, no. 5 (2015): 747–69.
Pérez Samper, María de los Ángeles. *Catalunya i Portugal el 1640: Dos pobles en una cruïlla.* Barcelona: Curial, 1992.
Pollmann, Judith. *Memory in Early Modern Europe, 1500–1800.* Oxford: Oxford Scholarship Online, 2017.
Por qué, para qué. S.l.: s.n., [1640].
[Rioja, Francisco de]. *Aristarco o Censura de la Proclamación Católica de los catalanes.* S.l.: s.n., [1641].
[Ros, Alexandre]. *La estrecha amistad.* S.l.: s.n., [1641].
Rubí de Marimon, Ramon. "Relación del lebantamiento de Cataluña." In *Cròniques de la Guerra dels Segadors*, edited by Antoni Simon Tarrés, 249–311. Barcelona: Fundació Pere Coromines, 2003.
[Sala, Gaspar]. *Proclamación Católica a la Magestad Piadosa de Felipe el Grande.* Barcelona: Sebastià and Jaume Matevat, 1640.
Sanabre, Josep. *La acción de Francia en Cataluña en la pugna por la hegemonía de Europa.* Barcelona: Librería J. Sala Badal, 1956.
Sarroca, Josep. *Política del Comte de Olivares, Contra Política de Cathaluña, y Barcelona.* Barcelona: Jaume Romeu, 1641.
Serra Puig, Eva. "1640: Una revolució política. La implicació de les institucions." In *La revolució catalana de 1640*, by Eva Serra Puig et al., 3–65. Barcelona: Crítica, 1991.
Simon Tarrés, Antoni. *1640.* Barcelona: Rafael Dalmau Editor, 2019.

———. "Un 'alboroto católico': El factor religiós en la revolució catalana de 1640." *Pedralbes: Revista d'Història Moderna* 23, no. 2 (2003): 123–46.

———. *Els orígens ideològics de la revolució catalana de 1640.* Barcelona: Publicacions de l'Abadia de Montserrat, 1999.

Sorel, Charles. *La Deffence des Catalans.* Paris: Nicolas de Sercy, 1642.

Torres Sans, Xavier. "De Tirlemont a Riudarenes: Política y religión en la crisis hispánica de 1640." *Hispania Sacra* 69, no. 139 (January–June 2017): 221–31.

———. "Nosaltres, els Macabeus: Patriotisme català a la Guerra dels Segadors." In *Una relació difícil: Catalunya i l'Espanya moderna (segles XVII–XIX)*, by Joaquim Albareda et al., 85–108. Barcelona: Base, 2007.

———. *La Guerra dels Segadors.* Vic: Eumo; Lleida: Pagès, 2006.

Traverso, Enzo. *El pasado, instrucciones de uso. Historia, memoria, política.* Barcelona: Marcial Pons, 2007.

Vopis, Francesc. *Ingenuidad Catalana Coronada de los Lilios.* Barcelona: Pedro Juan Dexen, 1644.

Zuloaga Hoyos, Gustavo. "La discusión sobre el canibalismo y los sacrificios en la disputa de Sepúlveda con Las Casas (1550–1551)." *Cuadernos de Filosofía Latinoamericana* 30, no. 100 (2009): 39–46.

NOTES

This work was supported by the project Power and Cultural Representations: Sensory Communities and Political Communication in the Hispanic World (16th–18th Centuries) (PID2020–115565GB-C21), funded by the Ministry of Science and Innovation of the Government of Spain, and by the project Rebellion and Resistance in the Iberian Empires, 16th–19th Centuries, funded by the European Union's Horizon 2020 research and innovation programme under the Marie Skłodowska-Curie Grant Agreement No 778076.

1. On the causes of the revolt and the events of the war, there are two classic references: John H. Elliott, *The Revolt of the Catalans: A Study in the Decline of Spain (1598–1640)* (Cambridge: Cambridge University Press, 1963); Josep Sanabre, *La acción de Francia en Cataluña en la pugna por la hegemonía de Europa* (Barcelona: Librería J. Sala Badal, 1956). For a more recent synthesis of the conflict, see Xavier Torres Sans, *La Guerra dels Segadors* (Vic: Eumo; Lleida: Pagès, 2006).

2. Because of its coincidence with the Corpus Christi holiday, this revolt is known today as the Corpus de Sang (Corpus of Blood) or the Corpus Christi Day revolt.

3. [Juan Adam de la Parra], *Súplica de la Muy Noble y Muy Leal Ciudad de Tortosa* (Tortosa: Pedro Martorell, 1640), 76r.

4. [Gaspar Sala], *Proclamación Católica a la Magestad Piadosa de Felipe el Grande* (Barcelona: Sebastià and Jaume Matevat, 1640), 68.

5. The *relaciones* were accounts of greatly varying length, both printed and handwritten, that reported events of all kinds (holidays, wars, religious and political events, etc.) and reached a large readership among the population during the seventeenth century.

6. Alain Hugon and Mathias Ledroit, "La bataille de l'imprimé en Catalogne à l'époque de la Guerre de Séparation (1640–1652)," *Histoire et civilisation du livre* 12 (December 2016): 361–76.
7. Pierre Nora, "Entre histoire et mémoire: La problématique des lieux," in *Les lieux de mémoire*, vol. 1, *La République*, ed. Pierre Nora (Paris: Gallimard, 1984), xix.
8. Enzo Traverso, *El pasado, instrucciones de uso. Historia, memoria, política* (Barcelona: Marcial Pons, 2007), 18.
9. Giovanni C. Cattini, "Myths and Symbols in the Political Culture of Catalan Nationalism (1880–1914)," *Nations & Nationalism* 21, no. 3 (July 2015): 445–60.
10. Judith Pollmann, *Memory in Early Modern Europe, 1500–1800* (Oxford: Oxford Scholarship Online, 2017); Erika Kuijpers et al., eds., *Memory before Modernity: Practices of Memory in Early Modern Europe* (Leiden: Brill, 2013).
11. Éva Guillorel, "La mémoire comme moteur de la révolte: Réflexions autour du rôle subversif des traditions orales dans l'Europe moderne," in *La mémoire des révoltes en Europe à l'époque moderne*, ed. Alexandra Merle, Stéphane Jettot, and Manuel Herrero (Paris: Classiques Garnier, 2018), 251–67.
12. An example is the comparison of the revolt of the Barretines in Catalonia (1688–1689) with that of the rebels of 1640, as a way to weaken the cause and chastise its protagonists who, just as forty years before, would surely lead the principality to disaster. Héloïse Hermant, "Les mises en récit du soulèvement des Barretines (1687–1690): Construction politique, construction culturelle, construction mémorielle," *Cahiers du CRHQ* 4 (2013): 1–30.
13. Alexandra Merle, Stéphane Jettot, and Manuel Herrero, eds., *La mémoire des révoltes en Europe à l'époque moderne* (Paris: Classiques Garnier, 2018), 11.
14. The Diputació del General was the institution in charge of upholding the Catalan constitutions, approved by agreement between the king and the kingdom in the Parliaments.
15. The Consell de Cent was the local council that governed Barcelona.
16. Many of these writings, promoted from the upper echelons of power, have been analysed in María Soledad Arredondo, *Literatura y propaganda en tiempo de Quevedo: Guerras y plumas contra Francia, Cataluña y Portugal* (Madrid: Vervuert, 2011), and María de los Ángeles Pérez Samper, *Catalunya i Portugal el 1640: Dos pobles en una cruïlla* (Barcelona: Curial, 1992), 314–95.
17. Francesco Benigno, *Specchi della rivoluzione: Conflitto e identità politica nell'Europa moderna* (Rome: Donzelli editore, 1999), 201.
18. Henry Ettinghausen, *La Guerra dels Segadors a través de la premsa de l'època* (Barcelona: Curial, 1993).
19. Torres Sans, *La Guerra dels Segadors*, 160.
20. The most recent analysis of the consequences of the billeting is Antoni Simon Tarrés, *1640* (Barcelona: Rafael Dalmau Editor, 2019).
21. The Catalans opposed the Count Duke of Olivares's project of fiscal and military centralization; his objective was to implement the Union of Arms either by consent or by force. On the defense of the Catalan contractual model and opposition to Olivares's project, see Antoni Simon Tarrés, *Els orígens ideològics de la revolució catalana de 1640* (Barcelona: Publicacions de l'Abadia de Montserrat, 1999); Joan

Lluís Palos, *Els juristes i la defensa de les Constitucions: Joan Pere Fontanella (1575–1649)* (Vic: Eumo, 1997); Eva Serra Puig, "1640: Una revolució política. La implicació de les institucions," in *La revolució catalana de 1640*, by Eva Serra Puig et al. (Barcelona: Crítica, 1991), 3–65.

22. Xavier Torres Sans, "De Tirlemont a Riudarenes: Política y religión en la crisis hispánica de 1640," *Hispania Sacra* 69, no. 139 (January–June 2017): 222.

23. Torres Sans, "Política y religión," 223–25.

24. Joan Busquets, "Revolta popular i religiositat barroca: L'excomunió de l'exèrcit espanyol a la catedral de Girona en 1640," in *Treballs d'història: Estudis de demografia, economia i societat a les comarques gironines*, by Ramon Alberch et al. (Girona: Patronat Eiximenis de l'Excma. Diputacio Provincial de Girona, 1976), 63–87.

25. On May 22, the *segadors* staged their first protest in Barcelona against the king's ministers, an act that prepared the ground for the assassination on Corpus Christi Day.

26. Xavier Torres Sans, "Nosaltres, els Macabeus: Patriotisme català a la Guerra dels Segadors," in *Una relació difícil: Catalunya i l'Espanya moderna (segles XVII–XIX)*, by Joaquim Albareda et al. (Barcelona: Base, 2007); Antoni Simon Tarrés, "Un 'alboroto católico': El factor religiós en la revolució catalana de 1640," *Pedralbes: Revista d'Història Moderna* 23, no. 2 (2003): 123–46.

27. This interpretation sought to allay the serious consequences that the murder of the king's representative would have for the Catalan authorities.

28. Francesc Vopis, *Ingenuidad Catalana Coronada de los Lilios* (Barcelona: Pedro Juan Dexen, 1644), chap. 27, 46.

29. [Sala], *Proclamación*, 66.

30. For an analysis of Sala's strategy in his narration of the viceroy's death, see Ivan Gracia-Arnau, "Els usos polítics de la Revolta dels Segadors: L'estratègia narrativa de Gaspar Sala a la *Proclamación Católica*," in *Actes del VIIIè Congrés d'Història Moderna de Catalunya "Catalunya i el Mediterrani,"* coord. Jaume Dantí, Xavier Gil, Diego Sola, and Ida Mauro (Barcelona: Edicions de la Universitat de Barcelona, 2019), 90–112.

31. Karsten Neumann, "La justificación 'ante el mundo': Difusión y recepción de la propaganda catalana en Europa en 1640," *Pedralbes: Revista d'Història Moderna* 18 (1998): 377–78.

32. [Francesc Martí Viladamor], *Noticia Universal de Cataluña* (s.l.: s.n., [1640]) 159–60; Antoni Marquès, *Cataluña Defendida de sus Émulos, Illustrada con sus Hechos, Fidelidad y Servicio a sus Reyes* (Lleida: Enrique Castañ, 1641), bk. 4, 60.

33. [Francesc Martí Viladamor], *Apoyos a la Verdad Catalana, Opugnada por un Papel que Comiença: Justificación Real* (s.l.: s.n., [1640]), paper 3, answer R.

34. Josep Sarroca, *Política del Comte de Olivares, Contra Política de Cathaluña, y Barcelona* (Barcelona: Jaume Romeu, 1641), 15r.

35. Although the French Crown made great efforts to accommodate the incorporation of Catalonia into the dynastic narrative of the House of Bourbon, other than Sorel's account there are few references to the events of the Corpus Christi Day of 1640. Daniel Aznar, "Cataluña y el rey: Representaciones y prácticas de la Majestad

durante el cambio de soberanía (1640–1655)" (PhD thesis, University of Barcelona, 2016).

36. Charles Sorel, *La Deffence des Catalans* (Paris: Nicolas de Sercy, 1642), 53.

37. The recent edition of the manuscript by M. Rosa Margalef contains three introductory studies on the biography and work of this artisan by James S. Amelang, Antoni Simon Tarrés, and Xavier Torres Sans. Miquel Parets, *Crònica*, ed. M. Rosa Margalef, 3 vols. (Barcelona: Barcino, 2011–2020).

38. Parets, *Crònica*, 1:363.

39. Parets, *Crònica*, 1:364.

40. Parets, *Crònica*, 1:363. The religious and punitive meanings of popular violence in early modern times have been assessed in depth. Here, for reasons of space, I will not further analyze this testimony, or the meanings of the practices of violence. Some classic references on rituals of violence are William Beik, *Urban Protest in Seventeenth-Century France* (Cambridge: Cambridge University Press, 1997); Denis Crouzet, *Les Guerriers de Dieu: La violence au temps des troubles de religion (vers 1525–vers 1610)* (Seyssel: Champ Vallon, 1990); Peter Burke, "The Virgin of the Carmine and the Revolt of Masaniello," *Past & Present* 99 (1983): 3–21; Natalie Z. Davis, "The Rites of Violence: Religious Riot in Sixteenth-Century France," *Past & Present* 59 (1973): 51–91. Other more recent studies include Christopher R. Friedrichs, "House-Destruction as a Ritual of Punishment in Early Modern Europe," *European History Quarterly* 50, no. 4 (2020): 599–624; Francesco Benigno, Laurent Bourquin, and Alain Hugon, eds., *Violences en révolte: Une histoire culturelle européenne (XIVe–XVIIIe siècle)* (Rennes: Presses Universitaires de Rennes, 2019); Graeme Murdock, Penny Roberts, and Andrew Spicer, eds., "Ritual and Violence," special issue, *Past & Present* 214, no. 7 (2012).

41. Christian Jouhaud, "Révoltes et contestations d'Ancien Régime," in *L'état et les conflits*, ed. Jacques Julliard, vol. 3 of *Histoire de France*, ed. André Burguière and Jacques Revel (Paris: Seuil, 1990), 71. Quoted in Benigno, *Specchi*, 178.

42. [Alexandre Ros], *La estrecha amistad* (s.l.: s.n., [1641]), 1. Attributed to Alexandre Ros, a former Jesuit in the service of the Spanish ambassador in Rome.

43. María Soledad Arredondo, "Noticia de la *Súplica de Tortosa* (1640), atribuida al Inquisidor Juan Adam de la Parra," *Cuadernos de Historia Moderna* 22 (1999): 141.

44. [Adam de la Parra], *Súplica*, 75v.

45. Simon Tarrés, *Els orígens ideològics*, 231–32.

46. [Alonso Guillén de la Carrera], *La Iustificació Real* (s.l.: s.n., [1640]), 1r.

47. Luca Assarino, *Delle Rivolutioni di Catalogna* (Genoa: Giovanni Maria Farroni, 1644), bk. 1, 139.

48. [Adam de la Parra], *Súplica*, 75.

49. Ramon Rubí de Marimon, "Relación del lebantamiento de Cataluña," in *Cròniques de la Guerra dels Segadors*, ed. Antoni Simon Tarrés (Barcelona: Fundació Pere Coromines, 2003), 274.

50. Francesc Pasqual de Panno, *Motines de Cataluña*, ed. Isabel Juncosa and Jordi Vidal (Barcelona: Curial, 1993), 139–40.

51. [Adam de la Parra], *Súplica*, 74r.

52. [Guillén de la Carrera], *Iustificació*, 1r.

53. *Por qué, para qué* (s.l.: s.n., [1640]), 2r.
54. [Francisco de Rioja], *Aristarco o Censura de la Proclamación Católica de los catalanes* (s.l.: s.n., [1641]), 26r.
55. [Ros], *La estrecha*, 5v.
56. [Ros], *La estrecha*, 7r.
57. William Arens, *El mito del canibalismo: antropología y antropofagia* (Mexico City: Siglo XXI, 1981), 46–55.
58. [Rioja], *Aristarco*, 22r.
59. Gustavo Zuloaga Hoyos, "La discusión sobre el canibalismo y los sacrificios en la disputa de Sepúlveda con Las Casas (1550–1551)," *Cuadernos de Filosofía Latinoamericana* 30, no. 100 (2009): 39–46. Practices such as opening the chest of victims and eating the heart were reported in widely circulated chronicles of the Indies, such as those of Francisco López de Gómara, Gonzalo Fernández de Oviedo, and Bernal Díaz del Castillo.
60. Violent practices that, as Judith Pollmann has shown, stemmed from transnational narratives of atrocity. "Remembering Violence: Trauma, Atrocities, and Cosmopolitan Memories," in *Memory in Early Modern Europe*, 160–85.
61. Manuel Peña Díaz, "La Inquisición y la memoria histórica de la revuelta catalana de 1640," *Bulletin of Hispanic Studies: Hispanic Studies and Researches on Spain, Portugal and Latin America* 92, no. 5 (2015): 747–69.
62. Hermant, "Barretines."

Chapter Six

Trauma and Postmemory in Martín Cortés's Uprising

Covadonga Lamar Prieto

The year 1565 marked an awakening for the conquerors' sons in Mexico City; they revolted against the authority of the Spanish Crown and were severely punished in return. After the fall of Tenochtitlán in 1521, the lands and riches of the Aztec empire were transferred to the Crown, but also into the hands of the conquerors in the form of encomiendas: grants of land and the labor of the people living on it. In 1542, Spain had tried to regain power over those conquerors with the *Leyes Nuevas*, or New Laws, which decreed the return of the encomiendas to the Crown "en la tercera vida" (in the third generation). In practical terms, this meant that upon their deaths, the conquerors' grandsons, the *tercera vida*, would be forced to revert their otherwise ill-gained lands to the Crown. Martín Cortés's uprising, however, marked a final readjustment of the Crown's policy toward those born in America (*criollos*). By 1565, the sons of the wealthier conquerors would be put on trial, condemned, and executed. Their crime? Lèse-majesté—attempting to put a new king on a new throne. Their leaders, brothers Alonso de Ávila and Gil González de Ávila, were beheaded. Martín Cortés and Martín Cortés, Hernán Cortés's two eldest sons (with the same name), suffered political repercussions and exile from America.

There are few eyewitness testimonies to the beheading of the Ávilas. The most vivid of them, examined in this chapter, is Juan Suárez de Peralta's "Tratado del descubrimiento de las Indias y su conquista," published in 1867 but probably written in the last decade of the sixteenth or the first decade of the seventeenth century.[1] The traumatic experience of the beheadings shifted his understanding of the world, and sent him on a voyage to Spain from which he never returned. That trauma traveled with him in the form of memories, remaining indelible and as accurate as when they first occurred. I agree with Bessel van der Kolk in his definition of these particular kinds of memories as "intrusive traumatic recollections of traumatic events."[2] Writing about them becomes not an exorcism, but a painful manifestation of their immanence.

The second testimony to be examined here, that of Luis de Sandoval Zapata, belongs to the next generation, reflecting those who were not present during the executions, but who nonetheless experienced the social consequences of the uprising. His text, the "Relación fúnebre a la infeliz trágica muerte de dos caballeros,"[3] likely written during the second quarter of the seventeenth century, was not published until 1863. I will argue in this chapter that Suárez de Peralta's work embodies a narrative of immediate trauma, while Sandoval Zapata depicts the effects, as described by Marianne Hirsch, of postmemory. Sandoval Zapata was not alive during the 1565 events, but he received the memories through social mores and possibly through oral testimonies and literature in a way of transgenerational pain. His memory of the trauma is societal; just like Don Quixote, he is making sense of the histories and stories that were present in his life through literature. At the same time, like Don Quixote's alter ego Alonso Quijano, he leaves a testimony of the social circumstances that forced him into that position.

The beheading of the Ávila brothers and the war against the conquerors' sons are at the heart of both Suárez de Peralta's and Sandoval Zapata's literary interpretations. In the time between the two authors, the Ávilas had become martyrs of the *criollo* cause. The uprising became, therefore, the symptom of a larger issue: the misalignment between the interests of the king (embodied in the *Leyes Nuevas*) and those of the conquerors' descendants, who had begun to flourish. The *criollos*' incipient sense of belonging, already palpable in Suárez de Peralta, thus collides with a European mistrust regarding all non-European bodies. Even when they were raised to consider themselves Spaniards, the dissonance between the *criollos*' behavior and the king's response shows they in truth existed in a third space: colonial subjects with a Spanish consciousness. Notwithstanding their self-definition, this new type of colonial subject was not considered for positions in colonial administration, as Shirley Cushing Flint points out, making it impossible for them to participate in the government of their land of birth.[4]

The term *criollo*, purposefully used in Spanish in this chapter, describes the American-born descendants of Spanish-born individuals. In this definition, America refers to the continent, while Spain refers to a European geographical entity. That entity is different from the political one that included territories in America (the continent) in its definition. At first, *criollo* and "creole" might seem equivalent in Spanish and English, but this is not exactly the case. The sociolinguistic realities and nuances of each term require extreme caution. There is a constant negotiation of identity that has been examined by critics,[5] an "indianization" according to Claudia Parodi,[6] that I propose to trace to the precise moment of the uprising led by Martín Cortés y Zúñiga. The trauma and the postmemory aftermath of that trauma, I ultimately argue, is the seed of identity from which eighteenth-century *criollismo* and a movement for independence would germinate.

SOURCES ABOUT THE UPRISING

There are three different sources regarding Martín Cortés's uprising. The first group are the legal and judicial documents from the period created by the Crown. The second are the autoethnographic and literary representations of experiences contemporary to the uprising, such as the *Monarquía indiana* by Fray Juan de Torquemada (1723)[7] and the "Tratado del descubrimiento" by Juan Suárez de Peralta, as well as the "Relación fúnebre" by Luis de Sandoval Zapata, which is close to the unrest but not immediate. The third contingent deals with Martín Cortés but contains texts written in the twentieth century, such as Luis González Obregón's interpretation of Suárez de Peralta (1904; 1906), Carlos Fuentes's interpretation in "Los hijos del conquistador" (1993),[8] and mainstream novels such as *Martín Ojo de Plata* by Matilde Asensi (2010).

Legal and Judicial Documents

The legal case against Martín Cortés y Zúñiga was compiled under the title *Proceso criminal contra don Martín Cortés, Marqués del Valle* (1566).[9] The case against the rest of the coconspirators can be found in the *Proceso general formado en la Audiencia de México contra todos los que resultaron cómplices en la rebelión de Nueva España* (1567).[10] Manuel Orozco y Berra published a compilation of some of the documents in his *Noticia histórica de la conjuración del Marqués del Valle* (1853),[11] where a list of the indicted can be read as a who's who of the most important families in the viceroyalty.[12] Even the viceroy, for instance, was allegedly destitute and forced to write a petition to the king (*Petición del Marqués de Falces*, 1566–1567). Orozco y Berra showed here his fascination with the emotional intensity of the story, reflecting upon the possibilities for fiction and the difficulty in attempting to rewrite the trauma.[13]

The most interesting confessions are those of Martín Cortés, the marquis, and Alonso de Ávila from 1566. During the trial, the two Ávila brothers, Alonso and Gil, insisted that they were innocent. Roland Schmidt-Riese has examined the brothers' confessions to see if there was any truth to either the accusation or the accused.[14] Schmidt-Riese, however, did not examine a third document, dated in 1566: *Confesión de Alonso de Avila Alvarado, preso y condenado a muerte como consecuencia de la conspiración para alzarse con el poder en Méjico, junto a Luis y Martín Cortés y otros*.[15] This document offers two contradictory testimonies by Alonso de Ávila. While in the first he insists that he is innocent and a worthy servant of his majesty, the context of the second creates a different opportunity for either remorse or acceptance of his circumstances. That second testimony was taken moments before his beheading, when he called a priest and, allegedly, confessed that he had always been guilty of treason. Suárez de Peralta does not acknowledge this second testimony, and his "Tratado del descubrimiento" is firm in the idea that the *criollos* were wrongfully convicted and died without guilt. He finesses his argument to assign a culprit, and claims the king was poorly served by those sent to act as judges. Suárez de Peralta brilliantly negotiates, therefore, the dichotomy between defending his friends and society while not criticizing the king, and, in doing so, diligently puts the blame on the viceregal administration. That administration, as I examine below, was not handled by locals, but by individuals sent from Spain.

While the legal documents report the official perspective on the uprising, the literary testimonies show a different interpretation. Suárez de Peralta plays with the rhythm of his narration in order to highlight the dissociated elements of those memories inflicted by trauma. However, as we will examine, Sandoval Zapata moves the scales yet more toward the development of a *criollo* identity emerging from the sixteenth to the seventeenth centuries, all the while foreshadowing later developments of the eighteenth century.

Literary sources

Suárez de Peralta, who lived the second half of his life in Castille stranded from most of his past in Mexico, configured his "Tratado del descubrimiento" according to the model of Alfonso X's *Estoria general*. Aiming for completeness, he succumbs to a horror vacui that reflects his attempt to convey America in its totality. While the text traces the origins of New Spain from the mythical past to its fifth viceroy, the memories of the uprising become, as I shall examine, akin to what Cathy Caruth would refer to as a voice that speaks from the wound: the text of the *Tratado* metamorphoses into "the other within the self that retains the memory of the 'unwitting' traumatic events of one's past."[16]

Sandoval Zapata's "Relación fúnebre" is a panegyric poem bordering on both martyrology and hagiography. The poem was lost to the general public until 1967, when José Pascual Buxó published it.[17] Buxó describes Sandoval as "uno de los poetas de más digno recuerdo entre los que bajo el nombre de tales se apretujan en la decimoséptima centuria novohispana" (one of the poets with a more dignified memory among those who are grouped together during the seventeenth century in New Spain) and as a follower of the "brillante y proteico estilo de Calderón" (brilliant and protean style of Calderón), while highlighting his ability to "revivir aquella vieja historia and proyectarla, con todas sus consecuencias, sobre sus lectores contemporáneos" (relive that old history and project it, with all its consequences, onto his contemporary readers).[18]

The idea of *revivir*, of *reliving* the consequences of the uprising, comes with a further reworking. While Suárez de Peralta ignored certain elements of this story, such as Alonso's final confession, Sandoval Zapata devised a more profound interpretation of the events that created a new memory informed, not only by the past, but also by the resentment after the uprising. And, even though Sandoval Zapata was not a witness, or precisely because he was not, his text is nevertheless imbued with the same despair as that of Suárez de Peralta.

JAIL, TORTURE, AND TRAUMA

The fragile political ecosystem of the viceroyalty shattered when the Crown authorized the return of Martín Cortés, the Marquis of the Valley of Oaxaca and Hernán Cortés's firstborn son from his Catholic marriage. Hernán's two sons named Martín had been born from different mothers; they had traveled with their father to Spain and remained there after their father's indictment. Hernán Cortés had initiated a battle with the Crown about the value and scope of his encomiendas. The numbers are astonishing: while claimed that he had been assigned 23,000 families, the king defended it was 23,000 souls. The marquis's return represented a glimpse of hope for the old conquistadores as they, along with their American-born sons, felt mistreated and dispossessed of honor and recognition and, as such, were already nursing a resentment against the Crown's deputies. L. N. McAllister, for instance, defines this as an inherited pain, a trauma transitioning into a postmemory, built upon old resentments that would be fed by the reactions against the uprising.[19] Furthermore, David Brading details that

> since the very beginning, the criollos seemed to have considered themselves dispossessed heirs, robbed of their birthright by an unjust Crown and by the usurping immigrants freshly arrived from the Iberian Peninsula. That resentment has its origins, in part, with men like Bernal Díaz del Castillo, who had blamed the Crown saying it had not properly rewarded their heroic service.[20]

The marquis would act as a magnet for the unhappy sons of the conquerors. As they were American born, they were de facto ineligible to work in the administration of the Viceroyalty, with their encomiendas reverting to the Crown after their sons, the conquerors' grandsons. At the same time, though, they were living off the efforts of the indigenous populations. The negotiation between entitlement and resentment consequently developed into the idea of eliminating the Crown's deputies and declaring the marquis the king of New Spain. The murmurs of these conversations reached the viceroy's palace, and he began an investigation, summoning individuals, some of whom eventually betrayed others, to confess their commitment to the uprising. As a result, the marquis, his brothers Martín and Luis, the Ávila brothers, the Guzmán brothers, the Quesada brothers, and the Herrera brothers, along with many others, were indicted.

Mexico did not have a jail in which it was deemed appropriate for these individuals of noble blood to await their sentences. Some were too powerful to be jailed, and as a result not all the indicted would endure jail time: the Cortés brothers would remain under house arrest in the viceregal palace while the rest, according to Suárez de Peralta, endured harsh conditions similar to those of the Inquisition's jails:

> Mandaron hazer una cárçel, temeraria, lo primero, á manera de las del santo offiçio, unas çeldas muy escuras, fortísimas y muy chicas, que solo estar en ellas un dia era gravísima pena, y estas no abia de aber en ellas y en cada una, sino uno ó dos presos. Quando se hazia la cárçel ybanla á ver munchos, y algunos de los que la estrenaron y della salieron para la muerte; dezíanse cosas de grandísima confusion, porque áun todavía creyan que venian los juezes en favor del marqués, y así estaban que no sabian qué hazerse.

> They built a fear-inducing jail, in the manner of those of the Inquisition, with very dark, solid, and small cells, so that being inside for even a day was a grave punishment, and they put in each cell no more than one or two prisoners. While the jail was being built, many people came to see it, and some of the first to be jailed were left there to face their death; there was a lot of confusion and gossip, because even then people were thinking that the judges who had been sent [from Spain] were favorable to the marquis, and with all that no one knew what to do.[21]

Even when he wrote his autobiography more than twenty years after the uprising, Suárez de Peralta still remembered with shocking clarity the confusion surrounding his counterparts' arrest, judgment, and imprisonment. None of them were expecting the Crown to act against them, or so harshly. After the *criollos* had been rounded up ("tiniendo ya muchos presos, llenas todas las carçeles" [there were so many prisoners that the jails were full]), the Crown's emissaries began torturing them, beginning with Baltasar de Aguilar: "desnudan y dánle el más bravo tormento que jamás se vió . . . Era lástima velle quál le dejaron hecho pedaços: volviéronle á la cárçel" (stripping and torturing him to an extent that had never been seen before . . . It was so painful to see him so worn out: they returned him to jail).[22] After him, the Quesada brothers, Cristóbal de Oñate, and even Alonso de Ávila's butler "que se llamaba Fulano Mendez, el qual dio grandísima lástima, porque era onrradísimo hombre en lo exterior, y estaba gotoso de los pies, que no podía andar sino con dos muletas y a caballo; era de ochenta años, la barba y la cabeça blanca, que no tenía pelo que no fuese blanco" (who was named John Doe, whose situation was particularly painful, as he behaved quite honorably, suffering from gout and only able to move around with crutches or on horseback; he was eighty, beard and hair both white, he did not have a hair that was not white).[23]

However, those in jail were not the only ones to suffer the consequences of the uprising, as the women from these families endured the social trauma and public shaming attached to the indictments. When Bernardino Pacheco Bocanegra was sentenced to death, for instance, his mother and wife became the center of a scene that, in Suárez de Peralta's memories, floats midway between Proust's madeleine and cinematic neorealism:

> Condenaron a muerte á Bernardino Pacheco de Bocanegra, el qual vi yo y todos tan á punto de sacalle, questaba ya confesado, y la mula á la puerta, y el Cristo y el verdugo y pregoneros. Este caballero era muy emparentado con lo prinçipal de la çiudad, y luego que lo supo su madre, y mujer y parientes, con los prelados de todas las órdenes fueron, ellas descalças y destocadas y descabelladas, cubiertas de luto, arrastrando por los suelos los mantos, sin atallos, llorando, que era la mayor compasion vellas, que jamás se vió, y desta manera entraron á los juezes, y puestas delante dellos se tendieron en el suelo pidiéndoles que por la pasion de Cristo Nuestro Señor otorgasen la suplicaçion á aquel, caballero, y no permitiesen matalle.

Bernardino Pacheco Bocanegra was sentenced to death, and I saw him, as I saw all of them, when he was about to be taken out [from the jail], and he had already confessed his sins, and the mule was waiting for him at the door, and the image of Christ, and the executioner, and the town's criers. This gentleman was kin to all the main families in the city, and when his mother, his wife, and his relatives knew about his sentence, with all the prelates from all the religious orders, they went there. The women were wearing no shoes or headdresses, and they had not combed their hair, they were all dressed in black, dragging their untied shawls along the floor, crying, and everyone felt compassionate after seeing them, as no one had seen anything like that before, and in that fashion they went in to see the judges, and they laid themselves on the floor in front of them begging the judges to have mercy on the gentleman, and to do it under Christ Our Lord's name, so that he might not be executed.[24]

Bernardino Pacheco Bocanegra's sentencing was the last one to be conducted in America. From then onward, the trial moved to Spain, with Martín Cortés, the marquis, and the Dean of the Cathedral of Mexico being judged in Madrid. Suárez de Peralta thus closes his memories about the uprising by negotiating the difficulty of acknowledging the Crown's authority while claiming that an injustice was perpetrated in the usurpation of the king's name: "Despues de salido de Mexico el liçençiado Muñoz, empeçó á gobernar la Audiençia; y ya no se hazian más dilijençias en lo del rebelion, porque abian dejado la tierra los juezes bien castigada y no se les abia quedado cosa por hazer" (After the departure of judge Muñoz from Mexico, the Audience began its rule. There were no more procedures related to the rebellion, as the judges had forced upon the land such punishments that not a thing remained to be pursued).[25] Distance, in time and space, was subsequently planted into the history—and the story—of the uprising.

TRAUMA AND MEMORY

The death of the Ávilas and the exile of the Quesadas, as well as other consequences—such as the forced attendance of mass wearing specific penitential garments (*capirotes*)—exemplified a public manifestation of torture and punishment. The repressive machinery that had controlled the bodies of the Aztecs by way of the conquerors now exerted, at the hands of new individuals from Spain, a similarly violent control over the bodies of the conquerors and their families.[26] The Ávilas' bodies generated a host of memories that Suárez de Peralta inhibited, repressed, and then transferred into an account of trauma. These memories, which focus primarily on Alonso, the older of the brothers, demonstrate an emotional intensity that he, in his writing, parallels in the rhythm of his narration.

In this manner, chapter 34 of the *Tratado del descubrimiento*, "Que trata de cómo se hizo justicia de Alonso de Ávila, y su hermano, y de lo que más sucedió" (Which deals with how justice was served to Alonso de Ávila and his brother, and other things that happened) is divided into different sections, each of which relates to the different stages of the Ávilas' case: their sentencing, notification of sentencing, beheading, and the aftermath. As a corollary, Suárez de Peralta reflects upon the misfortunes of the family after the death of the brothers.

Playing a game of hide-and-seek, he blames the marquis for the demise of the plan while fiercely defending him from additional attacks, claiming that he was not as shrewd as Suárez de Peralta could have wished: "que no quiero dello tratar y el descargo quél dió dello; el qual fué uno de los que más daño le hizieron, y áun la confision quel marqués hizo fué muy diferente de lo que prometia su entendimiento y viveza" (I don't want to talk about that, nor about the report that he gave on this topic, as that report was one of the more damaging elements for him, even the marquis's confession [of the crimes] was very different from what one could expect from his intelligence and cleverness).[27] The mark of injustice invades Suárez de Peralta's memories as he tries to self-censure: "En el negoçio pasaron munchas cosas, que las más dejo de tratar por ser de la calidad que es; sólo diré algunas que me pareçe hazen á mí propósito" (Many things happened in this respect, and I will not talk about them, as they pertain to a subject such as this; I will only talk about those related to what I want to talk about).[28]

In a constant back-and-forth, he complies with a forceful allegiance to the king and his ruling, while at the same time continuously trying to evoke the feelings of fragility and solitude that this trial brought on for the *criollos*: "los pobres caballeros no hallaban quien les ayudase, letrado, ni procurador, pensando deservian al rey, hasta que, con pena, mandaron les ayudasen (these poor gentlemen were unable to find any person who could help them, lawyer or defendant, as they [the legal representatives] were thinking that by helping the prisoners they were disloyal to the king until, finally and pitifully, they [the lawyers] were ordered to help the prisoners).[29] Not only that, but the text continues: "pues para presentar testigos, y que dijesen en su favor, y en las tachas de los que abian jurado contra ellos, no abia quien osase" (to bring forth witnesses, and speak in favor of the king, and ratify what they had said before against the prisoners, no one dared).[30] Suárez de Peralta seems to indicate, albeit sotto voce, that previous testimonies had been obtained under duress.

The alternation of description and directed dialogue in the chapter thereby serves to deflect responsibility while, more importantly, creating a space where those declared culprits can voice their suffering. When the narrator allows Alonso de Ávila to voice his own complaints, for instance, this same narrator is shielded from potential difficulties. Four decades had passed, neither the king nor New Spain was the same, but none of that was enough for Suárez de Peralta to break the cycle of hiding, and the social impact of the *criollos*' loss is yet another constant that continued to cause him pain: "No se vió jamás dia de tanta confusion y que mayor tristeza en jeneral ubiese de todos, hombres y mujeres, como el que vieron quando á aquellos dos caballeros sacaron á ajustiçiar: porque eran muy queridos y de los más prinçipales y ricos, y que no hazian mal a nadye, sino antes daban y onrraban su patria" (Never before had anyone, man or woman, seen a day filled with such general confusion and sadness, as the day when those gentlemen were taken to their executions: they were beloved, very well-related, and rich, and they did not cause any harm to anyone, on the contrary, they were generous and honored their homeland.)[31]

Writing about such acts for Suárez de Peralta is an anamnesis, where only through reminiscence from a previous experience can he know and learn. It is, following Lyotard, a "perlaboration" in which facts are not strictly historical, but a free chain of relations.[32] While the instances in which the narrator offers his opinion are scarce—"no hazian mal a nadye" (they did not cause any harm to anybody)—the notion of *patria* is noteworthy here, a word whose translation would be "homeland" or "mother/fatherland."[33] Where, then, is that *patria* the Ávilas were honoring with their actions?

If we read Suárez de Peralta closely, we could assume that with *patria* he is referring to New Spain instead of the general concept of imperial Spain. He was aware of the difference in social standing between Spanish-born and American-born subjects of the Crown, and he would let that idea emerge in the text. As a self-proclaimed memory keeper of his generation, he extends his voice to include those of the dead. In fact, after his death in Madrid, he was buried in the Gentlemen's Chapel, "la capilla de los caballeros," next to other New Spain-born subjects of the Crown. Even in the moment of their death, they intended to be with their own, surrounded by those with whom they shared, dare I say, a "patria": *criollismo* had been born.

Social panic increases in tone as we approach the beheadings. The judges deployed their soldiers, brought from Spain, with the objective of impeding people's movement. These soldiers took control of a main street, the one that would be used to move the Ávila brothers from the newly built jail to the gallows. The empire was providing its colonial subjects with first-row seats to their own liminality, as if it were cutting them down to size, reminding them that they were not Spanish-born: "vieran andar los hombres y las mujeres por las calles, todos espantados y escandalizados que no lo podian creer" (it was a sight to be seen, men and women walking in the streets, all of them terrified and in shock, unable to believe what was happening).[34] These *criollos* faced the sudden discovery of their place as intermediaries of the empire, but not entirely representative of the power of said empire. Some of them would become victims or victimizers, while all would be forced to defend the imperial order by policing one another:

> que fué neçesario mandar la audiençia saliese muncha jente á caballo, y de á pié, todos armados en uso de pelear, y la artillería puesta á punto; y así se hizo, que no quedó caballero, ni el que no lo era, que todos salieron armados y se recojeron en la plaza grande, frontero de las casas reales y de la cárçel, y tomaron todas las bocas de las calles, y desta manera aseguraron el temor, que le tenian grande. Pusieron jente de á caballo dende el tablado hasta la puerta de la cárçel,

de una parte y de otra, y luego jente de á pié, todos armados, delante de los caballos, y hecha una calçada ancha que podian caber más de seis hombres de á caballo: y sin atravesar ánima naçida.

> the government had to order people on horse and on foot into the streets, with their armor ready for combat, and artillery ready as well; and it was done in that way, and any gentleman, or even those that were not gentlemen, left their homes in complete armor and gathered together in the main square, next to the royal buildings and the jail; and they covered the entries from all streets, and in that way they felt reassured, as they were terrified. There were people on horseback from the gallows to the jail's door, from one side to the other, and then also people on foot in front of the horses, all of them armed, and this created a wide path upon which six people on horseback could pass, but no one dared to pass through there.[35]

The group of Spanish soldiers was not enough to contain the unrest. Local *criollos*—"caballeros, y los que no lo eran" (any gentleman, or even those that were not gentlemen)—would be made cannon fodder between the representatives of colonial power and the colonized subjects, both pre- and post-Columbian. These gentlemen on horseback or on foot, armed to the teeth, were the Ávilas' childhood friends, neighbors, and acquaintances. Considered "loyal," they knew they walked a very fine line, and that they could go, at any moment, from victimizers to victims. As Foucault puts it: "Generally speaking, all the authorities exercising individual control function according to a double mode; that of binary division and branding (mad/sane; dangerous/harmless; normal/abnormal)."[36]

Security was in the hands of the *criollos*, thus making them actionable elements of the same power mechanism that could run them over at the first opportunity. Additionally, if anything bad were to happen, such as any unrest, those sustaining the potential damage would be colonial subjects of different degrees of oppression: protesters, and those on the first line of violent response—population control and policing. This coercive assignment acts as a differential distribution in which each actor needs to learn and relearn their role: "who he is; where his must be; how he is to be characterized; how he is to be recognized; how a constant surveillance is to be exercised over him in an individual way, etc."[37]

The flashback of an image seems to return to Suárez de Peralta's mind, as the terror he felt next to the gallows permeates his description of the beheadings. That image at the same time hides his shame and shows his role in the maintenance of colonial rule:

> que me acaeçió detener el caballo, pasando por la plaça dondestaba la horca y en ella las cabeças destos caballeros, y ponérmelas á ver con tantas lágrimas de

> mis ojos, que no sé yo en vida aber llorado tanto, por solo considerar lo que el mundo abia mostrado en aquello que via presente, que no me pareçia ser cosa çierta, ni aber pasado, sino sueño y muy profundo, como quando un hombre está fuera de todo su sentido. . . . Çierto, en este punto, mestoy enterneçiendo con lo que la memoria me representa.

> I happened to stop my horse as I was passing through the square where the gallows were located, and there I saw the heads of these gentlemen, and as I looked there were so many tears in my eyes that I cannot recall in my whole life having cried that much, as I was considering what the world had shown itself to be capable of with those heads in front me at that point, and I was not able to believe it was true, but a nightmare from which it was very difficult to wake up, like a man who has gone completely mad. . . . In all honesty, at this point, I am moved by what my memory depicts for me.[38]

As Kolk explores, such a memory of trauma cannot come into existence until the individual is able to cope with the feelings caused by the traumatic event. Enough time had passed, and Suárez de Peralta had constructed a new life in Spain. At its start, Kolk says, the memory of trauma is only a dissociated memory (or a group of them), dislocated from the rest of the self-narrative and apparently only in fragments, such as the sensory and emotional flashbacks that Suárez de Peralta seems to have pieced together in the citation above. For, as Kolk posits:

> "memories" of the trauma tend to, at least initially, be experienced as fragments of the sensory components of the event; as visual images, olfactory, auditory, or kinesthetic sensations, or intense waves of feelings that patients usually claim to be representations of elements of the original traumatic event. What is intriguing is that patients consistently claim that their perceptions are exact representations of sensations at the time of the trauma. . . . [It] is in the very nature of traumatic memory to be dissociated, and to be initially stored as sensory fragments that have no linguistic components.[39]

The "Tratado del descubrimiento" increases in intensity and in descriptive quality in the chapters devoted to the 1565 uprising. The temporal line is fragile, while the spate of emotions creates a panorama that could not have been possible otherwise. Suárez de Peralta jumps from the neighing of his horse when it was scratched by the unfinished wood of the gallows to the Bocanegra women wailing, moving immediately to the aching view of an eighty-year-old man being dismembered and his blood in the streets. It is not possible to be sure of the reasons why Suárez de Peralta began writing down his memories, for we can assume he was not a young newlywed, as were his friends who faced the possibility of going to the gallows. If we follow the internal temporal references in the *Tratado*, we find that when he wrote his book, he was a recently married seventy-year-old and had a small child and an expectant wife. Although he had been in Spain for more than forty years, no records have been found about a potential return to New Spain during those decades. The memories from those few weeks during the uprising remained indelible in his mind: the streets on which he played as a young boy, the sound of the tearful multitudes, the visages of his friends emaciated by their confinement. But with more clarity than anything else, he recalls the executioner's axe, trying unsuccessfully to cut through his friend's neck:

> Sacaron primero á Gil Gonçalez y luego á su hermano, y desta suerte los llevaron derechos al tablado, sin traellos por las calles acostumbradas: fué la grita de llanto la que se dió, de la jente que los miraba, que era grima oillos, quando los vieron salir de la cárçel. Llegaron al tablado y se apearon y subieron en él, donde se reconçiliaron y retificaron en los dichos que abian dicho; y ya questaban puestos con Dios, hizieron á Gil Gonçalez que se tendiese en el tablado, abiendo el verdugo aperçebídose, y se tendió como un cordero, y luego le cortó la cabeça el verdugo, el qual no estaba bien yndustriado y fué haziéndole padeçer un rato, que fué otra lástima, y no poca. . . . Despues de cortada, con la grita y lloros, y solloços, volvió la cabeza Alonso de Ávila, y como vió á su hermano descabeçado dió un muy gran sospiro, que realmente no creyó hasta entonçes que abia de morir, y como le vió así, hincóse de rodillas y tomó á reconciliarse.

> They first brought Gil Gonçalez and then his brother, and in that manner they were taken to the gallows, but they were not passing through the usual streets: the wailing and weeping from those seeing the brothers leave the jail was frightening. They arrived at the gallows, dismounted, and climbed the stage, where they asked God for forgiveness and confirmed their testimonies; and when the brothers had already reconciled with God, the jailers made Gil Gonçalez lie on the wooden stage while the executioner got ready, and [Gil Gonçalez] lay there like a lamb, and then the executioner severed his head, but as the executioner was not skillful enough, he made [Gil Gonçalez] suffer for a while, and that was another pain to bear, and not the least of them. . . . After the beheading, with wailing and weeping and sobbing, Alonso de Ávila turned his head and, when he saw his beheaded brother, he let go a very deep sigh, as he had not really believed until that moment that he himself was going to die, and as he saw his brother, he fell on his knees and reconciled himself again.[40]

Suárez de Peralta hints as to his opinion regarding the beheadings when he says that Gil Gonçalez "laid himself like a lamb in the gallows" ("en el tablado . . . se tendió como un cordero"). This imagery, closely related to the idea of Jesus as sacrificial lamb, evokes powerful associations, as evident in the Gospel of John, of victimhood and innocence in the face of punishment: "Behold, the Lamb of God, who takes away the sin of the world" (John 1:29).

All this negotiation between blaming and hiding the blame, therefore, reveals a potential survivor's guilt, as his literary representation of suffering does not fall far from notions of post-traumatic stress disorder. As Kolk and McFarlane describe, it would not be impossible for those images, sounds, and emotions to have become an involuntary set of mental flashbacks from his trauma.[41]

Both Ávila brothers had insisted upon their innocence, and it was not until the very last moment, when his brother's head had been unskillfully severed, that Alonso repented, acknowledged the charges, retracted his testimony, and admitted that his death was just and fair. At that precise moment, Suárez de Peralta pressed his horse's head against the roughly cut planks of the gallows:

> Después de aber hecho justiçia de Alonso de Avila y su hermano, se dizian munchísimas cosas y ya no se trataba de otra, y munchos prometian de que abia de costar caro aquellas muertes, porque abian muerto sin culpa. Glosando sus confisiones, así las del proçeso, como las que abían hecho retificándose en el tablado quando murieron (que llanamente condenaron al marqués y á su hermano don Luis Cortés), y lo que el frayle dijo antes que cortasen la cabeça á Alonso de Ávila, que lo oi yo, porquestaba tan çerca del tablado que tenia mi caballo la frente pegada á él, y lo ví y oí todo, que era de los que fuimos con el jeneral huardándolos, y dijo las palabras atrás referidas: "que aquellos caballeros morían justamente, y que lo que abian jurado en sus confisiones era verdad."

> After justice had been served to Alonso de Ávila and his brother, many things were said about it, and it was the only thing to talk about, and many were promising that those deaths would cost dearly, as they had died without fault. Glossing their confessions, as well as those of the case, and the ones they had made while on the gallows where they changed their testimonies right before dying (fully blaming the marquis and Luis Cortés, the marquis's brother), and what the friar had said right before Alonso de Ávila's beheading, that I heard, as I was so close to the wooden gallows that my horse had its forehead touching it, and I saw and heard everything, as I had gone there with the general safeguarding them, and he [the friar] said the words that I mentioned before: "that these gentlemen had been justly sentenced to death, and that they had sworn in their confessions that the truth was that [they had been fairly sentenced]."[42]

That last confession ratified the institutional machinery of blame: he had confessed, he was guilty, justice had been served. There is, however, a divergence between the trial as it was recorded in the government archives and Suárez de Peralta's literary memories. In recalling the uprising, for instance, he says:

> el frayle se volvió al pueblo y dijo: "Señores, encomienden á Dios á estos caballeros, quellos dizen que mueren justamente." Y se volvió á Alonso de Ávila y le dijo: "¿No lo dize vuesa merçed así?" Y él dijo que sí, y se hincó de rodillas, bajándose el cuello del jubon y camisa: y era de ver lo que temia la

muerte. Atáronle los ojos con una venda, y ya que yba á tenderse, alçó la mano, y se descubrió y dijo de secreto al frayle çiertas palabras; y luego le tornaron á vendar, y se puso como se abia de poner, y el cruel verdugo le dió tres golpes, como quien corta la cabeça á un carnero, que á cada golpe que le daba ponia la jente los gritos en el çielo. De esta manera acabaron estos desdichados caballeros, dejando la tierra muy lastimada y confusa si morian con culpa ó sin ella.

the friar turned around to face the people and said: "Gentlemen, keep these other gentlemen in your prayers, as they themselves say they will die justly." And he turned to Alonso de Ávila and asked him: "Is that not what you'd say, sir?" And he [Alonso] agreed, and knelt while lowering the neckline of his shirt, and it was palpable how afraid he was of death. They covered his eyes with a blindfold and, as he was about to lie on the floor he raised his hand, uncovered his eyes and told secretly to the friar some things; and then they blindfolded him again, and he was put where he should be, and the cruel executioner hit him three times, as if he were cutting the head of a sheep, and with each blow the indignation of those present increased. This is the way in which the story of these unfortunate gentlemen ended, and the land remained very hurt and confused, not knowing if they were, in truth, guilty or not.[43]

The main divergence between the public record and Suárez de Peralta's version is Alonso's last words told to the priest. In any case, the land, maybe the *patria* (fatherland), remained "muy lastimada y confusa" (very damaged and confused), ready for the seeds of memory to bloom into postmemory.

MEMORY AND POSTMEMORY

Traumatic and traumatized memories echo in Sandoval Zapata's poem "Relación fúnebre," reconfiguring it, I argue, into a postmemory. Even though the Baroque style of the Indies has been traditionally described around the ideas of abundance, movement, and brusqueness, elements this poem shares with Suárez de Peralta's work, Sandoval Zapata presents an entirely Baroque version of what had been only a mannerist twist in Suárez de Peralta.

While Suárez de Peralta deals with emotional horror vacui and chiaroscuro, Sandoval Zapata builds a scaffolded Baroque interpretation departing from the memories that he received. For instance, Suárez de Peralta had sown in his text the seeds of doubt: suspicion of the innocence of the Ávilas, of the king, and more importantly, of the difference between American-born and Spanish-born. Not part of the generation forced to attend the beheading and that suffered the immediate social and structural consequences of the uprising, Sandoval Zapata had planted these suspicions in his text as cultural memories, first assumed as folklore—in opposition to an official narrative—and then transformed into what Marianne Hitsch would call "postmemories."[44] The memory of what was lost or what could have been, confounded in the resentment caused by the violence exerted over the *criollos*, found its way into the reality of the self-construction and society of the next generation.

This is evident, for example, in the confusion that Suárez de Peralta had already foreshadowed in his work: "Otro dia era juizio ver los que echaban todos, diziendo yban mártires y que no debian la muerte. . . . Hablaban con muncha desenvoltura, y no echaban las palabras en un pozo, que huardáronlas para tiempo, que las pagaron munchos muy pagadas" (On the next day it was remarkable to see how everyone was swearing, saying that they [the Ávilas] were martyrs and that a death sentence was excessive. . . . They were talking freely, and their words were not unheard, as they were listened to [by the government] and many of those who talked paid a heavy price for speaking out).[45]

The emotional temperament of Sandoval Zapata's poem coincides with the beheading, as the executioner's lack of dexterity comes to the forefront in an even more painful way than what we find in Suárez de Peralta. Though we cannot be sure if Sandoval Zapata read the *Tratado del descubrimiento*, a close analysis of both texts finds expressions, emotions, and turns of phrase that permit us to listen to the voice of the first author through the second. In so doing, Sandoval elevates the Ávilas to the altar of *criollo* martyrs, with Buxó claiming that: "*Relación* . . . declara con raro atrevimiento que fueron las envidias y las malas pasiones de los gobernantes, y no la presunta rebeldía contra un decreto real, la causa de su desastrosa muerte" (The *Relación* posits, with peculiar candor, that the cause of death [of the Ávilas] was envy and unscrupulous zeal on the part of those in power, and not an alleged revolt against a royal decree).[46] Sandoval Zapata, in other words, is not hesitant to give his point of view:

> A la pasion que govierna
> a la invidia que os acusa
> a lo ciego que os procesa.
> Diciendo que merecéis
> por ofender la diadema
> del invicto Rey de España
> que os derriben las cabezas.
> Que en público vil cadahalso
> mano bárbara y pleveya
> de un fementido verdugo
> se tiña en tan nobles venas
> que apriesa acusa la embidia
> y la indignacion que apriesa
> sabe fulminar la muerte

qué apriesa corre la envidia
y la indignación que aprisa.⁴⁷

To the passion that governs / to the envy that accuses you / to the blindness that prosecutes you. / Saying that you deserve / to get your heads severed / for offending the diadem / of the undefeated King of Spain. / In public, in vile gallows / a savage ignoble hand / of a phony executioner / will be tainted with your noble blood. / How fast envy is, / how fast indignation / death will end you / as fast as envy / and indignation seize you.

By the seventeenth century there was already a sense of a colonial past, both for Europeans and *criollos*, with Bernal Díaz del Castillo's resentful tone (via Suárez de Peralta) sublimating itself into a foundational myth for Sandoval Zapata. While Suárez de Peralta refers to his own biographical past, Sandoval Zapata alludes here to his emotional, shared experience of a past. It is, as Hirsch has described it, a "postmemory": a "structure of inter- and trans-generational transmission of traumatic knowledge and experience. It is a consequence of traumatic recall but (unlike post-traumatic stress disorder) at a generational remove."⁴⁸ In addition, it implies an emotional reworking of the facts; a story and history that have been received.

A postmemory of the uprising, as opposed to a historical reconstruction—an important distinction here—therefore manifests itself in Sandoval Zapata through intertextuality. In 1906, when Luis González Obregón took Suárez de Peralta's text and reworked its context, there was no emotion involved, no amplification of pain or regret. As González Obregón indicates, with a faith in history that reveals his own biases and candor, all he refers to are "históricos, copiados textualmente de las constancias procesales y de los libros que he consultado; . . . pero omito citas para no interrumpir la narración a cada paso" (historical events, copied verbatim from the legal documents and books I have consulted, . . . although some quotes will not be included to avoid stopping the narration every so often).⁴⁹ The omitted "citas" (quotes) that he references here are the direct quotes from the "Tratado del descubrimiento" where Suárez de Peralta is bitter and reacts against the Crown's response.

In complete opposition to González Obregón, Sandoval Zapata deals with intertextuality by creatively reading and supplementing the text of the "Tratado." There are three moments in his work that show how his inventive augmentation feeds on the pain of trauma: the depiction of the young *criollos*' pastimes; the moment in which the destroyed homes of the Ávilas are sown with salt; and the description of the beheadings. There are also occasional verses in which the text of the *Tratado* echoes in Sandoval Zapata. In those, it is Suárez de Peralta who is speaking from the wound, which, as Caruth describes, involves "the story of a wound that cries out, that addresses us in an attempt to tell us of a reality or truth that is not otherwise available."[50] The voice of Suárez de Peralta is the only reality of these first *criollos* available to Sandoval Zapata, and his insertion of direct quotes as verses into the poem acts as a suppuration from a generational and social wound that has not healed. For instance, when the always-elegant Ávilas first emerge from captivity toward the gallows, both authors describe them as wearing "tristes valletas," (distressed clothes for cleaning). In essence, the writers not only refer to the materiality of the cloth, in all its sad ("triste") roughness, but to the Ávilas' status, as well as that, more generally, of the *criollos*. A commentary on this status becomes more evident in three specific instances from these authors' writings.

Suárez de Peralta's interest in horses, for instance, is noteworthy in the *Tratado del descubrimiento,* but even more so in his two other manuscripts that have reached us: the *Libro de albeitería* and the *Tratado de la caballería, de la gineta y de la brida*. This latter text, for instance, focuses on the ways in which young male *criollos* passed their time by engaging in equestrian activities. In a subtle way, therefore, Suárez de Peralta blames the *criollos*' naïveté before the uprising on Viceroy Luis de Velasco, as, according to the story, the viceroy was keen on constantly organizing festivities and celebrations.[51] Sandoval, on the other hand, puts the focus on the Ávilas, who in Suárez de Peralta's text were only some of the participants in the entertainment. Horse riding and horsemanship competitions, bullfights and music abound in the lives of the young Ávilas. As *charrería* (Mexican horse[wo]manship) was approaching the definition we have today as an inherently Mexican pastime, depicting the Ávilas as *charros* transforms them immediately into popular figures:

> Dando ley en la palestra
> al mas generoso bruto,
> y ía en las públicas
> a los soplos del clarín
> que sonora vida alienta
> vlandieudo el fresno ó la caña
> y en escaramuzas diestras
> corren en vivientes rayos
> volas en aladas flechas.[52]

They were masters in the ring / taming the most generous beasts / and in public spaces / when the bugle sounded / for a more spirited life / brandishing a wooden rod or jousting / skillful in dressage / they ran on lightning bolts / they flew on winged arrows.

The second of the intertexts refers to the erasure of the Ávilas from the historical record by means of demolishing their homes, tearing down their coats of arms from buildings, and sowing salt on their lands: "los sentençiaron [a] perdimíento de todos sus bienes, y las casas sembradas de sal y derribadas por el suelo, y en medio un padron en él escrito con letras grandes su delito, y que aquel sestuviese para siempre jamás, que nayde fuese osado á quitalle ni borralle letra sopena de muerte" (they were sentenced to the loss of all their possessions, and their homes sown with salt and demolished to the ground, and in middle of all this, on a plaque their crime was written in large letters, and this was upheld for ever and ever, so that nobody might dare remove or erase the letters under penalty of death).[53] To this day, there is a plaque to remind those visiting the remains of the Aztec Templo Mayor in Mexico City that, during the first decades after the Spanish conquest, the homes of the Ávilas had been built there. Luis González Obregón indicates that the original plaque was at the Museo Nacional at the beginning of the twentieth century.[54]

If we examine the Ávilas' sentencing alongside that of the Távoras, a Portuguese noble family indicted by the Marquis of Pombal in the attempted regicide of José I in 1758, the similarities are striking:

> E considerando—se que a mais conforme a Direito hé a de escurecer, e desterrar por todos os modos da lembrança o nome, e a recordação de tão enormes delinquentes: condemnão outro sim ao mesmo Reo não só nas penas de Direito commum para serem derribadas, e picadas todas suas armas, e escudos em quaisquer lugares em que se acharem postas, e as cazas, materiais, e edificios da sua habitação demolidos, arrazados de sorte, que delles não fique signal, reduzidos a campo, e salgados

> And it needs to be taken into account that it is within the scope of the law to darken and banish from memory in all manners possible the name or the remembrances of such perilous delinquents: in addition, the accused is subject not only to the normal punishment, but also their coats of arms will be demolished, wherever these are located; their houses and buildings of any kind will be demolished as well, laid waste to the extent that no sign will remain of their existence and they return to be open land, and sown with salt.[55]

Sandoval's version follows the same structure: buildings, coats of arms, salt in the ground. However, he adds his own emotional temperament to the description ("estrago," "ignominia," "estéril," "horrible," "afrentoso") as a means of augmenting its emotional impact:

> Sus casas todas soberbias
> las derriban por estrago
> de la mas humilde tierra

por ignominia las aran
y de estéril sal las siembran.
... Decreto horrible decreta,
y con los duros relieves
del cincel en una piedra
padron afrentoso erige
que con inmortales letras
está acusando su culpa.[56]

All their proud homes / torn down and spoiled / turned into humble earth / plowed with disgrace. / A horrible decree was ordered, / and with the harsh corners / of a chisel against stone / humiliating news is spread / on an erected plaque / words that cannot be taken back / as they are blamed without guilt.

The memory of the judgments has been transformed, reworked by the pressure of emotions, something that becomes even clearer in the stanzas devoted to the gallows, where the shocking moment of the attempts to behead Gil takes preeminence:

Ya sobre el cuello del uno
con sangrienta lixereza,
descarga el furor del golpe
e intrépido lo degüella
y para poder quitar
de los ombros la cabeza
una y otra vez repite
la fulminada dureza
y al ver tan aleves golpes
el otro hermano se queja.[57]

With bloody nimbleness / he is on the neck of one of them / and lets the fury of a blow fly / and dauntlessly cuts his throat / and for finally separating / the shoulders from the head / he repeats his blows again and again / with surprising strength / and when he sees the blows / the other brother moans.

Here, Sandoval Zapata insists on Alonso de Ávila's pain, making it visible by bringing it into his very own present. Buxó affirms that Sandoval "[d]esborda los tópicos literarios oficiales" (goes beyond official literary clichés) to show "cómo bajo la gruesa cubierta de las celebraciones oficiales persistía y aun se encontraba ese resquemor criollo" (how under the heavy cover of official celebrations this *criollo* resentment persisted and even festered).[58] He singles out the "Relación fúnebre" and its difference from other contemporary works in their crudeness: "La muerte de los hermanos Ávila, dice, es un brutal espectáculo de horror y violencia, la vívida descripción del

desgarramiento de miembros humanos y de las reacciones de una empavo-
recida multitud hipnotizada por el canibalesco espectáculo" (The death of
the Ávila brothers, he says, is a brutal spectacle of horror and violence, the
vivid description of the tearing of human limbs and the reactions of a terrified
crowd mesmerized by the cannibalistic spectacle).[59]

The reworking of this memory reaches its climax by the end of the poem,
where Sandoval Zapata distills the *criollos*' resentment. Going beyond memory, he commends himself to God, and asks for a settling of the score with
those who were unjust to the *criollos*:

>   mas no importa que hay Dios grande
>   cuya eterna providencia
>   ofendidos desagravia
>   con sus cárceles eternas
>   en cuyas justas balanzas
>   aun leves culpas se pesan
>   que hara delitos tan graves
>   que matan vida y nobleza
>   ninguno de los mortales
>   desde el más augusto César
>   asta el pleveyo más vil
>   puede escusar la presencia
>   del divino Entendimiento.[60]

Rest assured, as God is great / His eternal mercy / defends those disrespected /
with His eternal jails / where fair scales weigh / even benign sins / what would
they do to such severe offenses / that kill life and rank / no mortal / from the
most august Caesar / to the lowest of the peasants / can avoid the judgement /
of divine understanding.

Martín Cortés's uprising mobilized those who believed themselves to be
the upper echelon of colonial society in New Spain, as they suddenly came
to realize that their social position was not what they had thought. The power
of the state made it abundantly clear that there was a new group, *criollos*,
who were neither Indians nor Spaniards. I argue, therefore, that it is possible
to track independence movements from this mutual realization, and that the
criollo movements of the eighteenth century have their roots in the actions,
memories, and postmemories described in Sandoval Zapata's text.

While the center of the uprising is Martín Cortés, the marquis, he was also
the one who suffered the ripple effects of the convictions. He was forced
to move back to Europe, while the *criollo* society in New Spain mourned
the loss of their social prestige and the deaths of the condemned, souring
and boiling in rage and resentment that impelled their movement toward

independence. The response to the uprising is framed by Suárez de Peralta and his counterparts as the breaking of a promise. Their fathers, as the first conquerors, had felt that the Crown was falling short in acknowledging their merits, rights, and status. However, they seem to have raised their sons with the mentality of being the owners of the land that they had usurped. I have not found Mexican testimonies to the uprising, as if the commoners were not part of this political maneuver. The *criollos* seemed surprised when, after plotting to kill all representatives of the Crown, they were indicted. The entitlement is blinding.

Both the "Tratado del descubrimiento" and the "Relación fúnebre" defend a line of thought that goes beyond the idea of justice. Their resentment and the description of social resentment in their society—added to the fear that emerges from Suárez de Peralta's words—opened the field to a different framing of the conspiracy. The response from the Crown and its effects on this society speak to the trauma of the brutal violence waged against them. Was this, however, the same violence that they had thrust upon the original inhabitants of the Americas? By finding themselves with the short end of the stick, they seem to have discovered that what is fair and just is defined downward through power structures. Violence, trauma, and postmemory act hand in hand.

WORKS CITED

Adorno, Rolena. "El sujeto colonial y la construcción cultural de la alteridad." *Revista de crítica literaria latinoamericana* 14, no. 28 (1988): 55–68.
Alberro, Solange. *El águila y la cruz: Orígenes religiosos de la conciencia criolla; México, siglos XVI–XVII*. México: FCE, 1999.
———. *Inquisición y sociedad en México, 1571–1700*. México: FCE, 1990.
Brading, David A. *Orbe indiano: De la monarquía católica a la república criolla, 1492–1867*. México: FCE, 1992.
———. *The Origins of Mexican Nationalism*. Cambridge: Cambridge University Press, 1985.
Cañizares-Esguerra, J. "New World, New Stars: Patriotic Astrology and the Invention of Indian and Creole Bodies in Colonial Spanish America, 1600–1650." *American Historical Review* 104 (1999): 33–68.
Cardiel Reyes, Raúl. *La primera conspiración por la independencia de México*. México: FCE, 1982.
Caruth, Cathy. *Unclaimed Experience: Trauma, Narrative and History*. Baltimore: Johns Hopkins University Press, 1996.
"Cédula de recomendación de don Fernando Cortés dada en Madrid el 26 de marzo de 1606." Archivo General de la Nación, México, 383, 100: Reales Cédulas, vol. 5, exp. 212, fol. 51, 1606.

Cheetham, Nicolas. *New Spain: The Birth of Modern Mexico*. London: Victor Gollancz, 1974.
"Confesión de Alonso de Avila Alvarado, preso y condenado a muerte como consecuencia de la conspiración para alzarse con el poder en Méjico, junto a Luis y Martín Cortés y otros." Archivo Histórico Nacional, México, Diversos-Colecciones 43, 10, 1566.
"Confesión de Martín Cortés, marqués del Valle de Oaxaca, sobre la cospiración para alzarse con el poder en Méjico, junto a su hermano D. Luis, y Alonso de Avila entre otros." Archivo Histórico Nacional, México, Diversos-Colecciones 43, 10, July 18, 1566.
"Diligencias hechas por don Juan de Ortega, alcalde mayor del partido de Tula y del de Tetepango en cumplimiento del mandamiento que le hizo don Luis Enríquez de Guzmán, duque de Alburquerque para que averigüe qué personas matan ganado cabrío y ovejuno. Se concedió la licencia a don Lorenzo Suárez de Peralta o a la persona que tuviera su poder para que pueda matar mil cabras y mil ovejas viejas e inútiles. Asimismo a Jacome Martín para matar mil setecientas cabras y ovejas. Tula, Pueblo." Archivo General de la Nación, 39, 1: Abasto y panaderías, vol. 3, exp. 10, fol. 56r–v, August 17–September 20, 1653.
"Expediente de concesión de licencia para pasar a Nueva España a favor de Lorenzo Suárez de Peralta." Archivo General de Indias, Indiferente, 2076, 150, 1617.
"Expediente de información y licencia de pasajero a indias de Lorenzo Suárez de Peralta, natural de Madrid, hijo de Juan Suárez de Peralta y de Isabel Hurtado de Mendoza, con su criado Pedro de Colmenares, hijo de Francisco de los Casares y de Francisca de Colmenares, a Nueva España." Archivo General de Indias, Contratación, 5369, 42, 1619.
Flint, Shirley Cushing. "Treason or Travesty: The Martin Cortes Conspiracy Reexamined." *Sixteenth Century Journal* 39, no. 1 (2008): 23–44.
Foucault, Michel. *Vigilar y castigar: Nacimiento de la prisión*. México: Siglo XXI, 1999.
García Icazbalceta, Joaquín. *Colección de documentos para la historia de México: Versión actualizada; Leyes y ordenanzas nuevamente hechas por su Magestad para la gobernación de las Indias y para la conservación y buen tratamiento de los Indios*. México: Antigua Librería Robredo, 1866.
González Boixo, José Carlos. "Los cronistas de Indias, iniciales tratadistas de la identidad de América." *Ínsula* 3–4 (1992): 549–50.
———. "Reflexiones sobre la 'literariedad' de las crónicas de Indias (a propósito del 'Proemio' a la *Historia* de Fernández de Oviedo)." In *La crítica literaria española frente a la literatura latinoamericana*, edited by Fleming Leonor and María Teresa Bosque Latra, 199–210. México: UNAM, 1993.
González Obregón, Luis. "Los primeros mártires de la Independencia mexicana." *El mundo ilustrado* 11, 12 (September 18, 1904): 275–78.
———. *Los precursores de la independencia de México en el XVI*. México: Librería de la viuda de C. Bouret, 1906.
González Stephan, Beatriz. "Sujeto criollo/conciencia histórica: La historiografía literaria en el periodo colonial." In *Ruptura de la conciencia hispanoamericana*

(época colonial), edited by José Anadón, 15–57. México: FCE; University of Notre Dame, 1998.

Hernández Monroy, Rosaura. "Rasgos de identidad nacional en la conciencia novohispana." In *Identidades y nacionalismos: Una perspectiva interdisciplinaria*, edited by Lilia Granillo Vázquez, 79–112. México: Universidad Autónoma Metropolitana, 2008.

Hirsch, Marianne. "The Generation of Postmemory." *Poetics Today* 29, no. 1 (2008): 103–28.

———. "Postmemory." https://www.postmemory.net.

Kolk, Bessel A. van der. "Trauma and Memory." *Psychiatry and Clinical Neurosciences* 52, no. 1 (1998): 52–64.

Kolk, Bessel A. van der, and Alexander C. McFarlane. "The Black Hole of Trauma." In *Literary Theory*, edited by Julie Rivkin and Michael Ryan, 487–99. Malden, MA: Blackwell, 2010.

Konetzke, Richard. "La condición legal de los criollos y las causas de la Independencia." *Estudios americanos* 2, no. 5 (1950): 31–54.

———. "Estado y sociedad en las Indias." *Estudios americanos* 3, no. 8 (1951): 33–58.

Lamar Prieto, Covadonga. "La lectura posmoderna de Carlos Fuentes en 'Los hijos del conquistador' sobre Suárez de Peralta." *Estudios mexicanos/Mexican Studies* 32, no. 1 (2016): 29–55.

Leal, Luis. *El cuento mexicano: De los orígenes al modernismo*. Buenos Aires: Universidad de Buenos Aires, 1966.

Leonard, Irving A. *Los libros del conquistador*. México: FCE, 1996.

Liss, Peggy K. *Orígenes de la nacionalidad mexicana: 1521–1556; La formación de una nueva sociedad*. México: FCE, 1975.

Lorente Medina, Antonio. *La prosa de Sigüenza y Góngora y la formación de la conciencia criolla mexicana*. México: FCE, 1996.

Lyotard, Jean François, and John Ronan. "Anamnesis of the Visible 2." *Qui parle* 11, no. 2, (1999): 21–36.

Mangan, Jane E. "Moving Mestizos in Sixteenth-Century Peru: Spanish Fathers, Indigenous Mothers, and the Children In Between." *William and Mary Quarterly* 70, no. 2 (2013): 273–94.

Manrique, Jorge Alberto. "La visión de Hernán Cortés en los criollos mexicanos." In *Hernán Cortés y su tiempo*, 1:497–99. Mérida: Junta de Extremadura, 1987.

McAlister, L. N. "Social Structure and Social Change in New Spain." *Hispanic American Historical Review* 43, no. 3 (1963): 349–70.

Orozco y Berra, M. *Noticia histórica de la conjuración del marqués del Valle: Años de 1565 a 1568; Formada en vista de nuevos documentos originales, y seguida de un estracto de los mismos documentos*. México: Tipografía de R. Rafael, 1863.

Ortega y Medina, Juan A. "Indigenismo e hispanismo en la conciencia historiográfica mexicana." In *Cultura e identidad nacional*, edited by Roberto Blancarte, 44–72. México: CONACULTA-FCE, 1994.

Parodi, Claudia. "The Indianization of Spaniards in New Spain." *Contributions to the Sociology of Language* 91 (2006): 29–52.

———. "La semántica cultural: Un modelo de contacto lingüístico y Las Casas." In *Visiones del encuentro de dos mundos en América*, edited by Karen Dakin, Mercedes Montes de Oca, and Claudia Parodi, 19–46. México: UNAM/UCLA-CECI, 2009.

———. "La semántica cultural y la indianización en América: Un análisis del contacto lingüístico." In *Actas del XV Congreso de la AIH "Las dos orillas,"* edited by Beatriz Mariscal and María Teresa Miaja de la Peña, 211–24. Mexico: FCE, 2007.

Pascual Buxó, José. "Luis de Sandoval Zapata: La poética del fuego y las cenizas." In *Obras de Luis de Sandoval Zapata*, edited by José Pascual Buxó, 1–17. México: Fondo de Cultura Económica, 1986.

———. "Sobre la 'Relación fúnebre a la infeliz, trágica muerte de dos caballeros' de Luis de Sandoval Zapata." In *Actas del Segundo Congreso Internacional de Hispanistas*, edited by Jaime Sánchez Romeralo and Norbert Poulussen, 473–80. Nimega: Instituto Español de la Universidad de Nimega, 1967.

"Petición del marqués de Falcés, Gastón de Peralta, virrey de Nueva España al Consejo de Indias, solicitando se remedie el agravio que ha padecido al ser destituido de su cargo, como consecuencia de la conspiración de Alonso y Gil de Avila, en México, la cual reprimió y no intentó favorecer." Archivo Histórico Nacional, Diversos-Colecciones 34, 4, 1566–1567.

Picón-Salas, Mariano. *De la conquista a la independencia: Tres siglos de historia cultural hispanoamericana*. México: FCE, 1944.

"Proceso criminal formado por el doctor Francisco de Sande, fiscal de la Audiencia de México, contra don Martín Cortés, Marqués del Valle, uno de los reputados cómplices en la rebelión de Nueva España. Resulta de este proceso que siendo virrey de Nueva España don Francisco Velasco, se presentó en la Audiencia de México, en 3 de mayo de 1566, una petición por el cabildo y regimiento de esta ciudad, exponiendo haber sido apresados en las Casas Reales don Martín Cortés, don Luis y don Martín, sus hermanos, y, en la cárcel de corte, Alonso Dávila Alvarado y su hermano Gil González Dávila, como cómplices en la Rebelión; piden se averigüe el hecho y se les castigue. Siguió la Audiencia la causa y sentenció a muerte a los mencionados Dávila." Archivo General de Indias, Patronato, 208, r. 1, 1566.

O proceso dos Távoras. Edited by Pedro de Azevedo. Lisbon: Publicações da Biblioteca Nacional, Inéditos I, 1921.

"Proceso general formado en la Audiencia de México contra todos los que resultaron cómplices en la rebelión de Nueva España. Resultaron cómplices don Martín Cortés, Marqués del Valle, don Luis y don Martín, sus hermanos, Alonso Dávila Alvarado y su hermano Gil González Dávila, don Juan y don Alonso de Guzmán, los hermanos Bocanegra, don Alonso y don Luis de Herrera, Alonso de Estrada, Alonso de Cabrera, el deán de México, y otros." Archivo General de Indias, Patronato 203, r. 6, 1567.

Sandoval Zapata, Luis. "Relación fúnebre a la infeliz trágica muerte de dos caballeros de lo más ilustre de esta Nueva España, Alonso de Ávila Alvarado y Gil González de Ávila, degollados en la nobilísima ciudad de México a 3 de agosto de 1566." In Orozco y Berra, *Noticia histórica de la conjuración*, 491–502.

Schmidt-Riese, Roland. "Glosando las confesiones de los hermanos Ávila: Discurso e identidad en la Nueva España a finales del siglo XVI." *Lexis* 26, no. 1 (2002): 3–78.

Schwaller, Robert C. "The Importance of Mestizos and Mulatos as Bilingual Intermediaries in XVI New Spain." *Ethnohistory* 59, no. 4 (2010): 713–38.

"Solicitud de matrimonio, viudo y soltera. Contrayentes: Andrés de Cervantes, 38 años; Mariana de Hoyo, 28 años. Testigos y ocupación: Lorenzo Suárez de Peralta, Gonzalo Sánchez de Herrera." Matrimonios, Catedral de México, Archivo General de la Nación, 220451, 69: vol. 19, exp. 38, folios 133–36, 1645

Suárez de Peralta, Juan. *Noticias históricas de la Nueva España*. Madrid: Justo Zaragoza, 1876.

———. "Tratado del descubrimiento de las Yndias y su conquista, y los ritos y sacrificios y costumbres que los yndios, y los birreyes y gobernadores, que los an gouernado espeçialmente en la nueva españa y del suçeso del marqués del valle segundo don martin cortes: del rebelion que se le ynputo de las justiçias y muertes que hizieron en Mexico los juezes comisarios que para ello fueron por su magestad y rrompimiento de los yngleses y del prinçipio que tubo Francisco Draque para ser declarado enemigo. Compuesto por Don Joan Suárez de Peralta, vecino y natural de México." Manuscript 302. Toledo: Biblioteca de la Junta de Comunidades de Castilla la Mancha, s/d.

Torquemada, Fray Juan de. *Los veintiún libros rituales y la Monarquía Indiana, re-producida a partir de la segunda edición de Madrid, 1723*. Edited by Miguel León Portilla. México: Porrúa, 1969.

NOTES

1. Juan Suárez de Peralta, "Tratado del descubrimiento de las Yndias y su conquista, y los ritos y sacrificios y costumbres que los yndios, y los birreyes y gobernadores, que los an gouernado espeçialmente en la nueva españa y del suçeso del marqués del valle segundo don martin cortes: del rebelion que se le ynputo de las justiçias y muertes que hizieron en Mexico los juezes comisarios que para ello fueron por su magestad y rrompimiento de los yngleses y del prinçipio que tubo Francisco Draque para ser declarado enemigo. Compuesto por Don Joan Suárez de Peralta, vecino y natural de México," s/d, Manuscript 302, Biblioteca de la Junta de Comunidades de Castilla la Mancha, Toledo.

2. Kolk, "Trauma and Memory," 54.

3. Luis Sandoval Zapata, "Relación fúnebre a la infeliz trágica muerte de dos caballeros de lo más ilustre de esta Nueva España, Alonso de Ávila Alvarado y Gil González de Ávila, degollados en la nobilísima ciudad de México a 3 de agosto de 1566," in *Noticia histórica de la conjuración del Marqués del Valle. Años 1565 a 1568; Formada en vista de nuevos documentos originales, y seguida de un estracto de los mismos documentos*, ed. Manuel Orozco y Berra (Mexico City: 1863), 491–502.

4. Shirley Cushing Flint, "Treason or Travesty: The Martin Cortes Conspiracy Reexamined," *Sixteenth Century Journal* 39, no. 1 (2008): 27.

5. José Carlos González Boixo, "Los cronistas de Indias, iniciales tratadistas de la identidad de América," *Ínsula* 3–4 (1992): 549–50; José Carlos González Boixo, "Reflexiones sobre la 'literariedad' de las crónicas de Indias (a propósito del 'Proemio' a la *Historia* de Fernández de Oviedo)," in *La crítica literaria española frente a la literatura latinoamericana*, ed. Fleming Leonor and María Teresa Bosque Latra (México: UNAM: 1993), 199–210; Richard Konetzke, "La condición legal de los criollos y las causas de la Independencia," *Estudios americanos* 2, no. 5 (1950): 31–54; Richard Konetzke, "Estado y sociedad en las Indias," *Estudios americanos* 3, no. 8 (1951): 33–58; Juan A. Ortega y Medina, "Indigenismo e hispanismo en la conciencia historiográfica mexicana," in *Cultura e identidad nacional*, ed. Roberto Blancarte (México: CONACULTA-FCE, 1994), 44–72. On the cultural construction of the subject, see Rolena Adorno, "El sujeto colonial y la construcción cultural de la alteridad," *Revista de crítica literaria latinoamericana* 14, no. 28 (1988): 55–68; Solange Alberro, *El águila y la cruz: Orígenes religiosos de la conciencia criolla; México, siglos XVI–XVII* (México: FCE, 1999); Beatriz. On race, see Jane E. Mangan, "Moving Mestizos in Sixteenth-Century Peru: Spanish Fathers, Indigenous Mothers, and the Children In Between," *William and Mary Quarterly* 70, no. 2 (2013): 273–94. For work dealing with *criollo* consciousness, but at a later time, see J. Cañizares-Esguerra, "New World, New Stars: Patriotic Astrology and the Invention of Indian and Creole Bodies in Colonial Spanish America, 1600–1650," *American Historical Review* 104 (1999): 33–68; Antonio Lorente Medina, *La prosa de Sigüenza y Góngora y la formación de la conciencia criolla mexicana* (México: FCE, 1996). The first moments of Mexican nationalism are discussed in Peggy K. Liss, *Orígenes de la nacionalidad mexicana: 1521–1556; La formación de una nueva sociedad* (México: FCE, 1975); David A. Brading, *The Origins of Mexican Nationalism* (Cambridge: Cambridge University Press, 1985); Nicholas Cheetham, *New Spain: The Birth of Modern Mexico* (London: Victor Gollancz, 1974). This is not, by any means, an exhaustive list.

6. Claudia Parodi, "The Indianization of Spaniards in New Spain," *Contributions to the Sociology of Language* 91 (2006): 34–7.

7. Fray Juan de Torquemada, *Los veintiún libros rituales y la Monarquía Indiana, re-producida a partir de la segunda edición de Madrid, 1723*, ed. Miguel León Portilla (México: Porrúa, 1969).

8. Covadonga Lamar Prieto, "La lectura posmoderna de Carlos Fuentes en 'Los hijos del conquistador' sobre Suárez de Peralta," *Estudios mexicanos/Mexican Studies* 32 (2016): 29–55.

9. "Proceso criminal formado por el doctor Francisco de Sande, fiscal de la Audiencia de México, contra don Martín Cortés, Marqués del Valle, uno de los reputados cómplices en la rebelión de Nueva España. Resulta de este proceso que siendo virrey de Nueva España don Francisco Velasco, se presentó en la Audiencia de México, en 3 de mayo de 1566, una petición por el cabildo y regimiento de esta ciudad, exponiendo haber sido apresados en las Casas Reales don Martín Cortés, don Luis y don Martín, sus hermanos, y, en la cárcel de corte, Alonso Dávila Alvarado y su hermano Gil González Dávila, como cómplices en la Rebelión; piden se averigüe el hecho y

se les castigue. Siguió la Audiencia la causa y sentenció a muerte a los mencionados Dávila," Patronato, Archivo General de la Nación, 208, r. 1, 1566.

10. "Proceso general formado en la Audiencia de México contra todos los que resultaron cómplices en la rebelión de Nueva España. Resultaron cómplices don Martín Cortés, Marqués del Valle, don Luis y don Martín, sus hermanos, Alonso Dávila Alvarado y su hermano Gil González Dávila, don Juan y don Alonso de Guzmán, los hermanos Bocanegra, don Alonso y don Luis de Herrera, Alonso de Estrada, Alonso de Cabrera, el deán de México, y otros," Patronato, Archivo General de la Nación, 203, r. 6, 1567.

11. Orozco y Berra, *Noticia histórica de la conjuración*.

12. Orozco y Berra in *Noticia histórica de la conjuración* includes the trials against the twelve indicted: Alonso de Ávila Alvarado and Gil González (1); Marín Cortés, the marquis (55); Martín Cortés (217); Diego Arias and Baltasar de Sotelo (247); Cristóbal de Oñate (279); Baltasar de Quesada and Pedro de Quesada (329); the lawyer Rodrigo de Carvajal (347); Pero Gómez de Cáceres (363); Juan de Valdivieso (379); Antonio Ruiz de Castañeda (399); the viceroy Marqués de Falces (411); and García de Albornoz (441).

13. "He formado la relación que acaba de leerse, sacada de los documentos originales, con el mayor cuidado que me ha sido posible: sin falsa modestia, no estoy satisfecho de ella; la creo con menos interés del que pudiera dársele, . . . preferí ser exacto, á amontonar palabras que dieran una falsa luz á mis personajes; no quise inventar situaciones verosímiles que hubieran hecho romancesco mi trabajo, no me aventuré á adivinar pensamientos que le hubieran dado variedad, por no forjar un cuento y apartarme del respeto que se debe á la historia." Orzoco y Berra, *Noticia histórica de la conjuración*, 67.

14. Roland Schmidt-Riese, "Glosando las confesiones de los hermanos Ávila: Discurso e identidad en la Nueva España a finales del siglo XVI," *Lexis* 26, no. 1 (2002): 3–78.

15. "Confesión de Alonso de Avila Alvarado, preso y condenado a muerte como consecuencia de la conspiración para alzarse con el poder en Méjico, junto a Luis y Martín Cortés y otros." Archivo Histórico Nacional, México, Diversos-Colecciones 43, 10, 1566.

16. Cathy Caruth, *Unclaimed Experience: Trauma, Narrative and History* (Baltimore: John Hopkins University Press, 1996), 3, 8.

17. Orozco y Berra mentioned this work in relation to the uprising, although it was unpublished.

18. José Pascual Buxó, "Sobre la 'Relación fúnebre a la infeliz, trágica muerte de dos caballeros' de Luis de Sandoval Zapata," in *Actas del Segundo Congreso Internacional de Hispanistas*, ed. Jaime Sánchez Romeralo and Norbert Poulussen (Nimega: Instituto Español de la Universidad de Nimega, 1967), 473, 475. All translations are mine, unless otherwise noted.

19. L. N. McAlister, "Social Structure and Social Change in New Spain," *Hispanic American Historical Review* 43 (1963): 361; Irving A. Leonard, *Los libros del conquistador* (México: FCE, 1996), 158.

20. David A. Brading, *Orbe indiano: De la monarquía católica a la república criolla, 1492–1867* (México: FCE, 1992), 323. The quote is a translation from the original: "Desde el principio, los criollos parecen haberse considerado como herederos desposeídos, robados de su patrimonio por una Corona injusta y por la usurpación de emigrantes recientes, llegados de la Península. En parte, su resentimiento se derivaba de los conquistadores, de hombres como Bernal Díaz del Castillo, quienes acusaron a la Corona de no haber sabido recompensar adecuadamente sus heroicos servicios."

21. Juan Suárez de Peralta, *Noticias históricas de la Nueva España* (Madrid: Justo Zaragoza, 1876), 236–37.

22. Suárez de Peralta, *Noticias históricas*, 238–39.

23. Suárez de Peralta, *Noticias históricas*, 240.

24. Suárez de Peralta, *Noticias históricas*, 245.

25. Suárez de Peralta, *Noticias históricas*, 247.

26. Michel Foucault, *Vigilar y castigar: Nacimiento de la prisión* (México: Siglo XXI, 1999), 32.

27. Suárez de Peralta, *Noticias históricas*, 214.

28. Suárez de Peralta, *Noticias históricas*, 214.

29. Suárez de Peralta, *Noticias históricas*, 214.

30. Suárez de Peralta, *Noticias históricas*, 214–15.

31. Suárez de Peralta, *Noticias históricas*, 218.

32. Jean François Lyotard and John Ronan, "Anamnesis of the Visible 2," *Qui parle* 11, no. 2 (1999): 24.

33. Suárez de Peralta, *Noticias históricas*, 218.

34. Suárez de Peralta, *Noticias históricas*, 219.

35. Suárez de Peralta, *Noticias históricas*, 219.

36. Foucault, *Vigilar y castigar*, 123.

37. Foucault, *Vigilar y castigar*, 203.

38. Suárez de Peralta, *Noticias históricas*, 217–18.

39. Kolk, "Trauma and Memory," 55.

40. Suárez de Peralta, *Noticias históricas*, 218. In a general sense, the term "gallows" refers to a crossbeam and noose. The Ávila brothers were not hanged; they had been deemed traitors, and were thus beheaded by axe, the punishment reserved for that type of crime. In my translation, I have used "gallows" to refer to the wooden platform where the executions took place.

41. Bessel A. van der Kolk and Alexander C. McFarlane, "The Black Hole of Trauma," in *Literary Theory*, ed. Julie Rivkin and Michael Ryan (Malden, MA: Blackwell, 2010), 489. As Kolk says here: "Most people who have been exposed to traumatic stressors are somehow able to go on with their lives without becoming haunted by the memories of what has happened to them. That does not mean that the traumatic events go unnoticed. After exposure to a trauma, most people become preoccupied with the event; having involuntary repeated replaying of upsetting memories serves the function of modifying the emotions associated with the trauma."

42. Suárez de Peralta, *Noticias históricas*, 227.

43. Suárez de Peralta, *Noticias históricas*, 229.

44. "'Postmemory' describes the relationship that the 'generation after' bears to the personal, collective, and cultural trauma of those who came before—to experiences they 'remember' only by means of the stories, images, and behaviors among which they grew up. But these experiences were transmitted to them so deeply and affectively as to seem to constitute memories in their own right. Postmemory's connection to the past is thus actually mediated not by recall but by imaginative investment, projection, and creation. To grow up with overwhelming inherited memories . . . is to be shaped, however indirectly, by traumatic fragments of events that still defy narrative reconstruction and exceed comprehension." Marianne Hirsch, "Postmemory," https://www.postmemory.net.

45. Suárez de Peralta, *Noticias históricas*, 222.

46. Pascual Buxó, "Sobre la 'Relación,'" 475.

47. Sandoval Zapata, "Relación fúnebre," lines 74–89.

48. Marianne Hirsch, "The Generation of Postmemory," *Poetics Today* 29, no. 1 (2008): 106.

49. Luis González Obregón, "Los primeros mártires," 275.

50. Caruth, *Unclaimed Experience*, 4.

51. We read in Suárez de Peralta: "Vivian todos tan contentos con él que no se trataba de otra cosa sino de regozijos y fiestas, y las que lo eran de huardar salia él en su caballo á la jineta, á la carrera . . . todos trataban de caballos, justas, sortijas, juegos de cañas, carrera pública; y estaban con esto tan contentos." *Noticias históricas*, 172.

52. Sandoval Zapata, "Relación fúnebre," lines 56–64.

53. Suárez de Peralta, *Noticias históricas*, 219.

54. González Obregón, "Los primeros mártires," 277.

55. *O proceso dos Távoras*, ed. Pedro de Azevedo (Lisbon: Publicações da Biblioteca Nacional, 1921), 52.

56. Sandoval Zapata, "Relación fúnebre," lines 328–33, 340–45.

57. Sandoval Zapata, "Relación fúnebre," lines 347–54.

58. Pascual Buxó, "Sobre la 'Relación,'" 476–77.

59. Pascual Buxó, "Sobre la 'Relación,'" 479.

60. Sandoval Zapata, "Relación fúnebre," lines 165–177.

PART THREE
The Dutch Republic

Chapter Seven

Hendrick Goltzius's *Lucretia* and the Eighty Years' War

Rachel Wise

The Dutch War of Independence, or the Eighty Years' War (1568–1648), was an uprising initiated by the Iconoclastic Fury of 1566, which matured into a fight for land, religious toleration, and governmental control between the northern rebels and Philip II, the Habsburg king of Spain (1527–1598; reign as Spanish King, 1556–1598). The war would ultimately result in the permanent cleaving of the Dutch Republic from the southern Netherlands. At the beginning of the second decade of this conflict (1577), virtuosic printmaker Hendrick Goltzius (1558–1617) arrived in the city of Haarlem, an area that had recently won autonomy from Spain and joined the rebels. There he set to work designing and engraving four plates (ca. 1578–1580) recounting the ancient story of Lucretia (Figs. 7.1–7.4). His *Lucretia* series was published in Antwerp by Philips Galle (1537–1612) and printed with inscriptions derived and adapted from Ovid's (43 BCE–17/18 CE) telling of the ancient tale.[1] The first plate of the series depicts a banquet scene, the second Lucretia and her handmaids demurely spinning, the third Lucretia's rape, and the final her suicide.

There has been contention over the interpretation of these engravings. David Kunzle views the last plate of the series, where Lucretia has taken a dagger to her own chest, in the context of political changes brought about by a significant event in the Dutch Revolt—the Union of Utrecht in 1579, which formally allied the northern provinces against the Spanish.[2] In his advocacy for political significance, though, Kunzle does not examine the other three plates of Goltzius's series. There are some scholars, however, who have bristled at marrying Netherlandish politics with Goltzius's formulation of the Roman story. In her analysis of the series, Karin Hanika finds the political

Figure 7.1 Hendrick Goltzius, *The Banquet of Sextus Tarquinius*, **plate 1** from *Lucretia* series, 1578–80. Engraving, 209 x 247 mm, Rijksmuseum, Rijksprentenkabinet, Amsterdam, inv. no. RP-P-OB-10.085. Source: Image © by courtesy Rijksmuseum, Amsterdam.

resonances hollow because, she asserts, the prints are more an explication of the male characters' actions and homosocial relationships, specifically those between Tarquin and Collatinus, than about Lucretia and her virtue.[3] Huigen Leeflang, in a 2003 exhibition catalog on Hendrick Goltzius, has also rejected using a wartime lens on the engravings because the series was published by Philips Galle in Antwerp, where it was destined for an international audience.[4]

An international audience, however, does not foreclose the possibility of allusions to a local war. Moreover, in 1580 Goltzius did not yet have his own shop and was dependent on publishing his works with Galle in Antwerp. While Tarquin and Collatinus are actors in Goltzius's series, their relationship does not overshadow or occlude the true protagonist of the engravings: Lucretia. Rather, the engravings primarily support the literary topos of Lucretia's virtue, which because of her suicide remains untainted and inspires political upheaval.

Figure 7.2 Hendrick Goltzius, *Lucretia and Her Handmaids Spinning*, **plate 2** from *Lucretia* series, 1578–80. Engraving, 210 x 249 mm, Rijksmuseum, Rijksprentenkabinet, Amsterdam, inv. no. RP-P-OB-10.086. **Source: Image © by courtesy Rijksmuseum, Amsterdam.**

This chapter argues that it is no coincidence that Goltzius produced the series while the Union of Utrecht was being signed and that consequently the four engravings proffer a political reading.[5] A close examination of all four engravings—not just the last plate—reveals an artist invested in both the Roman and contemporary political potential of the Lucretia narrative. Goltzius's *Lucretia* is the "first and last" Netherlandish series formulated around the narrative of her life.[6] It was rare for Goltzius to dedicate a full series to a pagan subject in general—he usually only used the format for biblical heroines.[7] Sixteenth-century depictions of Lucretia almost exclusively imagined her as a solitary figure, plunging the knife into her breast—in other words, devoid of the plotline trappings of her tale. Why would Goltzius lavish attention on the fuller narrative of her life? Portraying Lucretia's account as a series—a format also employed frequently by printmakers to track the events of the Eighty Years' War[8]—allowed Goltzius to explicate and draw parallels between Lucretia's narrative and the Dutch Revolt, implicating his burin in

Figure 7.3 Hendrick Goltzius, *The Rape of Lucretia*, plate 3 from *Lucretia* series, 1578–80. Engraving, 211 x 248 mm, Rijksmuseum, Rijksprentenkabinet, Amsterdam, inv. no. RP-P-OB-10.087. Source: Image © by courtesy Rijksmuseum, Amsterdam.

the rendering of the violence and redemption of the tale. Goltzius deliberately localized the ancient tale to the sixteenth century, validating and encouraging political interpretations by Netherlandish audiences living through the war: Lucretia's demise as a symbol of the provinces allying against Spain and the heroine herself as Belgica, the personification of the Netherlands. For international audiences with less investment in the Low Countries' troubles, the political allusions would have been more opaque.

By using an allegorical, transhistorical framework, Goltzius's *Lucretia* series buttressed and updated the perception and understanding of the Eighty Years' War. The trauma of the Revolt was mediated through the physical assault of Lucretia's rape, and the coalescing of ancient and contemporary time as well as literary and present traumas makes the four-plate series an insightful interpretive framework for understanding and processing the Eighty Years' War.

Figure 7.4 Hendrick Goltzius, *The Suicide of Lucretia*, plate 4 from *Lucretia* series, 1578–80. Engraving, 205 x 248 mm, Rijksmuseum, Rijksprentenkabinet, Amsterdam, inv. no. RP-P-OB-10.088. Source: Image © by courtesy Rijksmuseum, Amsterdam.

LUCRETIA

As told by Livy (59 BCE–17 CE) in his *History of Rome* (27 BCE–9 BCE) and later by Ovid in his *Fasti* (8 CE), the rape of Lucretia takes place during King Tarquinius Superbus's siege of Ardea (510 BCE), an ancient city south of Rome.[9] While Roman legions surround the town, the king's son Sextus Tarquinius (Tarquin) drinks and dines with friends—including Lucretia's husband, Collatinus—and they boast of their wives' virtue. Upon returning to Rome after their merriment, the men find themselves proven wrong as their women are "draped with garlands, keeping their vigils over the wine."[10] Only Lucretia is discovered modestly dressed at home, spinning wool while also bemoaning her husband's absence at war. Enraptured by Lucretia's beauty, but also her virtue, the king's son resolves to assault her, and so, "in the guise of a guest,"[11] comes again to her residence and dines with her.[12] He then forces his way to her chamber, informing her that if she refuses his advances, he will murder her, "kill a slave," and spread rumors that she was caught with the man—the most offensive form of adultery.[13] Lucretia, as Goltzius's text describes, "submit[s] out of fear for her good name" and is subsequently raped.[14] The following day, Lucretia summons her father and husband to tell them of her assault. Then, "without flinching," she pierces her heart with a dagger.[15] In the aftermath, Brutus, nephew of the king, displays Lucretia's wounded and lifeless body to the citizens of Rome, and in a call to arms, demands that Tarquinius be deposed of his kingship. Avenging Lucretia's rape, Brutus abolishes the tyrant from Rome and founds the Roman Republic.

Where Livy brings focus to Lucretia's virtue and suicide, instrumental in creating republicanism from kingship, the Ovidian version accentuates Lucretia's suffering and the sexual nature of Rome's foundation myth.[16] Although Goltzius draws from Ovid's account for the inscriptions accompanying his *Lucretia* series, he also specifically picks Ovid's more political couplets so that the fall of tyrannical kings undergirds his visual formulation.[17]

The story of Lucretia has historically been used to strengthen the founding myths of republics, including the Florentine and French Republics.[18] Scenes of rape catered to erotic tastes and overtures of power: raping a woman could be easily allegorized and analogized into exerting one's political prowess.[19] Indeed, the concept of rape was, as Amanda Pipkin notes, "flexible" and multivalent, and when deployed as an allegory, the personal violation of rape was discounted or ignored.[20] Like the tale of Lucretia, the "heroic rape" of the Sabine women also pervaded Renaissance visual culture. Here, the rape of women was a legitimized abduction: newly founded Rome needed a population, prompting orders for the Romans to "abscond" with the Sabine women to be their wives and bear their children. These rapists were therefore heroic victors. Lucretia's rape, in contrast, modeled a type of ravishment wherein the action was deemed punishable: Tarquin breached the private space of a married woman's home and defiled her.[21] Even so, Lucretia's innocence is still in doubt until she plunges the dagger into her chest and dies, thereby annulling questions over whether she consented to adultery and inspiring her male family to avenge the crime against her.

Lucretia's rape justified the "necessary" violence of republican founders, while also proving that tyrannical power exploits and violates private autonomy in the same way that assault desecrates the female body.[22] Sextus Tarquinius acts out the role of tyrant and claims his father's throne by raping Lucretia.[23] His assault violates her father's and husband's control of her body as well as their political authority and autonomy. Lucretia's suicide is thereby, as Melissa Matthes argues, instrumental in halting a continuation of Superbus's line of tyrant kings, as her assault and rape give way to the birth of a republic.[24] Depictions of Lucretia showcased the morality of the heroine, an antithesis to the lascivious appetites of the men who dared to challenge her innocence. Indeed, it was her virtue that provoked Tarquin to rape her.

From a Christian perspective, Augustine (354–430) was troubled by the tale of Lucretia, querying how, if she were guilty of adultery—as she gave "consent" to Tarquin to avoid murder and a framed assignation with a slave—she could be upheld in society as a model for women. And why, if she was chaste, did she have to die?[25] To Augustine, Lucretia's suicide was not a brave act, but in actuality, a murder. Despite Augustine's protestations, Lucretia was championed during the Renaissance as the model wife, gracing books on marriage, decorating chests for new brides, and inspiring what Daniela Hammer-Tugendhat calls a "Lucretia fever."[26] In paintings of this chaste woman, aphorisms suggested death over shame, her tale favoring suicide as the solution to the stain of adultery.

Sixteenth-century depictions of Lucretia typically portray her committing suicide. Walter Stechow describes three categories of Lucretia images: episodes from her life combined in one composition, the rape episode, and, most common, Lucretia alone, stabbing herself.[27] In the Netherlands, examples of her felo-de-se abound, simultaneously upholding Lucretia as a virtuous paragon but also allowing for an intimate encounter with an eroticized, half-nude woman.[28] Albrecht Dürer, Hans Baldung, Jan van Scorel, Pieter Coecke van Aelst, and Lucas Cranach, among others, ushered in a visual flood of these Lucretia suicide images.[29] The isolated depictions, Hammer-Tugendhat argues, are devoid of the political implications of the Lucretia story.[30] Exceptions to portraying her as a single figure are mostly found in prints, such as Hendrick Goltzius's series, where the political undertones come to the fore.[31]

RAPE AND THE REVOLT

In the 1560s and 1570s, rebel propagandists deployed allegories of women held hostage by the Duke of Alva (1507–1582), a deputy sent by King Philip II of Spain to rein in the heretics, in order to sharply criticize the Habsburg overlords. By the 1580s, writers began connecting sexual violence with violations of political abuse.[32] During the Eighty Years' War, Prince Maurits (1567–1625) and Frederik Hendrik (1584–1647) had soldiers who committed rape hanged,[33] though there was no law criminalizing rape in the northern Netherlands in the sixteenth and seventeenth centuries.[34] As early as 1581, William of Orange's *Apology*, penned by Orangists, directly attacked King Philip II of Spain for the unspeakable misdeeds of his soldiers: "We do not wish to relate the raping, ransoming, and arson that the Spanish have inflicted."[35] While King Philip II may not have been a literal rapist, he was responsible for the actions of his troops, who pillaged and raped their way through cities. Moreover, rape stood as an analogy for his defilement of political order.[36]

During the Oudewater Massacre in 1572, Spanish troops slaughtered three thousand citizens of the city. They also raped women of all ages, and in one of the most heinous actions, hanged a pregnant woman and tore the child from her womb. These atrocities against women were memorialized in a Frans Hogenberg etching (1574–ca. 1578) (Fig. 7.5), where the woman's corpse hangs from the doorway in the left foreground.[37]

The caption sets the scene: "Here you can see what tyranny and cruelty took place in Oudewater by God and infamous felons. They killed, spoiled, and violated, both virgins and married women. One of which they hanged naked, tore the fruit from her womb, and threw it away like filth."[38] Soldiers chase women with windswept hair, in the left and right foreground, as a prelude to their assault.[39] This violent and traumatic scene effectively registered the horror of war, and the trope of the murdered pregnant woman became a regular feature of the Black Legend of Spanish aggression.[40] The grisly presentation of the woman's body accentuates the violence of the soldiers, and it forms a corollary for Brutus's display of Lucretia's body to rally the Romans, and by extension, the Dutch rebels.

Figure 7.5 Frans Hogenberg, *Death in Oudewater 1575*, 1574–ca. 1578. Etching, 214 x 274 mm, Rijksmuseum, Rijksprentenkabinet, Amsterdam, inv. no. RP-P-OB-78.785–89. Source: Image © by courtesy Rijksmuseum, Amsterdam.

When a cruel leader violates the rights of subjects, that violation can be analogized in sexual terms—as rape.[41] Goltzius's *Lucretia* series belongs to the early phase of Orangist propaganda, which used gendered violence to construct a shared enemy. Indeed, it was in the late 1560s that William of Orange began a propaganda campaign to inspire a sense of "Dutch cohesion," a "supra-provincial identity," as a strategy to unite the provinces against Spain, employing images and texts using sexual assault to build an identity around a common violator.[42] The Pacification of Ghent in 1576 had allied the disparate provinces over the mutinous behavior of the Spanish army. But this coalition frayed fast, and two years later the Union of Utrecht began the formal process of politically dividing the northern and southern Netherlands. William of Orange, however, continued to advocate for a united fatherland, and he refused to sign the Union of Utrecht until it was clear that the Walloon provinces would support the Spanish king. The text of the Union of Utrecht, however, still made an explicit pronouncement of unity for its signatories: that these "provinces shall ally, confederate, and unite . . . to hold together eternally in all ways and forms as if they were but one province."[43] In 1581 these provinces formalized their declaration of independence from Spain with the Act of Abjuration.[44]

The tale of Lucretia's assault appealed to audiences' feelings of horror and righteous indignation.[45] At the rhetoric societies in Leiden (1596) and Rotterdam (1599), Tarquinius, Phalaris, and Caligula were all called companions of the tyrannical Spanish king.[46] Indeed, in 1609 a tableau vivant of the deposing of Tarquinius Superbus was performed in Amsterdam's Dam Square in celebration of the signing of the Twelve Years' Truce, which brought a temporary halt to the war's proceedings.

THE SIEGE OF HAARLEM

Executed thirty years before the Truce, Goltzius's *Lucretia* inaugurated the ancient tale as a corollary for the emerging autonomy of the northern provinces. Goltzius foregrounds the transfer of power from kingship to republicanism in the last line of the Ovidian inscription accompanying Lucretia's suicide: "That day meant the end of the rule of kings."[47] This inscription invites a Netherlandish audience to view the termination of monarchical power as an agitation for their own breaking away from Habsburg Spain. Furthermore, just as King Tarquinius Superbus besieged Ardea, so too did the Spanish occupy Haarlem from 1572 to 1573, an analogy Goltzius accommodates in his series. The first line of Goltzius's text on the first plate foregrounds the Roman blockade as the backdrop to the narrative: "While the besieged Ardea is surrounded by Roman legions and has to withstand a lengthy siege, the young Tarquin entertains his friends with a lavish meal."[48] For a Netherlandish audience, the comparison between the siege of Ardea and their contemporary blockades would have been apparent.

In Haarlem, the citizens starved during the Spanish siege of their city. For months Haarlem had been attempting to forge a neutral position between the rebels and Spanish loyalists. Their careful equivocating, however, was all for naught. Leaving a path of burned cities and piles of bodies in their wake, Spanish troops laid siege to Haarlem on December 11, 1572. With a garrison of about three thousand troops (mostly German mercenaries, under the direction of Captain Wigbolt Ripperda) the city prepared itself for the attack.[49] The Spanish troops pummeled the city with cannons and constructed tunnels to blow up the town walls. Haarlem withstood the assault with help from William of Orange, the leader of the rebels, who managed to orchestrate an elaborate food-smuggling operation over the frozen Haarlemmermeer. Nonetheless, by May there was no more bread, the city's defensive walls had crumbled, and townspeople were reduced to the pitiable state of eating vermin and animal hides. Haarlem surrendered on July 13, 1573, and opened the city to marauding soldiers, who executed the entirety of the garrison, imprisoned citizens, and levied fines.

Since ancient times, the conquest of cities through siege warfare has been described in violent sexualized terms.[50] The taking of a city by a foreign army was a rape, a plunder, a violation of the "maiden." Lucretia's assault, then, is mirrored in the siege violence wrought by the Romans in Ardea, and by analogy, the Spanish in Haarlem. Her violation also stands as a more general symbol of Spanish oppression throughout the Netherlandish provinces.

A MODERN BANQUET

Goltzius modernizes the Lucretia story by costuming the figures in the first plate in contemporary clothes, a fact that caught the eye of Karel van Mander (1548–1606), a biographer of Netherlandish and German painters, and prompted him to state: "There was a banquet into which he had very subtly inserted some modern costumes, which contributed very much to its good appearance, and to my mind it was quite different from what was usually done by us Netherlanders."[51] It is striking that Van Mander's only comment on a series dedicated to Roman history is reserved for Goltzius's projection of the Lucretia story into "modern" times. Adorned in clothes of the day, the characters notably transpose the Roman tragedy to the current moment.[52] Dressing up Lucretia's story in early modern fashion prepared the viewer to read the allegory of Lucretia—from its first plate—in the contemporary moment. It was not just through costume that Goltzius brought the Lucretia tale into the sixteenth century, however. He further localized the series in the last plate, where Lucretia's aggrieved father is likely based on his own father's visage: Jan Goltzius, a citizen of Haarlem, of whom he engraved a portrait the year prior, in 1578.[53]

Not all the characters in the banquet scene are in modern clothes, however. The background soldiers observing the revelry are portrayed in antique armor. Goltzius's scene presents inebriated women and men seated around a candlelit table and entertained by musicians and a dancing couple.[54] On the left of the composition, a knife is prominently placed at the head of the table, threateningly close to a piece of fruit, directing the viewer's eyes down the diagonal of the table. The blade foreshadows Tarquin's attack on Lucretia and the dagger she will take to her breast. In the initial preparatory drawing Goltzius made for the banquet scene, the knife is smaller and deemphasized on the table, indicating that he wanted to heighten its symbolic import in the print.[55] The knife holds the additional connotation of Goltzius's burin, used to gouge and cut the metal plates with the story of Lucretia. With his engraver's tool, Goltzius has expertly rendered the effect of candlelight at the table, which casts a glow on the seated figures and creates exaggerated shadows on the draped wall behind. He also introduces the barrel-vaulted arch motif in the background, which he employs in the subsequent engravings to advance the narrative; here, an arch frames the soldiers in antique dress observing the scene.

But whose banquet are they watching: Tarquin's lavish meal, where the men boast of their wives' virtue? Or is it the scene of their wives making merry in their absence? There is no consensus in the literature.[56] Goltzius's inscriptions seem to indicate that it is Tarquin's meal at the royal palace: "The young Tarquin entertains his friends with a lavish meal; they talk about the love between them and their wives. Each man praises his own wife. They all go straight away to the royal palace and drink wine there all night."[57] But if so, the men are hypocritically consorting with other women while praising the constancy of their spouses. Hanika suggests that the men in the foreground are Tarquin, seated at the end of the table with his arm around a well-dressed woman, and Collatinus, who sits with his back to the servant.[58] But who, then, are the soldiers in the archway?

While Goltzius's inscription does not describe spying on the king's daughters-in-law, the scene may be of the indecorous wives, "necks draped with garlands, keeping their vigils over the wine."[59] The presence of the soldiers in the back archway, then, makes sense: they are Collatinus and Tarquin, who again appear in the doorway of the next plate, observing Lucretia. Ovid's text, however, does not describe the wives consorting with men,[60] so perhaps Goltzius has taken this liberty to heighten the polarity between the lascivious women and the demure Lucretia. While the specifics of the scene remain ambiguous, the costumes are not, and the five elegantly attired women at the banquet are rendered so as to contrast with the next plate, where a quintet of plainly robed women are industriously occupied. Perhaps the scene's multivalence is intentional on Goltzius's part, abbreviating the story by overlaying two meals, both of which insinuate morally dubious behavior.

LUCRETIA AND HER HANDMAIDS SPINNING

In the spinning scene, a veiled Lucretia demurely winds a ball of yarn, a commonplace activity in the northern provinces dependent on the textile trade.[61] These women symbolized domestic virtue and industry, and they alluded to the Virgin Mary, who spun the thread of life and served as the ultimate paragon of virtue.[62] Goltzius's composition was inspired by the first engraving from Dirck Volkertsz. Coornhert's (1522–1590) series *Praise of the Virtuous Wife* (1555), based on Proverbs 31:10–31 (Fig. 7.6).

Figure 7.6 Dirck Volckertsz. Coornhert after Maarten van Heemskerck, *The Virtuous Woman Spins*, plate 1 from *Praise of the Virtuous Wife* series, 1555. Engraving, 251 x 203 mm, Rijksmuseum, Rijksprentenkabinet, Amsterdam, inv. no. RP-P-1894-A-18302. Source: Image © by courtesy Rijksmuseum, Amsterdam.

In this engraving, the wife—a woman who even while seated dwarfs her companions—is positioned centrally, spinning wool and linen, with two onlookers placed in a doorway. She is an exemplum of Solomon's words— "She seeketh wool, and flax, and worketh willingly with her hands."[63] Likewise, Goltzius renders a slightly enlarged Lucretia in the center of the composition, drawing upon the medieval hieratic scale afforded to the Virgin Mary. She is portrayed sedulously rolling yarn, while her maids are engaged in a variety of tasks: spinning, using the wool winder, and sewing a piece of cloth. Working by candlelight late into the night in contrast to the alcohol-fueled banquet of the first engraving, Lucretia cements her chaste reputation and upholds her virtuous industry.[64] A coterie of Roman soldiers—including Lucretia's husband and Tarquin—watch these models of domesticity and morality from an archway in the background. Tarquin is likely the soldier gazing intently toward Lucretia; he, Ovid writes, is "transported by blind love."[65] One of Lucretia's servants looks over her shoulder to acknowledge their presence while holding a pair of scissors. Juxtaposed against the men, the scissors foreshadow the weapon and phallus of Tarquin and the dagger Lucretia plunges into her heart. Of note is the diminutive size of the scissors in the preparatory drawing for the print, just as the knife in the banquet scene drawing was deemphasized.[66] In the realization of the engraving, Goltzius exaggerated the blades to anticipate the coming sexual scene, or, perhaps even to denote a symbol of castration.[67] On the right of the composition, an open door reveals Lucretia's bed, also portending her coming ravishment.

LUCRETIA'S RAPE

The final two prints of the series portray the assault and suicide of Lucretia, familiar territory for northern artists, though Goltzius does not rely upon their standardized imagery. Tarquin lunges toward a now nude Lucretia on her bed, dagger suggestively raised in threat of murder and rape. Lucretia's transformation from a demure and modestly clad wife to a disrobed and threatened woman is stark, and it marks the intrusion of blatant eroticized violence into the series. The composition of the engraving derives from a 1571 print by Cornelis Cort (ca. 1533–1578) (Fig. 7.7) based on Titian's ca. 1571 painting *Tarquin and Lucretia* (Fig. 7.8); Titian (ca. 1488–1576) supervised Cort's reproduction.[68]

Ironically, Titian painted this lewd scene for the archenemy of the Dutch, King Philip II of Spain, for whom he executed twenty-five paintings during his tenure as a court painter. Focusing on the scene of the rape, Titian vividly renders the assault with Tarquin, dressed in shades of red, falling

Figure 7.7 Cornelis Cort after Titian, *Lucretia and Sextus*, 1571. Engraving, 371 x 266 mm, Rijksmuseum, Rijksprentenkabinet, Amsterdam, inv. no. RP-P-1951–541. Source: Image © by courtesy Rijksmuseum, Amsterdam.

Hendrick Goltzius's Lucretia *and the Eighty Years' War* 181

Figure 7.8 Titian, *Tarquin and Lucretia*, **ca. 1571. Oil on canvas, 1889 x 1451 mm, Fitzwilliam Museum, Cambridge, inv. no. 914. Source: Image © by courtesy Fitzwilliam Museum, Cambridge.**

toward a weeping and bejeweled Lucretia, while a slave holds back the curtains to reveal the scene. Peter Humfrey notes that while Titian relied on Livy's account of the tale, he eliminated the political thrust of the story. Rather, Titian's canvas foregrounds the tension between unchecked desire and morality.[69] Under Titian's brush, the action takes place on a bed devoid of even the context of a bedroom. Norman Bryson likewise calls Titian's painting a nobleman's crime against a woman of his rank, with no political frame of reference.[70]

Cornelis Cort's engraving of the scene, however, expands the cropped canvas on all sides, giving greater description to the bed, body of the slave, steps leading up to the scene of the rape, and Lucretia's cast-off shoes. Where Cort's engraving was executed in reverse of the original, Goltzius's print follows the direction of Titian's painting.[71] Under Goltzius's burin, narrative abounds beyond Cort's insertions. Goltzius's scene allows a view of Tarquin and Lucretia's candlelit meal in the left background, where Tarquin can be discerned holding a knife, continuing the trope of omnipresent sharp instruments in the series. A scene of intimate nocturnal dining, the vignette recalls the couples at the banquet of the first plate, already tainting the reputation of the industrious Lucretia by visual association. In the bedroom, Lucretia's clothes have been discarded on the table—perhaps suggestive of Tarquin removing them himself. The aggressor steps onto a footstool to gain access to Lucretia, who sits on a bed mounded with sheets and pillows.

Goltzius has made a few modifications to Tarquin's dress: his stockings have slipped down, he wears a medal around his neck, his doublet is unbuttoned on the side, and an earring dangles from his ear rather than from Lucretia's. Where Titian relied on red paint to emphasize Tarquin's violent actions, Goltzius portrays a disarrayed oppressor. Nude and angled frontally, so that the viewer can fully see her body, Lucretia's vulnerability is the center of attention, and her hair is down, a telltale sign that a woman is under sexual threat.[72] Furthermore, her flowing hair is also reminiscent of depictions of the penitent Mary Magdalene, suggesting that Lucretia's guilt has begun even before her assault.[73] Tarquin pounces forward, a vein in his neck bulging with exertion. There is no slave in Goltzius's rendering, despite his presence in the caption: "He even threatened murder and involved a slave in his crime."[74] The rape, rather than Tarquin's threat of murder, is the climax of the engraving. Goltzius has repositioned the dagger from Titian's composition to the center of the scene, now unmistakably aligned with Tarquin's phallus.

Lucretia raises her arm in despair as Tarquin reaches to touch her left breast, the spot where on the coming day she will stab herself. Goltzius thus explicitly acknowledges the interconnectedness of Tarquin's rape and Lucretia's self-destruction. Lucretia has knocked over a chamber pot at the foot of the bed, the spilled urine correlating with the married woman's "breached body";[75] the servant, in the right corner foreground of the first plate, foreshadows the overturned chamber pot in pouring spirits from a cistern for the carousing Romans.[76] Goltzius's additions to the scene—the discarded clothes, overturned basin of urine, sphinx heads carved into the furniture, and evening meal in the background—bring genre-like details to the episode and emphasize the narrative context of the story so that the rape of Lucretia cannot be interpreted in isolation.

Goltzius's signature, "Henricus Goltzius inuentor et sculptor," appears beneath Tarquin's outstretched legs and knife, center foreground, and Philips Galle's name is engraved beneath his foot. This is the only plate Goltzius signed in the first state, intimating, according to Leeflang, that Goltzius initially devised this engraving with the intention to sell it in isolation.[77] Often in a series, however, one print carries most of the signatures, so this is not absolute proof of separate issue. Nonetheless, the prominence of the signatures correlates the engraver and publisher with the tyrant, giving Goltzius's burin erotic charge.[78] Just as Tarquin wields his knife and phallus to rape Lucretia, Goltzius uses his burin, with virtuosity, to render Lucretia naked, vulnerable, and unchaste. Even if Philips Galle sold the rape print separately, its meaning changes when viewed in the context of the entirety of the series, where the scene is not just one of ravishment, but a pivotal step in the creation of the Roman Republic. Where Titian's canvas is a schematic, lewd illustration of unchecked immorality, Goltzius's engraving is purposed for constructing the grand narrative of the overthrow of tyranny; under Goltzius's burin, Tarquin is the villain who overrides Lucretia's self-defense.

Sitting on the edge of the bed, facing forward, Lucretia's nude body is gratuitously displayed for the viewer so that they might, like Tarquin, take pleasure in the contours of her form, rendered with networks of cross-hatched lines. The viewer, then, is made complicit in the attack on Lucretia, but the erotic appeal of her body is made acceptable by the moral of the tale. The spectacle of Lucretia's body also foreshadows its display in the background of the final scene (Fig. 7.9).

In the print detailing her assault, her body is presented for sexual gratification, but in the last plate the viewer is denied a full-frontal view: instead, the corpse is barely visible in the back left corner, her body articulated with minimal line and the dagger still thrust into her chest. This display of her diminutive, lifeless form will now inspire the overthrow of tyranny.

SUICIDE AND THE SUFFERING BELGICA

Lucretia's suicide invokes the visual tradition of allegorical representations of the Low Countries. It is morning, and she sits in her bedchamber before her canopied bed—the site of her rape—having just plunged the dagger into her breast, her left arm extended in pain. Her bodily positioning is mirrored by the man on the right, who empathically touches his breast and reaches his foreshortened arm out to the audience, drawing them into the scene and

Figure 7.9 Detail of Figure 7.4.

manifesting Lucretia's sacrifice and pain. Goltzius relies upon Livy's account in his inclusion of four men, for Ovid only mentions her father and husband at her suicide. Hanika suggests that the gesticulating soldier in classical garb might be Brutus, who, as Livy writes, witnessed her self-murder alongside Collatinus, her father, and Publius Valerius.[79] Brutus overlaps with the man behind him—Collatinus—so that they meld into one being with three legs, perhaps, as intimated by Hanika, suggestive of their future role as the first two consuls of the Republic.[80] Publius Valerius stands in front on the left, with Lucretia's father behind. The arch in the back left corner displays a view onto the revolt inspired against King Tarquinius Superbus, justifying Lucretia's self-sacrificing action and again functioning as a narrative portal. Brutus displays Lucretia's body to the Roman people, "inaugurat[ing] a political community founded upon seeing and being seen," for it is observing Lucretia's passive and violated body that motivates the citizens into action to form a republic.[81]

Surrounded by men observing her pierced heart, Lucretia parallels the assaulted Belgica in Hans Collaert I's (ca. 1525–1580) *Lament Over the Desolation of the Netherlands* (ca. 1570–1580) (Fig. 7.10).

Figure 7.10 Hans Collaert I after Ambrosius Francken, *Lament over the Desolation of the Netherlands*, ca. 1570–1580. Engraving, 434 x 572 mm, Museum Plantin-Moretus / Prentenkabinet, Antwerp, inv. no. PK.OP.18283. Source: Image © by courtesy Museum Plantin-Moretus, Antwerp–UNESCO, World Heritage / Photo: Peter Maes.

Belgica personified the Low Countries and, from the first decade of the Eighty Years' War, appeared in paintings, poems, plays, triumphal arches, and tableaux vivants.[82] In this print, four soldiers rob and assault Belgica, ripping off her clothes, pulling her hair, and tearing her heart from her body.[83] Cities burn and soldiers terrorize peasants in the background, while Belgica is juxtaposed against a ruinous building.[84] Designed by Ambrosius Francken (1544–1618), the print was inspired by the Spanish Fury of 1576, when mutinying Spanish troops laid waste to the city of Antwerp. Whereas Lucretia stabs her own heart as a repeated assault on her body, Belgica's heart is grasped like a fondled right breast. Collaert's scene is a confluence of Lucretia's assault in narrative and suicide in composition: while Lucretia is surrounded by angered male family members and friends in the last print, Belgica is swarmed by grasping and harassing soldiers; Belgica mirrors Lucretia's body positioning during her rape, with her left arm extended over her head in distress. The personifications of Ambition and Greed represent the soldiers' motivation to assault, while Distrust and Envy, in the form of harpies, pull the seventeen provinces apart. Lucretia's assault, by comparison, instead alludes to the uniting of the provinces through the founding of the Republic. She has found resoluteness in suicide—to clear her name of unfaithfulness.

When Goltzius set out designing and engraving his plates, the future of the Low Countries was uncertain. William of Orange's advocacy for a common Netherlands had been tempered by the Union of Utrecht, though it was not until 1585, with the Spanish takeover of Antwerp, that the possibility of a northern-southern fatherland was foreclosed.[85] Goltzius's visualization of the *Lucretia* series can be interpreted as a call for *all* the provinces to throw off the yoke of monarchical oppression, just as Belgica symbolized the full seventeen provinces. For a viewer from Holland or Zeeland, the two most prominent provincial advocates for the Union of Utrecht, however, the

Figure 7.11 Anonymous, *Maid of Holland and the Departure of the Duke of Alva from the Netherlands*, **1573. Copper, 30 mm diameter, Rijksmuseum, Amsterdam, inv. no. NG-VG-3-448. Source: Image © by courtesy Rijksmuseum, Amsterdam.**

Lucretia series could also have provided an interpretation of just the northern provinces allying against Spain.

As a potential symbol of the unification of the northern provinces, Lucretia additionally recalls the imagery of the Maid of Holland, who likewise signified chastity and Dutch independence.[86] In her early depictions in the Revolt, the stoic Maid of Holland is portrayed in a wattle-fenced hortus conclusus, like the impenetrable Virgin Mary (Fig. 7.11).

She wears the Hat of Liberty—a symbol of freedom for Roman slaves who earned their emancipation—and brandishes a sword. The Maid of Holland was used by Amsterdam, Dordrecht, Haarlem, and Alkmaar as their civic symbol of resistance.[87] As a seated, chaste woman, weapon in hand, the Maid of Holland shares a visual vocabulary with Lucretia—especially, as in Goltzius's context, where the Roman woman can be interpreted as a symbol of the northern provinces or, more specifically, the city of Haarlem. When breached by a tyrannical Tarquin (symbol of Spain), Lucretia takes the dagger and uses it on herself to bring republicanism and freedom to the Netherlands.

Mieke Bal notes the inherent problem of depicting rape, for it cannot be visualized because the physical act covers the victim, and it also obscures the victim's "self-image" and "subjectivity."[88] Instead, rape depends upon metaphor. In this case, the suicide of Lucretia operates as a metaphor for and consequence of the rape itself.[89] In Dutch, the word for suicide, dating from the seventeenth century, is *zelfmoord*, or self-murder.[90] The blade pierces her heart, just as the men in the Collaert engraving grab the heart of Belgica as a sign of rape. But by invoking her rape with a dagger to the heart, Lucretia reverses her taking by Tarquin, and her personal assault becomes political.

Where knives threaten sexual violence in the print of Lucretia's rape and allude to Goltzius's burin disrobing the heroine and rendering the assault, the dagger takes on redemptive meaning in the final plate. Submerged almost to the hilt, the weapon has undone what Tarquin did to Lucretia: stain her reputation. Brutus presents her lifeless body to the people, the blade still protruding from her chest, and the populace, in response, hold up their weapons. For Goltzius, Lucretia's knife becomes a metaphor for his own burin, which, in presenting this detailed account of her life, justifies the rebellion against Spain and the alliance of the provinces.

CONCLUSION

Out of the ravishment and suicide of Lucretia, a new republic was born, thus offering an overriding message of optimism to the war-torn city of Haarlem and, more broadly, to the rebels, while simultaneously masking the personal violation of rape in favor of political abstraction. Goltzius's adaptation of the Lucretia narrative into a four-part series format was unique, and under his burin, the tragic tale of Lucretia became an allegory for the Netherlands, reflecting the renunciation of the Spanish king and the hope for a unified Netherlands freed from Spanish tyranny. It is instructive to note that Goltzius produced numerous portraits of rebels during the 1580s and 1590s: most importantly, William of Orange and his third wife, Charlotte de Bourbon (1546/47–1582), but also military leaders, a variety of known Orangist supporters, and influential foreign leaders vested in the Dutch people's cause against Spain.[91] Beyond political portraits of leaders in the Revolt, various attempts have been made in Goltzius's historiography to find political commentary in his allegorical, mythological, and ancient history works.[92] The *Lucretia* series should be the first among his works to be viewed as connecting Roman history and contemporary politics, at least for a local audience living through and coping with the traumas of the Eighty Years' War.

WORKS CITED

Arnade, Peter J. *Beggars, Iconoclasts, and Civic Patriots: The Political Culture of the Dutch Revolt.* Ithaca, NY: Cornell University Press, 2008.

Ayumi, Yasui. "Belgica: Personification of the Low Countries in Prints during the Eighty Years' War." *Bulletin of Kanazawa College of Art* 53 (2009): 11–23.

Bal, Mieke. *Looking In: The Art of Viewing.* London: Routledge, 2001.

Boogman, J. C. "The Union of Utrecht: its Genesis and Consequences." *BMGN—Low Countries Historical Review* 94, no. 3 (1979): 377–407.

Bryson, Norman. "Two Narratives of Rape in the Visual Arts: Lucretia and the Sabine Women." In *Rape: An Historical and Social Enquiry*, edited by Sylvana Tomaselli and Roy Porter, 152–73. Oxford: Blackwell, 1989.

Carroll, Margaret D. "The Erotics of Absolutism: Rubens and the Mystification of Sexual Violence." *Representations* 25 (Winter 1989): 3–30.

———. *Painting and Politics in Northern Europe: Van Eyck, Bruegel, Rubens, and Their Contemporaries.* University Park: Pennsylvania State University, 2008.

Cuneo, Pia F. "Jörg Breu the Elder's *Death of Lucretia*: History, Sexuality, and the State." In *Saints, Sinners, and Sisters: Gender and Northern Art in Medieval and Early Modern Europe*, edited by Jane L. Carroll and Alison G. Stewart, 26–43. Burlington, VT: Ashgate, 2003.

Diels, Ann, and Marjolein Leesberg, comps. *The New Hollstein: Dutch and Flemish Etchings, Engravings and Woodcuts, 1450–1700: Collaert Dynasty.* Edited by Marjolein Leesberg and Arnout Balis. Part 5. Ouderkerk aan den Ijssel: Sound and Vision, 2005–2006.

Donaldson, Ian. *The Rapes of Lucretia: A Myth and Its Transformations.* Oxford: Clarendon Press, 1982.

Duke, Alastair. "The Elusive Netherlands: The Question of National Identity in the Early Modern Low Countries on the Eve of the Revolt." *BMGN—Low Countries Historical Review* 119 (2004): 10–38.

———. "In Defense of the Common Fatherland: Patriotism and Liberty in the Low Countries, 1555–1576." In *Networks, Regions, and Nations*, edited by Robert Stein and Judith Pollmann, 217–39. Leiden: Brill, 2010.

Fishman, Jane Susannah. *Boerenverdriet: Violence between Peasants and Soldiers in Early Modern Netherlandish Art.* Ann Arbor: UMI Research Press, 1979.

Franits, Wayne E. *Paragons of Virtue: Women and Domesticity in Seventeenth-Century Dutch Art.* Cambridge: Cambridge University Press, 1993.

Golan, Steven Robert. "Scenes from Roman Republican History in Seventeenth-Century Dutch Art." PhD diss., Wittenberg University, 1984.

Grewe, Cordula. "Shaping Reality through the Fictive: Images of Women Spinning in the Northern Renaissance." *RACAR: Canadian Art Review* 19, no. 1 (1992): 6–19.

Hammer-Tugendhat, Daniela. *The Visible and the Invisible: On Seventeenth-Century Dutch Painting.* Translated by Margarethe Clausen. Berlin: De Gruyter, 2015.

Hanika, Karin. "Lucretia als 'Damenopfer' patriarchaler Tugendkonzeptionen: Die vier Kupferstiche des Hendrik Goltzius." In *Eros, Macht, Askese: Geschlechterspannungen als Dialogstruktur in Kunst und Literatur*, edited by Helga Sciurie and Hans-Jürgen Bachorski, 396–422. Trier: Wissenschaftlicher Verlag Trier, 1996.

Holman, Beth. "Goltzius's Great Hercules: Mythology, Art, and Politics." *Netherlands Yearbook for History of Art* 42–43 (1991–92): 397–412.

Horst, Daniel. *De Opstand in zwart-wit: Propagandaprenten uit de Nederlandse Opstand (1566–1584).* Zutphen: Walburg Pers, 2003.

Hults, Linda C. "'Lucretia': Speaking the Silence of Women." *Signs* 16, no. 2 (Winter 1991): 205–37.

Humfrey, Peter. *Titian.* London: Phaidon, 2007.

Judson, J. Richard. *Dirck Barendsz., 1534–1592.* Amsterdam: Vangendt, 1970.

Korazija, Eva. *Eros und Gewalt Hendrik Goltzius und der niederländische Manirismus* [sic]. Zürich: Graphische Sammlung der Eidgenössischen Technischen Hochschule Zürich, 1982. Exhibition catalog.

Kossmann, Ernst Heinrich, comp. and ed. *Texts Concerning the Revolt of the Netherlands.* London: Cambridge University Press, 1974.

Kuijpers, Erika. "The Creation and Development of Social Memories of Traumatic Events: The Oudewater Massacre of 1575." In *Hurting Memories and Beneficial Forgetting: Posttraumatic Stress Disorders, Biographical Developments, and Social Conflicts*, edited by Michael Linden and Krzysztof Rutkowski, 191–201. New York: Elsevier, 2013.

Kunzle, David. *From Criminal to Courtier: The Soldier in Netherlandish Art 1550–1672.* Leiden: Brill, 2002.

Leeflang, Huigen. "The Life of Hendrick Goltzius." In *Hendrick Goltzius: Drawings, Prints, and Paintings (1558–1617)*, edited by Ger Luijten et al., 13–32. Zwolle: Waanders, 2003. Exhibition catalog.

———. "Various Manners of the Best Masters." In *Hendrick Goltzius: Drawings, Prints, and Paintings (1558–1617)*, edited by Ger Luijten et al., 33–56. Zwolle: Waanders, 2003. Exhibition catalog.

Livy. *A History of Rome: Selections.* Translated and with an introduction by Moses Hadas and Joe P. Poe. New York: Modern Library, 1962.

Lowenthal, Anne W. "Wtewael's Netherlandish History Reconsidered." *Netherlands Yearbook for History of Art* 38 (1987): 215–25.

Matthes, Melissa. *The Rape of Lucretia and the Founding of Republics: Readings in Livy, Machiavelli, and Rousseau.* University Park: Pennsylvania State University Press, 2000.

McGrath, Elizabeth. "A Netherlandish History by Joachim Wtewael." *Journal of the Warburg and Courtauld Institutes* 38 (1975): 182–21.

Mielke, Ursula, comp. *The New Hollstein: Dutch and Flemish Etchings, Engravings and Woodcuts, 1450–1700: Frans Hogenberg: Broadsheets.* Edited by Ger Luijten. Ouderkerk aan den Ijssel: Sound & Vision, 2009.

Newlands, Carole Elizabeth. *Playing with Time: Ovid and the Fasti.* Ithaca, NY: Cornell University Press, 1995.

Onuf, Alexandra. "Old Plates, New Impressions: Local Landscape Prints in Seventeenth-Century Antwerp." *Art Bulletin* 96, no. 4 (December 2014): 424–40.

Ovid. *Ovid's Fasti.* Edited and translated by James George Frazer. Cambridge: Harvard University Press, 1959.

Peacock, Martha Moffitt. "The Maid of Holland and Her Heroic Heiresses." In *Women and Gender in the Early Modern Low Countries*, edited by Sarah Joan Moran and Amanda Pipkin, 68–127. Leiden: Brill, 2019.

Pedrocco, Filippo. *Titian: The Complete Paintings.* London: Thames & Hudson, 2001.

Peeters, Natasja. "'Den quaden tyt'? The Artistic Career of the Young Ambrosius Francken before the Fall of Antwerp." *Oud Holland* 121, no. 2 (2008): 99–116.

Pipkin, Amanda. *Rape in the Republic: Formulating Dutch Identity.* Leiden: Brill, 2013.

———. "'They were not humans, but devils in human bodies': Depictions of Sexual Violence and Spanish Tyranny as a Means of Fostering Identity in the Dutch Republic." *Journal of Early Modern History* 13 (2009): 229–64.

Pollmann, Judith. *Memory in Early Modern Europe, 1500–1800.* Oxford: Oxford University Press, 2017.

Rublack, Ulinka. "Wench and Maiden: Women, War and the Pictorial Function of the Feminine in the German Cities in the Early Modern Period." *History Workshop Journal* 44 (Autumn 1997): 1–21.

Sandberg, Brian. "'Generous Amazons Came to the Breach': Besieged Women, Agency and Subjectivity during the French Wars of Religion." *Gender and History* 16, no. 3 (November 2004): 654–88.

Schubert, Dietrich. "Halbfigurige Lucretia-Tafeln der 1. Hälfte des 16. Jahrhunderts in den Niederlanden." *Jahrbuch des Kunsthistorischen Instituts der Universität Graz* 6 (1971): 99–110.

Schuler, Carol M. "Virtuous Model/Voluptuous Martyr: The Suicide of Lucretia in Northern Renaissance Art and Its Relationship to Late Medieval Devotional

Imagery." In *Saints, Sinners, and Sisters: Gender and Northern Art in Medieval and Early Modern Europe*, edited by Jane L. Carroll and Alison G. Stewart, 7–25. Burlington, VT: Ashgate, 2003.
Sellink, Manfred, comp. *The New Hollstein Dutch and Flemish Etchings, Engravings and Woodcuts, 1450–1700: Cornelis Cort*. Edited by Huigen Leeflang. Part 3. Rotterdam: Sound and Vision, 2000.
Spies, Marijke. "Verbeeldingen van vrijheid: David en Mozes, Burgerhart en Bato, Brutus en Cato." *De Zeventiende Eeuw* 10, no. 1 (1994): 141–58.
Stechow, Walter. "Lucretia Statua." In *Essays in Honor of Georg Swarzenski*, edited by Oswald Goetz, 114–24. Chicago: Henry Regnery, 1951.
Stone-Ferrier, Linda A. *Images of Textiles: The Weave of Seventeenth-Century Dutch Art and Society*. Ann Arbor: UMI Research Press, 1985.
Tanis, James, and Daniel Horst. *Images of Discord: A Graphic Interpretation of the Opening Decades of the Eighty Years' War*. Bryn Mawr, PA: Bryn Mawr College Library, 1993. Exhibition catalog.
Van der Heijden, Manon. "Women as Victims of Sexual and Domestic Violence in Seventeenth-Century Holland: Criminal Cases of Rape, Incest and Maltreatment in Rotterdam and Delft." *Journal of Social History* 33 (2000): 623–44.
Van Mander, Karel. *The Lives of the Illustrious Netherlandish and German Painters . . . With an Introduction and Translation*. Volume 1. Edited by Hessel Miedema. Translated by Derry Cook-Radmore. Doornspijk, Netherlands: Davaco, 1994–99.
Van Winter, P. J. "De Hollandse Tuin." *Netherlands Yearbook for History of Art* (1957): 29–121.
Veldman, Ilja M. "Lessons for Ladies: A Selection of Sixteenth and Seventeenth-Century Dutch Prints." *Simiolus: Netherlands Quarterly for the History of Art* 16, no. 2 (1986): 113–27.
Vetter, Ewald. *Maria im Rosenhag*. Dusseldorf: Schwann, 1956.
Wolfthal, Diane. *Images of Rape: The "Heroic" Tradition and Its Alternatives*. Cambridge: Cambridge University Press, 1990.

NOTES

1. Ovid, *Ovid's Fasti*, ed. and trans. James George Frazer (Cambridge: Harvard University Press, 1959), 2.725–852. Text cited according to book number and verse numbers.

2. Initially the treaty was signed by Holland, Zeeland, Utrecht, and the Ommelanden of Groningen. Later, Friesland, Overijssel, Drenthe, Flanders, and Brabant joined. The southern constituents were never more "than honorary external members," however. J. C. Boogman, "The Union of Utrecht: Its Genesis and Consequences," *BMGN—Low Countries Historical Review* 94, no. 3 (1979): 388. David Kunzle, *From Criminal to Courtier: The Soldier in Netherlandish Art 1550–1672* (Leiden: Brill, 2002), 188–89. Kunzle's viewpoint coincides with the catalog entry for the same plate from the 1982 exhibition *Eros und Gewalt: Hendrik Goltzius und*

der Niederländische Manierismus, which likewise verifies a connection between Lucretia's suicide and the founding of the Dutch Republic. Eva Korazija, *Eros und Gewalt Hendrik Goltzius und der niederländische Manirismus* [sic], exh. cat. (Zürich: Graphische Sammlung der Eidgenössischen Technischen Hochschule Zürich, 1982), 54–55, cat. 4.

3. Karin Hanika, "Lucretia als 'Damenopfer' patriarchaler Tugendkonzeptionen: Die vier Kupferstiche des Hendrik Goltzius," in *Eros, Macht, Askese: Geschlechterspannungen als Dialogstruktur in Kunst und Literatur*, ed. Helga Sciurie and Hans-Jürgen Bachorski (Trier: Wissenschaftlicher Verlag Trier, 1996), 396–422, esp. 419–21.

4. Huigen Leeflang, "Various Manners of the Best Masters," in *Hendrick Goltzius: Drawings, Prints, and Paintings (1558–1617)*, ed. Ger Luijten et al., exh. cat. (Zwolle: Waanders, 2003), 42, cat. 8.

5. For a comparative analysis of politics at play in Jörg Breu's *Lucretia*, see Pia F. Cuneo, "Jörg Breu the Elder's *Death of Lucretia*: History, Sexuality, and the State," in *Saints, Sinners, and Sisters: Gender and Northern Art in Medieval and Early Modern Europe*, ed. Jane L. Carroll and Alison G. Stewart (Burlington, VT: Ashgate, 2003), 26–43.

6. Steven Robert Golan, "Scenes from Roman Republican History in Seventeenth-Century Dutch Art" (PhD diss., Wittenberg University, 1984), 16.

7. Leeflang, "Various Manners of the Best Masters," 42.

8. Beginning in 1569, artists such as Frans Hogenberg and his son Abraham set their etching needles to work, narrating the events of the conflict from an "objective" perspective.

9. Livy, *A History of Rome: Selections,* trans. and with introduction by Moses Hadas and Joe P. Poe (New York: Modern Library, 1962), 1.57–60. Text cited according to book number and verse numbers. Ovid, *Fasti*, 2.725–852. For a summary of classical accounts of Lucretia, see Ian Donaldson, *The Rapes of Lucretia: A Myth and Its Transformations* (Oxford: Clarendon Press, 1982), 5–8.

10. Ovid, *Fasti*, 2.739–40.

11. Ovid, *Fasti*, 2.787.

12. Ovid, *Fasti*, 2.784.

13. Ovid, *Fasti*, 2.809. See Linda C. Hults, "Dürer's 'Lucretia': Speaking the Silence of Women," *Signs* 16, no. 2 (Winter 1991): 206n2.

14. Translation of accompanying captions provided in Leeflang, "Various Manners of the Best Masters," 40. Translation modified.

15. Leeflang, "Various Manners of the Best Masters," 40.

16. For a comparison of the two versions, see Carole Elizabeth Newlands, *Playing with Time: Ovid and the Fasti* (Ithaca, NY: Cornell University Press, 1995), 146–74, esp. 146–48.

17. Hanika contends that Goltzius's reliance on Ovid's words obfuscates a political reading of the series. Hanika, "Lucretia als 'Damenopfer,'" 420.

18. Amanda Pipkin, *Rape in the Republic: Formulating Dutch Identity* (Leiden: Brill, 2013), 4.

19. This idea is extrapolated upon by Diane Wolfthal, *Images of Rape: The "Heroic" Tradition and Its Alternatives* (Cambridge: Cambridge University Press, 1990), 23n90, though she gives credit to Margaret Carroll. See Margaret Carroll, "The Erotics of Absolutism: Rubens and the Mystification of Sexual Violence," *Representations* 25 (Winter 1989): 3–30.

20. Pipkin, *Rape in the Republic*, 18; Wolfthal, *Images of Rape*, 1–6.

21. Pipkin, *Rape in the Republic*, 18.

22. Amanda Pipkin, "'They were not humans, but devils in human bodies': Depictions of Sexual Violence and Spanish Tyranny as a Means of Fostering Identity in the Dutch Republic," *Journal of Early Modern History* 13 (2009): 235n15. Melissa Matthes, *The Rape of Lucretia and the Founding of Republics: Readings in Livy, Machiavelli, and Rousseau* (University Park: Pennsylvania State University Press, 2000), 4–5.

23. See rape as royal prerogative in Carroll, "The Erotics of Absolutism," 3–30; Cuneo, "Jörg Breu the Elder's *Death of Lucretia*," 26–43.

24. Matthes, *Rape of Lucretia*, 28.

25. Augustine discusses Lucretia in his *City of God* (ca. 413 CE). For further discussion of Augustine's writings on Lucretia, see Donaldson, *Rapes of Lucretia*, 28–39.

26. Daniela Hammer-Tugendhat, *The Visible and the Invisible: On Seventeenth-Century Dutch Painting*, trans. Margarethe Clausen (Berlin: De Gruyter, 2015), 63; Ilja M. Veldman, "Lessons for Ladies: A Selection of Sixteenth and Seventeenth-Century Dutch Prints," *Simiolus: Netherlands Quarterly for the History of Art* 16, no. 2 (1986): 120–21.

27. Walter Stechow, "Lucretia Statua," in *Essays in Honor of Georg Swarzenski*, ed. Oswald Goetz (Chicago: Henry Regnery, 1951), 114.

28. Dietrich Schubert, "Halbfigurige Lucretia-Tafeln der 1. Hälfte des 16. Jahrhunderts in den Niederlanden," *Jahrbuch des Kunsthistorischen Instituts der Universität Graz* 6 (1971): 99–110.

29. For analysis of these images in light of devotional imagery, see Carol M. Schuler, "Virtuous Model/Voluptuous Martyr: The Suicide of Lucretia in Northern Renaissance Art and Its Relationship to Late Medieval Devotional Imagery," in *Saints, Sinners, and Sisters: Gender and Northern Art in Medieval and Early Modern Europe*, ed. Jane L. Carroll and Alison G. Stewart (Burlington, VT: Ashgate, 2003), 7–25.

30. Hammer-Tugendhat, *The Visible and the Invisible*, 68.

31. Hammer-Tugendhat, *The Visible and the Invisible*, 65n148.

32. This argument is made in Pipkin, *Rape in the Republic*, 45–55, with a concise summary of her arguments on 81.

33. Pipkin, *Rape in the Republic*, 21n73.

34. Hammer-Tugendhat, *The Visible and the Invisible*, 72, n173; Manon van der Heijden, "Women as Victims of Sexual and Domestic Violence in Seventeenth-Century Holland: Criminal Cases of Rape, Incest and Maltreatment in Rotterdam and Delft," *Journal of Social History* 33 (2000): 624.

35. Quoted and translated in Pipkin, *Rape in the Republic*, 51–52n48.

36. Pipkin, *Rape in the Republic*, 70. The anonymous treatise *Political Education* and Hugo Grotius's tract *Commentary on the Law of Prize and Booty* (1604–05) more concretely connect the king's subjugation with sexual assault, as noted by Pipkin, 52–53. See also Peter J. Arnade, *Beggars, Iconoclasts, and Civic Patriots: The Political Culture of the Dutch Revolt* (Ithaca, NY: Cornell University Press, 2008), 222–25.

37. Ursula Mielke, comp., *The New Hollstein: Dutch and Flemish Etchings, Engravings and Woodcuts, 1450–1700: Frans Hogenberg: Broadsheets*, ed. Ger Luijten (Ouderkerk aan den Ijssel: Sound & Vision, 2009), cat. B102.

38. Translated in Erika Kuijpers, "The Creation and Development of Social Memories of Traumatic Events: The Oudewater Massacre of 1575," in *Hurting Memories and Beneficial Forgetting: Posttraumatic Stress Disorders, Biographical Developments, and Social Conflicts*, ed. Michael Linden and Krzysztof Rutkowski (New York: Elsevier, 2013), 194.

39. Pipkin, *Rape in the Republic*, 63.

40. Kuijpers, "The Creation and Development of Social Memories," 195. Judith Pollmann also discusses the print in *Memory in Early Modern Europe, 1500–1800* (Oxford: Oxford University Press, 2017), 170–71.

41. Pipkin, *Rape in the Republic*, 70.

42. Pipkin, *Rape in the Republic*, 40.

43. Ernst Heinrich Kossmann, comp. and ed., *Texts Concerning the Revolt of the Netherlands* (London: Cambridge University Press, 1974), 166.

44. For a further discussion of the Netherlandish fatherland during the early years of the Revolt, see Alastair Duke, "In Defense of the Common Fatherland: Patriotism and Liberty in the Low Countries, 1555–1576," in *Networks, Regions, and Nations*, ed. Robert Stein and Judith Pollmann (Leiden: Brill, 2010), 217–39.

45. Pipkin, "'They were not humans,'" 236.

46. Leeflang, "Various Manners of the Best Masters," 42n43; Marijke Spies, "Verbeeldingen van vrijheid: David en Mozes, Burgerhart en Bato, Brutus en Cato," *De Zeventiende Eeuw* 10, no. 1 (1994): 151–52.

47. Leeflang, "Various Manners of the Best Masters," 40.

48. Leeflang, "Various Manners of the Best Masters," 40.

49. For a brief history of the siege, see Arnade, *Beggars*, 236–40.

50. Ulinka Rublack, "Wench and Maiden: Women, War and the Pictorial Function of the Feminine in the German Cities in the Early Modern Period," *History Workshop Journal* 44 (Autumn 1997): 1–21; Brian Sandberg, "'Generous Amazons Came to the Breach': Besieged Women, Agency and Subjectivity during the French Wars of Religion," *Gender and History* 16, no. 3 (November 2004): 654–88.

51. Karel van Mander, *The Lives of the Illustrious Netherlandish and German Painters . . . With an Introduction and Translation*, ed. Hessel Miedema, trans. Derry Cook-Radmore (Doornspijk, Netherlands: Davaco, 1994–99), vol. 1, fol. 284r, 30–31.

52. J. Richards Judson suggests that Goltzius might have "borrowed" the idea of using modern clothes from Dirck Barendsz., who had used contemporary Venetian costume in *Mankind Awaiting the Last Judgment*, ca. 1581, pen and brown ink drawing, 336 x 490 mm, inv. no. DYCE.442, Victoria & Albert Museum, London. J. Richard Judson, *Dirck Barendsz., 1534–1592* (Amsterdam: Vangendt, 1970), 33nn1–4.

53. This is suggested by Leeflang, "Various Manners of the Best Masters," 42. Hendrick Goltzius, *Jan Goltz II*, 1578, engraving. 14.9 x 10 cm, Princeton University Art Museum, Princeton, inv. no. x1934-631.

54. Goltzius likely derived the diagonal table from Venetian prototypes. Leeflang, "Various Manners of the Best Masters," 41n35.

55. Hendrick Goltzius, *The Banquet of Sextus Tarquinius*, ca. 1578-80, pen in gray and black, brush in gray, brown in foreground over black chalk, 193 x 253 mm, inv. no. Z 235, Herzog Anton Ulrich-Museum, Graphische Sammlung, Braunschweig.

56. This is a fact also noted by Hanika, "Lucretia als 'Damenopfer,'" 412. For a summary of previous attributions, see Hanika, 412n18.

57. Leeflang, "Various Manners of the Best Masters," 40.

58. Hanika, "Lucretia als 'Damenopfer,'" 413.

59. Ovid, *Fasti*, 2.739-40.

60. Livy describes them "whiling their time away in luxurious banqueting with their young friends." Livy, *History of Rome*, 1.57.

61. Lucretia's textile work also recalls Homer's *Odyssey*, where daily, Penelope weaves a burial shroud for Odysseus's father, while waiting for the return of Odysseus.

62. Linda A. Stone-Ferrier, *Images of Textiles: The Weave of Seventeenth-Century Dutch Art and Society* (Ann Arbor: UMI Research Press, 1985), 83-95. The Madonna "spun" a body for Christ in her womb as a veil of flesh.

63. Proverbs 31:13. For another example of women engaged in textile activities, see Philips Galle after Pieter Bruegel, *Parable of the Wise and Foolish Virgins*, 1558-65, engraving, 223 x 290 mm, inv no. RP-P-OB-7381, Rijksmuseum, Amsterdam. For a brief discussion, see Veldman, "Lessons for Ladies," 115.

64. Cordula Grewe, "Shaping Reality through the Fictive: Images of Women Spinning in the Northern Renaissance," *RACAR: Canadian Art Review* 19, no. 1 (1992): 9-10. For a discussion of spinning and seventeenth-century moralizing tracts, see Wayne E. Franits, *Paragons of Virtue: Women and Domesticity in Seventeenth-Century Dutch Art* (Cambridge: Cambridge University Press, 1993), 29-31, 71-73.

65. Ovid, *Fasti*, 2.762.

66. Hendrick Goltzius, *Lucretia and the Women Spinning*, 1578, pen in black, gray wash, 195 x 249 mm, inv. no. Z 236, Herzog Anton Ulrich-Museum, Braunschweig.

67. Hanika, "Lucretia als 'Damenopfer,'" 407n11.

68. Filippo Pedrocco, *Titian: The Complete Paintings* (London: Thames & Hudson, 2001), 297, cat. 260.

69. Peter Humfrey, *Titian* (London: Phaidon, 2007), 186.

70. Norman Bryson, "Two Narratives of Rape in the Visual Arts: Lucretia and the Sabine Women," in *Rape: An Historical and Social Enquiry*, ed. Sylvana Tomaselli and Roy Porter (Oxford: Blackwell, 1989), 169.

71. There is a seventeenth-century engraved and enlarged copy in reverse published by Gian Giacomo de Rossi. Manfred Sellink, comp., *The New Hollstein Dutch and Flemish Etchings, Engravings and Woodcuts, 1450-1700: Cornelis Cort*, ed. Huigen Leeflang, part 3 (Rotterdam: Sound and Vision, 2000), no. 191.

72. Pipkin, *Rape in the Republic*, 63.

73. Hanika, "Lucretia als 'Damenopfer,'" 401.

74. Leeflang, "Various Manners of the Best Masters," 40.
75. Hults, "Dürer's 'Lucretia,'" 222–23.
76. J. Richardson Judson notes that the kneeling figure is related to the servant in the same pose in a print by Dirck Barendsz.: Jan Sadeler after Dirck Barendsz., *Mankind before the Flood*, ca. 1600, engraving, inv. no. R4852, Harvard Art Museums, Boston. See Judson, *Dirck Barendsz.*, 33n4.
77. Leeflang, "Various Manners of the Best Masters," 42. In the second state, the first plate of the series contains a title: LVCRETIAE ROMANE HISTORIA.
78. The association was first noted in Hanika, "Lucretia als 'Damenopfer,'" 402.
79. Hanika, "Lucretia als 'Damenopfer,'" 404.
80. Hanika, "Lucretia als 'Damenopfer,'" 404.
81. Matthes, *Rape of Lucretia*, 6. Translation modified.
82. Alastair Duke, "The Elusive Netherlands: The Question of National Identity in the Early Modern Low Countries on the Eve of the Revolt," *BMGN—Low Countries Historical Review* 119 (2004): 18n43. For her iconography, see Yasui Ayumi, "Belgica: Personification of the Low Countries in Prints during the Eighty Years' War," *Bulletin of Kanazawa College of Art* 53 (2009): 11–23; Elizabeth McGrath, "A Netherlandish History by Joachim Wtewael," *Journal of the Warburg and Courtauld Institutes* 38 (1975): 185. Joachim Wtewael produced a series of drawings narrating the history of the Netherlands with Belgica as the protagonist. McGrath dates them to 1610, but Anne W. Lowenthal contends that they were made between 1622 and 1625. Anne W. Lowenthal, "Wtewael's Netherlandish History Reconsidered," *Netherlands Yearbook for History of Art* 38 (1987): 215–25. Sometimes Belgica also takes on the attributes of Patientia.
83. The engraving has been discussed in passing. See Kunzle, *From Criminal to Courtier*, 145–46; Ann Diels and Marjolein Leesberg, comps., *The New Hollstein: Dutch and Flemish Etchings, Engravings and Woodcuts, 1450–1700: Collaert Dynasty*, ed. Marjolein Leesberg and Arnout Balis, part 5 (Ouderkerk aan den Ijssel: Sound and Vision, 2005–06), 198–90, no. 1213; James Tanis and Daniel Horst, *Images of Discord: A Graphic Interpretation of the Opening Decades of the Eighty Years' War*, exh. cat. (Bryn Mawr, PA: Bryn Mawr College Library, 1993), 105–06, no. 25; Natasja Peeters, "'Den quaden tyt'? The Artistic Career of the Young Ambrosius Francken before the Fall of Antwerp," *Oud Holland* 121, no. 2 (2008): 102–04; Daniel Horst, *De Opstand in zwart-wit: Propagandaprenten uit de Nederlandse Opstand (1566–1584)* (Zutphen: Walburg Pers, 2003), 179–81; Pipkin, *Rape in the Republic*, 73, who connects the scene of rape to Vondel's play *Gijsbrecht*; Alexandra Onuf, "Old Plates, New Impressions: Local Landscape Prints in Seventeenth-Century Antwerp," *Art Bulletin* 96, no. 4 (December 2014): 435. Dutch, Latin, and French inscriptions describe the horrors of war.
84. For a study of the violence wrought on peasants during the war, see Jane Susannah Fishman, *Boerenverdriet: Violence between Peasants and Soldiers in Early Modern Netherlandish Art* (Ann Arbor: UMI Research Press, 1979).
85. Duke, "Patriotism and Liberty," 239.
86. For the evolution of the Maid of Holland and the rise of female Dutch Revolt symbols, see Martha Moffitt Peacock, "The Maid of Holland and Her Heroic

Heiresses," in *Women and Gender in the Early Modern Low Countries*, ed. Sarah Joan Moran and Amanda Pipkin (Leiden: Brill, 2019), 68–127; P. J. Van Winter, "De Hollandse Tuin," *Netherlands Yearbook for History of Art* 8 (1957): 29–121. On the hortus conclusus, see Ewald Vetter, *Maria im Rosenhag* (Dusseldorf: Schwann, 1956). In 1595–1597 the city of Dordrecht donated a stained glass window of the Maid of Holland as a token of friendship to its fellow rebellious city of Gouda.

87. Peacock, "Maid of Holland," 78.

88. Mieke Bal, *Looking In: The Art of Viewing* (London: Routledge, 2001), 100–01. Bal also offers a rhetorical analysis of Lucretia's suicide through metonymy and synecdoche.

89. Bal, *Looking In*, 100.

90. Bal, *Looking In*, 99.

91. Others have noticed this Orangist trend. See Huigen Leeflang, "The Life of Hendrick Goltzius," in *Hendrick Goltzius: Drawings, Prints, and Paintings (1558–1617)*, ed. Ger Luijten et al., exh. cat. (Zwolle: Waanders, 2003), 16. Pro-Orangist figures include Jan van Broekhoven, Jan van Duvenvoorde, Françoise van Egmond, Jacques de la Faille, Josina Hamels, Gerrit de Jong, Adriaan Manmaker, Jaspar van Poelgeest, Jan Baptist van Renesse, Adriaen van Swieten, and Adriaen van Westcapelle. Foreign leaders espousing political leanings in favor of the Dutch include Frederik II, Henry IV, Robert Dudley (Earl of Leicester), and Heinrich von Rantzau.

92. Beth Holman, "Goltzius's Great Hercules: Mythology, Art, and Politics," *Netherlands Yearbook for History of Art* 42–43 (1991–92): 397–412. David Kunzle reads several of Goltzius's prints, such as his *Allegories of Faith* (1578) series and *Allegory of War* (1578), as politically motivated works. Kunzle, *From Criminal to Courtier*, 188–203.

Chapter Eight

Landscape and the Memory of Place in Claes Jansz. Visscher's Prints of Brabant

Alexandra Onuf

Claes Visscher's (1587–1652) title page for the *Regiunculae et Villae Aliquot Ducatus Brabantiae* introduces a series of landscape prints that he etched and published in Amsterdam in 1612 (Fig. 8.1).¹ Setting the tone for the

Figure 8.1 Claes Jansz. Visscher, Title page to *Regiunculae, et Villae Aliquot Ducatus Brabantiae . . .* series, 1612. Etching, 100 x 155 mm, Andrew W. Mellon Fund, National Gallery of Art, Washington, D.C., inv. no. 1975.59.1. Source: Image © by courtesy NGA Images.

images to follow, the title page presents a simple rustic scene. In the center stands a thatch-roofed barn with a large sheet tacked to the wall, on which is printed the series title and publication details in Latin. Translated, it reads "some places and villas of the duchy of Brabant, designed by P. Bruegel, and for the sake of painters etched and published by Nicolas Johannes Visscher, Amsterdam." The date 1612 is scratched into a rough dirt road just in front of the barn. Bordered by a dilapidated fence and a stand of trees, the road leads from the right foreground toward the left, passing over a slight rise and opening onto a vista of a larger farmstead with a dovecote in the distance. To the right of the barn stands an oversized peasant with a feathered cap, codpiece, and bagpipe, who leans on a walking stick and looks off along the roadway. For all its apparent simplicity, the title page is notable in several ways. First, the title's text states that the prints in the series present views of Brabant, a Netherlandish province far to the south of Amsterdam. Unlike the typical focus on imaginary or ideal landscape imagery, these prints purport to represent specific real locations—"places and villas"—in this distant Southern province. Second, the title page attributes the designs for the prints to the long-deceased Pieter Bruegel (ca.1525–1569), surely the most famed Brabantine artist of the sixteenth century. This attribution is underscored visually by the peasant at right, who follows a familiar Bruegelian type.[2] Bruegel was known for his peasant scenes and landscapes, both in paintings and prints, and by 1612 his artistic reputation and posthumous legacy were fully established.[3] This attribution "dates" the views to a previous era, even as the title page clearly states the series was published in 1612. Visscher's title page thus advertises his landscape series as representing both a distant region and an earlier time.

These apparent anomalies of place and time are explained by an important fact that the title page does not advertise: the prints in Visscher's series are not based on his own original designs but are rather carefully copied versions of an earlier set of landscape prints known as the *Small Landscapes*, first published in Antwerp in 1559 and 1561.[4] Visscher etched his own copies of these prints, carefully replicating the subjects and compositions of the original prints at a slightly reduced scale. Hieronymus Cock (1518–1570), the original publisher of the series, had also identified the prints as Brabantine, drawn "mostly around Antwerp."[5] He did not, however, attribute the designs to Bruegel, even though he worked closely with the artist and did publish several prints after his designs in precisely the same years.[6] Visscher likely made this connection to Bruegel to capitalize on the artist's posthumous legacy while also underscoring the authenticity of the local Brabantine scenes drawn by the most famous artist of the region.

Taken on its own, the *Regiunculae* series might be considered a commercial experiment, a bid made by a young printmaker and publisher to establish his nascent business. After all, Visscher had just set up his shop in the Kalverstraat in Amsterdam the previous year, in 1611.[7] However, this series was not a singular undertaking, but rather part of a larger effort to publish earlier Brabantine landscapes. In addition to his copies of the *Small Landscapes*, he reprinted two other sets of views of the rural surroundings of Brussels and Antwerp. These series had also been first published in Antwerp (though slightly later than the *Small Landscapes*) in the 1580s by the printmaker and publisher Hans van Luyck (1518–after 1595).[8] Visscher attributed the Brussels series, likewise unattributed in its initial publication, to the Flemish artist Hans Bol (1534–1593), second only to Bruegel in his fame in seventeenth-century Holland, probably with much the same intent to underscore the series' artistic value and topographic authenticity.[9] In the Antwerp series, Visscher maintained the original attribution to Jacob Grimmer (1525–1590), an artist native to Antwerp who was best known for his landscapes.[10] Taken together, Visscher's efforts resulted in the republication of over sixty sixteenth-century Brabantine landscape views in early seventeenth-century Holland, an extraordinary output for a relatively new genre of rural landscape imagery.[11]

Republishing older prints was in no way exceptional among seventeenth-century print publishers; in fact, Visscher himself rapidly expanded his stock through these means, not just with landscapes, but across many genres of imagery, including historical prints, cartographic images, biblical representations, and genre scenes.[12] Nonetheless, it is notable that one of Visscher's first major initiatives as a publisher was his campaign to reprint and reissue Brabantine landscapes originally published in the Southern Netherlandish printing capital of Antwerp in the middle of the previous century. Taken together, these three series represent a sudden and substantial revival of sixteenth-century Brabantine topographic landscape imagery in early seventeenth-century Holland. This begs the question: what was the impetus for Visscher's concerted publishing program of so many Brabantine landscape prints so long after their initial publication and in the new context of the nascent Dutch Republic?

Visscher's deliberate campaign was not simply an effort to establish a specialized field for himself as a print publisher; he also understood that these images would carry a particular topical resonance in the 1610s. This chapter will investigate Visscher's Brabantine landscape series within the historical and political moment in which he published them, namely during the fraught early years of the Twelve Years' Truce (1609–1621). Four decades into the Eighty Years' War between the Spanish Habsburg rulers and the Netherlandish rebels, the prints preserved and re-presented images of a

Brabantine countryside that no longer existed after long decades of violent revolt. In this respect, they actively participated in a larger negotiation of memory and meaning-making necessitated by the upheavals of the Dutch Revolt. Drawing upon the burgeoning field of early modern memory studies, this chapter considers these prints as active agents in this process.[13] The appearance of these reprinted landscapes of Brabant in Holland constructed visual loci for the dynamic construction of historical memory at precisely the juncture when, thanks to the truce, the northern United Provinces were effectively politically separated from their Southern Netherlandish counterparts, which remained under Spanish jurisdiction. But even as the prints functioned as sites of memory or nostalgia, they also served as conduits through which the past could be appropriated and employed in the present. As such, the prints visually underscore both the rupture and continuity between South and North at this critical and tendentious political moment. In registering the nuances and specifics of places now distant both in time and space, Visscher's reissued Brabantine prints were both retrospective and generative, affording audiences in seventeenth-century Holland a visual medium through which to negotiate past experiences of violence and displacement wrought by the Revolt into new narratives of political and geographic identity.

A PRECARIOUS PEACE: THE AMBIVALENCE OF THE TWELVE YEARS' TRUCE

The Twelve Years' Truce, signed in Antwerp in April 1609, brought a temporary peace in the long war between the Spanish Netherlands and the nascent Dutch Republic, which had been underway since 1566.[14] The Eighty Years' War, motivated by both political and confessional disputes, had been in essence both a civil war among factions within the seventeen Netherlandish provinces and a revolt against their Spanish rulers. The truce brought a welcome if temporary hiatus in the conflict and allowed travel and communication across borders that had long been treacherous or completely blocked. Moreover, the truce was the first official recognition of the seven independent Northern provinces, separate from the Southern ones that remained under Spanish rule. In coming to terms, the peace treaty confirmed a de facto political and territorial division between the Northern and Southern Netherlands even as it relaxed and opened the physical borders between them.

The signing of the truce occasioned jubilant celebrations in both the South and the North. Jasper van der Steen cites several contemporary accounts that record "bonfires, government proclamations of thanksgiving, bell-ringing, blazing tar barrels, celebratory sermons, commemorative prints and medals [that] demonstrated public relief about the laying down of arms in many cities in the Low Countries."[15] The States General in Holland sponsored such a day of thanksgiving "after such a long, incessant and bloody civil war of forty years."[16] Almost every part of the Netherlands had suffered from the ongoing hostilities. The Habsburg army and the rebels waged major campaigns and battles along the shifting front lines of the war, capturing and often sacking cities throughout the 1570s and 1580s. Major cities had suffered long and devastating sieges, including most notably Haarlem (1572–1573), Leiden (1573–1574), and later Antwerp (1584–1585), before the latter fell to Alexander Farnese's troops in 1585.[17] Soldiers, both under military orders and during periods of mutiny or desertion, laid waste to both cities and the countryside. The Sack of Antwerp (1576) is perhaps the most notorious instance of such devastation, but even the regular billeting and provisioning of garrisons on both sides proved costly and onerous for urban civilians and their rural counterparts alike.[18] Troops often ransacked homes and farms, confiscated property, and torched crops as they rampaged through the countryside.

This extreme and arbitrary violence led to popular outpourings of lament in popular song, verse, and imagery, as in this print designed by Ambrosius Francken (1544–1618) and engraved by Hans Collaert I (ca. 1525–1580), in

Figure 8.2 Hans Collaert I after Ambrosius Francken, *Lament over the Desolation of the Netherlands*, ca. 1570–1580. Engraving, 434 x 572 mm, Museum Plantin-Moretus / Prentenkabinet, Antwerp, inv. no. PK.OP.18283. Source: Image © by courtesy Museum Plantin-Moretus, Antwerp–UNESCO, World Heritage / Photo: Peter Maes.

which an allegorical figure of Belgica is beset by rapacious soldiers while cities burn and farmers fend off soldiers in the background landscape (Fig. 8.2).[19] This print is notable not just for the clear representation of the devastating consequences of war, but also because it includes the coats of arms of all seventeen provinces, strung along a cord at the top of the image. At the center, a figure of Fiducia (Trust) tries to hold the fraying cord together as figures of Dissidentia (Distrust) and Invidia (Jealousy) pull it apart at its two ends. The image suggests that war was not just wreaking havoc on cities, towns, and the countryside; it was pulling apart the provinces of the Netherlands that would otherwise be connected by some natural cord of unity.

It is therefore unsurprising that initially, many celebrated the Twelve Years' Truce not just because of the cessation of hostilities, but also because it offered the prospect of a newly peaceful and united Netherlands. In Antwerp, Judith Pollmann reports, a procession commemorating the peace treaty featured another figure of Belgica with a lion at her feet, proclaiming that the divided Netherlands had once more been made whole.[20] The perceived notion of renewed unity among the provinces was also commemorated in cartographic form. Claes Visscher, who published maps as well as landscape prints, issued a grand *Leo Belgicus* map in 1611, showing all seventeen provinces within the contours of the rampant lion (Fig. 8.3). The map is framed by the coats of arms of each province along the top border and small profile views of all the major Netherlandish cities along its sides. Allegorical figures of the Southern and Northern provinces embrace in the left corner as they trample Oude Twist (Old Dispute) beneath their feet. Opposite them, in the lower right corner, a figure of Slapende Oorlogh (Sleeping War) nods off, lulled by the newly established peace and harmony among the provinces. Several single-sheet prints published in this period likewise commemorated the truce as the triumph of unity and peace over strife and conflict.[21]

The notion of a united Netherlands had long been especially resonant among the enormous population of Southern émigrés who had moved to cities in Northern provinces since the start of the war. As Jan Briels has shown, Southerners began emigrating to the Northern provinces in huge waves from the 1570s on, seeking refuge from oppressive Spanish rule and religious persecution, economic hardship, and the ravages of war unleashed by the Revolt. Briels calculated that at least 46,000 people emigrated from Antwerp to the North between 1578 and 1589 alone, mostly settling in Amsterdam.[22] This unprecedented migration was significant enough to shift the mercantile and artistic center of gravity from Antwerp to Amsterdam, which had been something of a backwater in the sixteenth century but saw its commercial star rise in the seventeenth, particularly after it abjured the Spanish crown in 1578.[23] In some Northern towns and cities, Southern migrants as much as doubled the local population; for instance, in Haarlem the population had

Landscape and the Memory of Place   205

Figure 8.3 Claes Jansz. Visscher, *Novissima, et Accuratissima Leonis Belgici* . . . , ca. 1611. Etching and engraving, 480 x 580 mm, The David Rumsey Map Collection, Stanford University, inv. no. G6011.A5 1611.V5. Source: Image © by courtesy Stanford University.

been decimated by the Spanish siege in 1572–1573 and a devastating fire in 1576. But thereafter the city grew from 18,000 to roughly 40,000 inhabitants in 1622, largely on the strength of the migration of Southern linen weavers, yarn bleachers, and merchants.[24] In total, there may have been some 100,000 or more Flemish and Brabantine exiles in the Republic. Most of these exiles were Protestants forced to leave their hometowns after Alexander Farnese's campaign to retake the rebellious cities in the South in the 1580s. In Antwerp, for example, after the city's Calvinist government fell to Farnese's siege in 1585, citizens were given the option either to revert to Catholicism or to settle their affairs and leave the city within four years.[25]

Initially, these immigrants often perceived their relocation as temporary and did not necessarily or immediately adopt their residence in the North as a permanent resettlement. Indeed, as Johannes Müller has persuasively argued, this first generation of migrants often held out hope, even over decades, that they would one day be able to return to their lost homelands once their

Southern compatriots finally threw off the yoke of Spanish tyranny and the Netherlands were reunited.[26] The war, after all, was ongoing, and the tides had turned many times before. All the way up through the negotiation of the Twelve Years' Truce in 1609 and even in the years afterward, Southern exiles advocated vociferously for continued resistance to and war against Spain. For them, the restoration of the unified *patria* of the Netherlands was the only way to assure their own return home.

This rhetoric of unification had circulated throughout the first decades of the Revolt, as evident in the Francken print illustrated above. It drew upon pamphlets circulated by William of Orange (1533–1584) and his adherents in the 1560s that championed the notion of a united Netherlandish vaderland (fatherland), held together by a natural common bond and steadfast against the alien (Spanish) forces that threatened it, an argument that enjoyed a renewed and widespread popular appeal at the turn of the century.[27] In the early seventeenth century and especially in years leading up to the truce, the calls for reunification focused heavily on xenophobic attacks against the Spanish. These attacks emphasized not just the cruelty of Spain's military leaders and king, but also the very character of the Spanish people, drawing on and expanding the long tradition of the Black Legend to make the case that true patriots should continue to fight against the Spanish scourge.[28] Even continued war, with all its hardships, was preferable to a "crooked peace" with such unreliable adversaries.[29]

Thus, the implications of the truce were conflicted and complicated from its very outset. On the one hand, the truce was widely welcomed and celebrated, as the newly reopened borders allowed travel between cities and provinces in the North and Antwerp and other Southern locales for the first time in a generation. Trade resumed, forced military contributions and levies were curtailed, property could be reclaimed, and old financial dealings resolved. Beyond this, exiles hoped that the newly reopened borders and the renewed social and familial contacts they allowed might finally rally their Southern compatriots to their cause and convince them to cast off the yoke of Spanish rule. However, Judith Pollmann has demonstrated just how disorienting and fraught these renewed contacts actually were, as families and neighbors who had lived apart for decades came to recognize the degree to which they each had changed in the meantime: "yet such visits were of course also a confrontation with the different paths that the Northern and Southern Netherlands had taken since 1585," especially in confessional beliefs.[30] The myth of the unified *patria*, one of the key rhetorical mechanisms underlying the framing of the war effort and employed by exiles to maintain hope for an eventual homecoming, ran headlong into the reality that North and South had developed into two distinct and increasingly distant cultural and confessional communities. Müller argues that it was at precisely this juncture, after the signing of the truce and the reopening of the borders, that exiles in the North finally had to renounce their longstanding hopes of real reunification. For the exiles found that, despite their best efforts to wake up their compatriots to the tyrannical threat of their Spanish overlords, their Southern brethren were, on the contrary, perfectly content under their Spanish rulers and had no desire to throw off the supposed yoke of oppression. Ultimately, their campaign to demonize the Spaniards succeeded only in articulating the growing and increasingly unbridgeable distance between North and South, thus hastening the break they specifically sought to avoid and ameliorate. Thus, "exiles lived in no man's land between political reality and nostalgia for the past—a great river that now divided the Netherlands for which they claimed to have fought, a river that was at long last to become a divider of cultures."[31] The truce served, then, not as a means of reunifying the natural Netherlandish *patria*, but rather as the turning point that initiated the cleaving of the Netherlands into two separate polities.

However, the truce was by its very terms temporary, set to expire in 1621. Even as the truce reopened contact between the Southern and Northern Netherlands, causing exiles to re-examine their assumptions about and hopes for the future unity of the whole Netherlands, it also quickly became a period of intense internal political contestation *within* the Northern Netherlands. Without the immediate external military threat of the war against Spain, competing factions developed within the nascent Dutch Republic that argued for very different confessional, political, and military positions. While the struggle between the Remonstrants and the Counter-Remonstrants began as a fairly narrow dispute over the Protestant religious doctrine of predestination in 1610, it soon expanded to align with divergent political factions during the period of the truce. One faction favored peace with Spain (the Remonstrants) while the other advocated for continuing to prosecute the war (the Counter-Remonstrants), the position favored by most hardline exiles who sought the complete defeat and withdrawal of the Spaniards from their former homelands. This conflict led to the brink of civil war before the Counter-Remonstrants, with the of backing of Stadholder Maurice of Nassau, ultimately gained control and quashed the Remonstrant cause, executing, imprisoning, and exiling its leaders in 1618.[32] Thus, the duration of the truce was anything but a period of social harmony and political consensus—not between the Northern and Southern Netherlands, nor within the newly recognized Dutch Republic. Indeed, the goals and consequences of both the war and the truce had not yet cohered into a clear or singular narrative.

It is in this context that we turn to reconsider the role of Visscher's several series of Brabantine landscape prints, as they were all published at precisely this juncture of political uncertainty, volatility, and change. While art historians traditionally assessed the art of the Dutch Golden Age as a strictly art-historical development, following its own internal imperatives and separate from or only tangentially affected by the backdrop of these current political realities, more recent scholars have taken a broader view. Beginning with the work of Simon Schama, scholars have made the case that artistic development could both reflect contemporary political and cultural currents and indeed also help to shape them.[33] H. Perry Chapman has argued that in the particular context of the Twelve Years' Truce we see that artistic production—even and especially "private" art that has traditionally been excluded from such contextual political analysis—could indeed carry political resonances in a moment when public opinion was increasingly influenced by broadsheets, pamphlets, and propaganda prints, which often incorporated visual imagery.[34] In other words, images that we might assume were valued for their aesthetic qualities in a private context might well have also borne political implications, especially in this precarious and contentious moment in the nascent Dutch Republic.

In this sense, images could and did participate in a much broader cultural and political discourse. While broadsheets and similarly topical imagery responded to immediate contemporary events, images could also take up and recontextualize older compositions to consolidate and frame memories of the past, especially contested narratives related to the ongoing war. Indeed, Marianne Eekhout has gone further to demonstrate that all kinds of objects of material culture—not just images, but also physical objects like cooking pots and cannonballs—participated in discourses, both public and private, related to memorializing events of the war and determining their meanings.[35] Reissued and remediated, Visscher's Brabantine prints offered unique sites through which Southern exiles and native Hollanders alike were able simultaneously to dwell in places of the past and to negotiate the rapidly evolving political and social circumstances of the present.

BRABANTINE LANDSCAPES RENEWED

The original plates for the *Small Landscape* prints that Hieronymus Cock had issued in 1559 and 1561 remained in Antwerp in the hands of Philips Galle (1537–1612) and his heirs, who reissued three more editions of the series.[36] Undeterred, Claes Visscher etched his own slightly smaller copies of twenty-four of the original forty-four plates, to which he added the newly devised title page discussed above and one additional view not found in the original series. Visscher began his copied series with one of the only views that depicts an easily identifiable monument—the Roode Poort (Red Gate) of Antwerp (Fig. 8.4).

Figure 8.4 Claes Jansz. Visscher, Roode Poort, no. 2 from Regiunculae, et Villae Aliquot Ducatus Brabantiae . . . series, 1612. Etching, 104 x 158 mm, Andrew W. Mellon Fund, National Gallery of Art, Washington, D.C., inv. no. 1975.59.2. Source: Image © by courtesy NGA Images.

Like the title page that so clearly anchors the series in Brabant, this print further specifies the locale, namely Antwerp's northeastern gate.[37] It was through this very gate that Prince William of Orange entered the city in 1577, as commemorated in Frans Hogenberg's (1535–1590) news print published around that time and included in his series of *Nederlandse Gebeurtenissen, 1577–1583*, a widely disseminated set of images recording the important events of the period (Fig. 8.5).[38] The fact that Visscher chose to place this instantly recognizable and historically significant landmark at the start of his series indicates that he sought to stress the topographic content and historical import of the prints.

From there, the numbered sequence of views moves through rustic villages, past inns, by farmhouses, around ponds, over bridges, and along country lanes (Fig. 8.6). These are small, intimate views, measuring just 4" x 6", that invite slow, close perusal. The flat terrain and low horizon line rarely provide an outlet for the eye or a vista onto the distant horizon, while trees and rural buildings bound the images at their edges, keeping the viewer ensconced within the tranquil space of each view (Fig. 8.7). We encounter occasional figures strolling, resting, and fishing, their presence welcoming us to enter and pause within these pleasant spots. The slow, easy progression from print to print enacts a sort of visual journey, undertaken as though on foot but

Figure 8.5 Frans Hogenberg, *Entrance of Prince William of Orange into Antwerp, 1577*, from Series 8 of *Nederlandse Gebeurtenissen, 1577–1583*, 1577–79. Etching, 210 x 280 mm, Rijksmuseum, Amsterdam, inv. no. RP-P-OB-78.784–163. Source: Image © by courtesy Rijksmuseum, Amsterdam.

from the comfort of an armchair.[39] Though the countryside around Antwerp had suffered brutal devastation during the preceding decades of the revolt, Visscher included no trace of this recent history in his placid recreations of Antwerp's hinterlands. Instead, he opted to carefully replicate the rustic views as Cock had initially published them fifty years prior, arranging them into a succession of peaceful vistas that move from the city's gate out into and through the undisturbed villages and hamlets of the Brabantine countryside.

Visscher etched the *Regiunculae* series himself, but his task was easier with the *Environs of Brussels* and the *By Antwerpen* series, the other two sets of Brabantine landscape prints he published around the same time. He had acquired the plates for both these series from the estate sale of the bookseller and publisher Cornelis Claesz (1551–1609) in 1610 and likely published his editions shortly thereafter, though he did not date them.[40] The *Environs of Brussels* is a set of twenty-four views of villages and monuments around Brussels, each identified with an inscription at top. Visscher numbered the series and inscribed his own name as publisher in the lower right corner of the first plate (Fig. 8.8).[41] At the center bottom edge he added the inscription:

Figure 8.6 Claes Jansz. Visscher, *Village Road*, no. 4 from *Regiunculae, et Villae Aliquot Ducatus Brabantiae* . . . series, 1612. Etching, 100 x 155 mm, Andrew W. Mellon Fund, National Gallery of Art, Washington, D.C., inv. no. 1975.59.4. Source: Image © by courtesy NGA Images.

Figure 8.7 Claes Jansz. Visscher, *Country Village with Church and Bridge*, no. 15 from *Regiunculae, et Villae Aliquot Ducatus Brabantiae* . . . series, 1612. Etching, 99 x 155 mm, Andrew W. Mellon Fund, National Gallery of Art, Washington, D.C., inv. no. 1975.59.15. Source: Image © by courtesy NGA Images.

Figure 8.8 Hans Collaert I after Hans Bol, View of the Palace of Brussels, **no. 1 from** Environs of Brussels **series published Claes Jansz. Visscher, ca. 1612. Engraving, 138 x 199 mm, Rijksmuseum, Amsterdam, inv. no. RP-P-1889-A-15012. Source: Image © by courtesy Rijksmuseum, Amsterdam.**

"HBol delineavit ad vivum" (H. Bol designed [this] from life). Based on the evidence of surviving preparatory drawings for the series, scholars have questioned Visscher's attribution of the designs to Bol. However, like his attribution of the *Regiunculae* to Pieter Bruegel, this too was an astute choice—Hans Bol had spent the last years of his life in Amsterdam as an exile from the Southern Netherlands and would therefore have been well-known to Northern artists and collectors as a Southern Netherlandish master with a specialty in landscapes.[42] Visscher's further assertion that Bol made these drawings "from life" underscores the publisher's desire to assert the faithfulness with which these sites were depicted.[43]

Indeed, the *Environs of Brussels* is the most explicitly topographic of the three Brabantine landscape series Visscher published. The inscriptions identify several noteworthy castles and monuments of the Brussels region, including the first print in the series of the ducal palace at Coudenberg, identified as "Thof van Brussel"; the Castle of Carloo to the south of the city; and the Castle ter Rivieren to the northwest. However, even views without major landmarks are identified. These views depict the towns and villages in the surrounding region, among them Elsene to the southeast, Linthout in Schaerbeek to the east, and Stalle to the south (Fig. 8.9).

Landscape and the Memory of Place   213

Figure 8.9 Hans Collaert I after Hans Bol, *View of Stal*, no. 15 from *Environs of Brussels* series published Claes Jansz. Visscher, ca. 1612. Engraving, 138 x 199 mm, Rijksmuseum, Amsterdam, inv. no. RP-P-1889-A-15026. Source: Image © by courtesy Rijksmuseum, Amsterdam.

The terrain is hilly and forested, crisscrossed with roadways and paths, and dotted with fields, ponds, and streams. In every image, figures walk or rest, tend to livestock, carry water, wood, and other heavy loads, or simply meander at leisure through the countryside. Indeed, many of the spots depicted in these views had long been recreational destinations for Brussels' urban dwellers. Though these prints are only slightly larger than those in the *Regiunculae*, measuring almost 5 1/2" x 8", their compositions are more expansive, offering vistas over undulating hilly landscapes that extend into the deep distance. The figures are more dynamic and fully articulated as well, often grouped together as though in conversation, pointing to nearby sites, or hailing each other from across roadways and villages.

The *By Antwerpen* series includes twelve slightly smaller prints, measuring about 5" x 7 1/3", that showcase the rural surrounds of Antwerp.[44] Here Visscher maintained the original inscription on the first plate that indicates Jacob Grimmer was responsible for the designs and Adriaen Collaert (ca.1560–1618) engraved the plates (Fig. 8.10) Though the sites here are not identified with place-names as in the Brussels series, the rural structures—barns with thatched roofs, gabled stone houses, inns, church steeples—are rendered with careful precision. Occasionally, a large village, an impressive

Figure 8.10 Adriaen Collaert after Jacob Grimmer, *Landscape with Travelers*, no. 1 from the *By Antwerpen* series published Claes Jansz. Visscher, ca. 1612. Engraving, 126 x 186 mm, Rijksmuseum, Amsterdam, inv. no. RP-P-1919-2072. Source: Image © by courtesy Rijksmuseum, Amsterdam.

Figure 8.11 Adriaen Collaert after Jacob Grimmer, *Landscape with a River and a Windmill*, no. 8 from the *By Antwerpen* series published Claes Jansz. Visscher, ca. 1612. Engraving, 124 x 184 mm, Rijksmuseum, Amsterdam, inv. no. RP-P-1919–2079. Source: Image © by courtesy Rijksmuseum, Amsterdam.

manor house, or a church appears in the middle ground; far in the distance there are often glimpses of a river and rolling hills to the horizon (Fig. 8.11). These landscapes are also enhanced with figural groups—peasants, peddlers, and travelers traverse the roadways and waterways of the countryside as they go about their quotidian tasks. Compared to both the *Regiunculae* and the Brussels series, these views appear slightly more idealized and generic, with the villages and farmsteads pushed into the middle distance of more extensive views, and occasionally fantastical rock cliffs rising in the distance. The figural groups are sometimes granted a more narrative role, with one view even appearing to include the journey to Emmaus. These sorts of stylistic and compositional choices were quite typical of sixteenth-century landscape imagery, which tended toward more expansive and imaginary vistas. In this sense, the style and format of the views confirm their artistic legacy as authentic sixteenth-century Brabantine landscapes, even if they do not purport to accurately portray specific sites in the way the Brussels series does. Rather, these views evoke the Brabantine countryside more generally as a serene and bucolic expanse.

All three of the series are rendered in a clear, naturalistic style. However composed the landscapes may in fact be, there is little in the way of embellishment or ornament to distract from the plain immediacy of the views. Familiar rustic architectural structures mark these landscapes as specifically Brabantine, while their naturalistic mode of representation also encourages the viewer to experience these views directly, as if in the present. The diminutive size of all the series demands intimate and personal perusal; the viewer must lean in close to follow their pathways and make out their details. Most of the prints across all three series offer a sort of visual entry point at the threshold of each image, and from there the viewer can easily move along gentle zigzagging roads and paths, reinforced by trees and hillocks that guide the eye and attention. This compositional structure, repeated even as it is varied from print to print, activates the viewer's role in each view, underscoring the experience of an ongoing leisurely visual journey through each series. Despite the visual and compositional variety, in other words, there is a consistency across the series in viewing experience, a shared visual mode of entering and moving through the spaces of these views that carries over from scene to scene and from series to series.

TIME AND SPACE TRAVEL: BRABANTINE LANDSCAPES IN THE DUTCH REPUBLIC

The centering of the viewer within these landscapes enacts a kind of *emplacement*—a term the environmental philosopher Forrest Clingerman has employed as "an interpretative structure through which to understand time's depth in place."[45] He frames this as the spatiotemporal corollary to Paul Ricoeur's notion of how *emplotment* situates readers within a narrative.[46] For Clingerman, places and environments are not simply neutral settings for human experience but rather active constituents in dialectical dialogue with the memory and imagination of those who dwell there. He stresses that "places contain the trace of memory" and reminds us that memory itself is not fixed and constant but rather is "renewed and changed through the present. . . . We are led to forget certain elements of place, just as we remember others, as inevitable parts of our experience."[47] Ultimately, he argues, "by *re-placing the self* and remembering place, nature becomes more than a backdrop; *it is a participant in the narrative, an other that embodies memory, an other that locates imagination, and thereby an other that provides a constitutive element of selfhood.*"[48]

While Clingerman's contemporary hermeneutics of place does not explicitly offer a model for the historical interpretation of environments and landscapes, his conception of the intertwined relationship between memory and place opens a productive avenue through which to understand the reemergence of Brabantine landscape imagery in the Dutch Republic. At a moment when places of the past—understood not just as physical locales or territories but also as repositories of communal and political identity—were a subject of uncertain and contested significance, these print series invited viewers to revisit and remember the Brabantine countryside and to reenvision its meaning in the present.

The compositional immediacy of the print series "emplaces" viewers, enabling them to visually activate the landscape views through the agency of memory and experience. The views function as "legible landscapes," as the environmental philosopher Martin Drenthen has termed them, images of landscapes that "contain signs that can be 'read' like meaningful texts that tell a story about ourselves and our history, much in the same way that other texts from our cultural heritage do."[49] The Brabantine countryside views, as presented and re-presented in these printed series, thereby become—like other cultural texts—bearers of meaning borne through time. These meanings are not strictly iconographic or symbolic in the traditional art historical mode, that is, stable and fixed. Instead, the landscapes resonate with the rich, varied personal and collective historical narratives of the Brabantine past as they were carried forward and reconfigured, reconsidered, and redeployed in the present. For viewers in early seventeenth-century Holland, to be emplaced in these Brabantine country villages was to inhabit distant places and a time long since passed. The invitation to walk into and through the villages and countryside of Brabant proffered by the prints would have made this distant region visually present—a kind of early modern time and space travel—giving viewers the chance to see places of the past in the present and to actively engage with their implications at a moment of critical historical transformation.

For some exiles in the North, still eager to return to Brabant, Visscher's prints could keep the memory of their homeland alive. Such "armchair travel" was surely nostalgic, recalling a past before the countryside had been devastated by long years of war and violence. By eliding any reference to the strife and ruination that these actual places had endured for decades, Visscher's series made present a vision of Brabant's past, before the Revolt had reshaped its landscapes, and as many hoped it would one day once again become, transforming the reassuring and familiar memory of places of the past into an optimistic expectation for peaceful restoration and seamless reintegration in the future. By prompting memories of their lost homelands in the present, the prints allowed exiles to actively foster the prospect of their imminent return, however long it had been deferred and however improbable it increasingly seemed to become.

On the other hand, as discussed above, for many Dutch residents, exile and native alike, the Twelve Years' Truce had the inverse impact of finally foreclosing the possibility of a future restored and unified *patria*. Exposing the considerable political, religious, and cultural rifts that had gradually grown up between the Northern and Southern Netherlands during the war, the truce marked for many the recognition of a new kind of distance between North and South, and between the present and the past. It was at this juncture that some exiles and their descendants sought to establish new permanent communities and connections in their Northern homes.[50] A familiar example to art historians is Karel van Mander (1548–1606), a native of Meulebeke in West Flanders who had emigrated to Haarlem via Kortrijk and Bruges and actively embraced his new identity as a Haarlemer. The anonymous biography appended to the posthumous 1618 edition of his *Schilderboek* describes van Mander's departure from the South, where the biographer recounts, "the countryside was given over to destruction and decay."[51] Van Mander came to fully embrace his new home in Haarlem, however, writing two laudatory poems dedicated to extolling the city. In the first poem, entitled "Het Beelt van Haerlem" (The Image of Haarlem), van Mander claims that he had never encountered "a town so pleasant and well situated as Haarlem in fine Holland" and goes on to praise its local traditions and productive industries, but also especially the pleasant delights of its countryside, which he likens to an "earthly paradise."[52] He was one of many authors, poets, and rhetoricians to cultivate such narratives, highlighting a shift in focus from the Southern regions of the past to the comparable beauty, prosperity, and pleasures of the Northern countryside. In Haarlem and other Northern towns, Flemish and Brabantine chambers of rhetoric flourished, and these émigré authors and rhetoricians "disseminated new civic identities that inscribed the past of the exiles into the historical narrative of their host societies."⁵³ Exile and native playwrights alike extolled the contributions of the "new Haarlemers" to the revived glory of the city, stressing the common enmity both natives and newcomers shared for their common foe, the Spaniards.

For these audiences, the Brabantine views in Visscher's series served as visual memorials to a time past and place lost. Pierre Nora has argued that what he calls *milieux de mémoire*, or active sites of cultural memory that are inhabited and experienced in the present, as in ritual, can be transformed into *lieux de mémoire*, or fixed vestiges of a cultural past, when they are no longer actively experienced in the present. These *lieux de mémoire* are essentially commemorative, creating a discontinuity between the present and the past.⁵⁴ These prints, presenting as they do an idyllic picture of the Brabantine countryside, fixed in a distant prewar past, could serve as visual *lieux de mémoire*. This does not mean that the images ceased to shape new meaning and understandings of the past in the present; on the contrary, such visual testaments to past places and experiences could become a locus for consolidating memories of the past now severed from a present lived experience. Viewed in this light, the prints do not so much offer a way to restore or recreate a relationship to the Brabant of the past as they do a mechanism for transforming this past

Figure 8.12 Claes Jansz. Visscher, *Beacon at Zandvoort*, no. 2 from *Plaisante Plaetsen* series, ca. 1611–13. Etching, 102 × 145 mm, Rijksmuseum, Amsterdam, inv. no. RP-P-1879-A-3463. Source: Image © by courtesy Rijksmuseum, Amsterdam.

into a coherent narrative of historical memory that served to forge new communities out of the heterogenous populations of Flemings, Brabaners, and Hollanders in Haarlem and other cities of the nascent Dutch Republic.

Visscher himself may have read his Brabantine views this way. At the same time that he issued his Brabantine sets, he also published a series of views of the countryside around Haarlem, the *Plaisante Plaetsen*.[55] Visscher's carefully orchestrated sequence of local views is numbered and labeled on a table of contents with a view of Zandtvoort (Fig. 8.12).

The viewer is encouraged to explore the rural surroundings of Haarlem through a virtual tour of spots in the local countryside. The prints move in an arc through the rural outskirts of the city, offering views of dunes, inns, woods, and bleaching fields along the way. The viewer is invited to enter these places via roads leading out from the foreground, just as in the Brabantine series, and is, once again, accompanied by country folk walking, working, and resting. As in the Brussels series, Visscher includes significant monuments around the city, including the Leper Asylum and the ruins of the Huis ter Kleef, which were especially notable for having served, respectively, as a Spanish encampment and headquarters during the siege of Haarlem in 1573 (Fig. 8.13). The inclusion of these monuments adds a deliberate memorial resonance to the views of the landscape, which otherwise focus on the rustic architecture and the quotidian activities of the countryside.

Figure 8.13 Claes Jansz. Visscher, *Huis ter Kleef*, no. 12 from *Plaisante Plaetsen* series, ca. 1611–13. Etching, 103 x 158 mm, Rijksmuseum, Amsterdam, inv. no. RP-P-1879-A-3473. Source: Image © by courtesy Rijksmuseum, Amsterdam.

On a formal level, the Haarlem series is clearly indebted to the compositional logic and seemingly unfiltered naturalism of the Brabantine sets.[56] Visscher's transposition of the pictorial model of the Brabantine landscapes to Haarlem creates a visual continuity between South and North, perhaps to suggest their inherent and natural unity. But perhaps this visual analogy also suggests that Haarlem and its rural surrounds might be able to recuperate those places to the south in the incipient Dutch Republic. In 1612, Haarlem was a city filled with migrants—migrants who were beginning to rethink themselves as new citizens rather than foreign exiles. By reconstituting the image and visual vocabulary of Southern territories in Northern ones, the *Plaisante Plaetsen* series appropriates and subsumes the image of the Brabant of the past into a new lexicon of a specifically Northern Netherlandish landscape. We might understand this as an effort to salvage "time's depth in place" by relocating it and incorporating it into the very history and memory of Haarlem. The Twelve Years' Truce might have portended that the Netherlands would never become an ideally united *patria*, and that the exiles would never be able to return to their lost homes, but seen in conjunction with his three Brabantine series, the images in Visscher's *Plaisante Plaetsen* appear to propose that the notion of Netherlandishness could be forged anew, recentered and recuperated in the landscapes of the nascent Dutch Republic.

CONCLUSION

Claes Visscher's three Brabantine landscape print series, published in the first years of the Twelve Years' Truce, might appear at first glance to be straightforward local views, depicted in a direct, naturalistic style simply to record real places in print. This chapter has attempted to argue that these landscapes were not quite so transparent. Visscher's timely republication brought them into circulation in Holland in the 1610s, at exactly the moment when the places they depict—Antwerp, Brussels, the countryside of Brabant—were highly contested sites, not still fully part of an imagined Netherlandish *patria* but also not yet fully separated from the cultural, religious, and political communities taking shape in the new Dutch Republic. Despite their pleasant, peaceful vistas that look so immediate, these series were in their republication in Holland inevitably retrospective, traces of a remembered past before the dislocations and rupture of war. However, by offering up a visual tour through which to dwell in times long past and places now quite distant, they were also charged with the potential to realign and re-place prewar Brabant in seventeenth-century Holland. These images of Brabant could serve as the visual loci of memory upon which to imagine new identities and places of community in the Dutch Republic.

WORKS CITED

Adams, Ann Jensen. "Competing Communities in the 'Great Bog of Europe': Identity and 17th-Century Dutch Landscape." In *Landscape and Power*, edited by W. J. T. Mitchell, 35–76. Chicago: University of Chicago Press, 1994.
Alpers, Svetlana. "Bruegel's Festive Peasants." *Simiolus* 6, no. 3/4 (1972–73): 163–76.
———. *The Making of Rubens*. New Haven, CT: Yale University Press, 1995.
Asaert, Gustaaf. *1585: De val van Antwerpen en de Uittocht van Vlamingen en Brabanders*. Tielt: Lannoo, 2004.
Bassens, Maarten. *Bruegel: The Complete Graphic Works*. London: Thames & Hudson, 2019.
Briels, J. G. C. A. *Zuid-Nederlandse Immigratie 1572–1630*. Haarlem: Fibula-Van Dishoeck, 1978.
Chapman, H. Perry. "Propagandist Prints, Reaffirming Paintings: Art and Community during the Twelve Years' Truce." In *The Public and Private in Dutch Culture of the Golden Age*, edited by Arthur K. Wheelock Jr. and Adele Seeff, 43–63. Newark: University of Delaware Press, 2000.
Christie's. *Dutch, Flemish and German Drawings*. Sale catalog. Amsterdam, November 30, 1987.
Clingerman, Forrest. "Memory, Imagination, and the Hermeneutics of Place." In *Interpreting Nature*, edited by Forrest Clingerman, Brian Treanor, Martin Drenthen, and David Ulster, 245–63. New York: Fordham University Press, 2013.
Cosemans, Alex. "Het Uitzicht van Brabant op het einde der 16de eeuw." *Bijdragen tot de Geschiedenis van het Hertogdom Brabant* 27 (1936): 285–351.
De Bertier de Sauvigny, Reine. *Jacob et Abel Grimmer: Catalogue Raisonné*. Brussels: La Renaissance du Livre, 1991.
De Boer, Lisa. "Hogenberg and History: Popular Imagery of the Golden Age and the Making of Dutch History." In *The Arts, Community and Cultural Democracy*, edited by Lambert Zuidervaart and Henry M. Luttikhuizen, 214–32. Houndmills, Basingstoke, Hampshire: Macmillan Press, 2000.
De Kooker, H. W., and B. van Selm. *Boekcultuur in de Lage Landen, 1500–1800: Bibliografie van publicaties over particulier boekenbezit in Noord- en Zuid-Nederland, verschenen voor 1991*. Utrecht: HES, 1993.
Diels, Ann. "Hans Collaert I." In *Met Passer en Penseel: Brussel en het oude hertogdom Brabant in beeld*, edited by Véronique Van de Kerckhof, Helena Bussers, and Véronique Bücken, 206–10. Brussels: Dexia Bank, 2000.
Diels, Ann, and Marjolein Leesberg. *The New Hollstein: Dutch & Flemish Etchings, Engravings, and Woodcuts, 1450–1700, Volume 15: The Collaert Dynasty*, edited by Marjolein Leesberg and Arnout Balis. 8 parts. Ouderwerk aan den Ijssel: Sound & Vision in cooperation with the Rijksprentenkabinet, Rijksmuseum Amsterdam, 2005–2006.
Drenthen, Martin. "Reading Ourselves through the Land: Landscape Hermeneutics and Ethics of Place." In *Placing Nature on the Borders of Religion, Philosophy, and Ethics*, edited by Forrest Clingerman and Martin Dixon, 123–38. Farnham, UK: Ashgate, 2011.

Duits, Henk. "Het leven van Karel van Mander: Kunstenaarsleven of schrijversbiografie?" *De zeventiende eeuw* 9 (1993): 113–30.
Duke, Alastair. "The Elusive Netherlands: The Question of National Identity in the Early Modern Low Countries on the Eve of the Revolt." In *Dissident Identities in the Early Modern Low Countries*, edited by Judith Pollmann and Andrew Spicer, 9–55. Farnham, UK: Ashgate, 2009.
Eekhout, Maria Francisca Davina. "Material Memories of the Dutch Revolt: The Urban Memory Landscape in the Low Countries, 1566–1700." PhD diss., Leiden University, 2014. https://scholarlypublications.universiteitleiden.nl/handle/1887/29686.
Freedberg, David. *Dutch Landscape Prints of the Seventeenth Century*. London: The British Museum, 1980.
Gibson, Walter. "Bruegel and the Peasants: A Problem of Interpretation." In *Pieter Bruegel the Elder: Two Studies*, 11–52. Franklin Murphy Lectures 11. Lawrence: University of Kansas Spencer Museum of Art, 1991.
———. *Pleasant Places: The Rustic Landscape from Bruegel to Ruisdael*. Berkeley: University of California Press, 2000.
Hautekeete, Stefaan. Introduction to *The New Hollstein: Dutch and Flemish Etchings, Engravings, and Woodcuts 1450–1700, Volume 27: Hans Bol*, 2 parts, edited by Ger Luijten, 1:xxvii-ci. Ouderkerk an den Ijssel: Sound & Vision in cooperation with the Rijksmuseum, Amsterdam, 2015.
———. "Van Stad en Land: Het beeld van Brabant in de vroege topografische tekenkunst." In *Met Passer en Penseel: Brussel en het oude hertogdom Brabant in beeld*, edited by Véronique Van de Kerckhof, Helena Bussers, and Véronique Bücken, 46–57. Brussels: Dexia Bank, 2000.
Hollstein, F. W. H. *Dutch and Flemish Etchings, Engravings, and Woodcuts, ca. 1450–1700*. Amsterdam: M. Hertzberger, 1949–.
Israel, Jonathan. *The Dutch Republic: Its Rise, Greatness, and Fall, 1477–1806*. Oxford: Clarendon Press, 1998.
Kolfin, Elmer. "Amsterdam, stad van prenten: Amsterdamse prentuitgevers in de 17de eeuw." In *Gedrukt tot Amsterdam: Amsterdamse prentmakers en -uitgevers in de gouden eeuw*, edited by Elmer Kolfin, Jaap van Steen, and Jasper Hillefers, 11–57. Zwolle: Waanders, 2011.
Kuijpers, Erika, Judith Pollmann, Johannes Müller, and Jasper van der Steen, eds. *Memory before Modernity: Practices of Memory in Early Modern Europe*. Leiden: Brill, 2013.
Leeflang, Huigen. "The Sign of Claes Jansz Visscher and His Progeny: The History and Significance of a Brand Name." *Rijksmuseum Bulletin* 62 (2014): 241–68.
Levesque, Catherine. *Journey through Landscape in Seventeenth-Century Holland: The Haarlem Print Series and Dutch Identity*. University Park: Pennsylvania State University Press, 1994.
———. "Landscape, Politics, and the Prosperous Peace." *Nederlands Kunsthistorisch Jaarboek* 48 (1997): 222–57.
McGrath, Elizabeth. "A Netherlandish History by Joachim Wtewael." *Journal of the Warburg and Courtauld Institutes* 38 (1975): 182–217.

Michalsky, Tanja. "Die Natur der Nation: Überlegungen zur 'Landschaft' als Ausdruck nationaler Identität." In *Europa im 17. Jahrhundert: Ein Politischer Mythos und seine Bilder*, edited by Klaus Bussmann and Elke Anna Werner, 333–54. Stuttgart: Franz Steiner Verlag, 2004.

Müller, Johannes. *Exile Memories and the Dutch Revolt: The Narrated Diaspora, 1550–1750*. Leiden: Brill, 2016.

Nalis, Henk. *The New Hollstein: Dutch & Flemish Etchings, Engravings, and Woodcuts, 1450–1700, Volume 5: The Van Doetecum Family*, edited by Ger Luijten and Christiaan Schuckman. 4 parts. Rotterdam: Sound & Vision Interactive in cooperation with the Rijksprentenkabinet, Rijksmuseum Amsterdam, 1998.

Nora, Pierre. *Realms of Memory: The Construction of the French Past*. Edited by Lawrence D. Kritzman. Translated by Arthur Goldhammer. 3 vols. European Perspectives. New York: Columbia University Press, 1996.

Onuf, Alexandra. "Hans van Luyck and the Byways of Flemish Landscape Prints." In *Tributes to David Freedberg: Image and Insight*, edited by Claudia Swan, 203–17. London: Harvey Miller, 2019.

———. *The Small Landscape Prints in Early Modern Netherlands*. London: Routledge, 2018.

Orenstein, Nadine. *Hendrick Hondius and the Business of Prints in Seventeenth-Century Holland*. Rotterdam: Sound & Vision Interactive, 1996.

———, ed. *Pieter Bruegel the Elder: Drawings and Prints*. New Haven, CT: Yale University Press, 2001.

Orenstein, Nadine, Huigen Leeflang, Ger Luijten, and Christiaan Schuckman. "Print Publishers in the Netherlands, 1580–1620." In *Dawn of the Golden Age: Northern Netherlandish Art, 1580–1620*, edited by Ger Luijten and Arianne van Suchtelen, 167–200. Amsterdam: Rijksmuseum, 1993.

Parker, Geoffrey. *The Army of Flanders and the Spanish Road, 1567–1659: The Logistics of Spanish Victory and Defeat in the Cow Countries' Wars*. New York: Cambridge University Press, 1972.

Pollmann, Judith. *Memory in Early Modern Europe, 1500–1800*. Oxford: Oxford University Press, 2017.

———. "No Man's Land: Reinventing Netherlandish Identities, 1585–1621." In *Networks, Regions and Nations: Shaping Identities in the Low Countries, 1300–1650*, edited by Robert Stein and Judith Pollmann, 241–61. Leiden: Brill, 2010.

Richardson, Todd M. *Pieter Bruegel the Elder: Art Discourse in the Sixteenth-Century Netherlands*. Farnham, UK: Ashgate, 2011.

Ricoeur, Paul. "The Text as Dynamic Identity." In *Identity of the Literary Text*, edited by Mario J. Valdés and Owen Miller, 175–86. Toronto: University of Toronto Press, 1985.

———. *Time and Narrative*. 3 vols. Translated by Kathleen McLaughlin and David Pellauer. Chicago: University of Chicago Press, 1984–88.

Rutgers van der Loeff, J. D. *Drie lofdichten op Haarlem*. Haarlem: De Erven F. Bohn, 1911.

Schama, Simon. "Dutch Landscape: Culture as Foreground." In *Masters of 17th-Century Dutch Landscape Painting*, edited by Peter Sutton, 64–83. Boston: Museum of Fine Arts, 1987.

———. *The Embarrassment of Riches: An Interpretation of Dutch Culture in the Golden Age*. London: Collins, 1987.

Silver, Larry. *Peasant Scenes and Landscapes: The Rise of Pictorial Genres in the Antwerp Art Market*. Philadelphia: University of Pennsylvania Press, 2006.

Simon, M. "Claes Jansz. Visscher." PhD diss., University of Fribourg, 1958.

Smits-Veldt, Mieke B. "'Het vaderland' bij Hollandse rederijkers, circa 1580–1625: Grondgebied en identiteit." In *Vaderland: Een geschiedenis van de vijftiende eeuw tot 1940*, edited by N. C. F. van Sas, 83–107. Amsterdam: Amsterdam University Press, 1999.

Van de Kerckhof, Véronique, Helena Bussers, and Véronique Bücken, eds. *Met Passer en Penseel: Brussel en het oude hertogdom Brabant in beeld*. Brussels: Dexia Bank, 2000.

Van den Brink, Peter, ed. *Bruegel Enterprises*. Ghent: Ludion, 2001.

Van der Coelen, Peter. "Something for Everyone? The Marketing of Old Testament Prints in Holland's Golden Age." In *Patriarchs, Angels and Prophets: The Old Testament in Netherlandish Printmaking from Lucas Van Leyden to Rembrandt*, edited by Peter van der Coelen, 37–61. Amsterdam: Museum Het Rembrandthuis, 1996.

Van der Steen, Jasper. "A Contested Past: Memory Wars during the Twelve Years Truce (1609–21)," in Kuijpers, Pollmann, Müller, and Van der Steen, *Memory before Modernity*, 45–61.

———. *Memory Wars in the Low Countries, 1566–1700*. Leiden: Brill, 2015.

Vande Weghe, Robert. *Geschiedenis van de Antwerpse straatnamen*. Antwerp: Mercurius, 1977.

Van Eeghen, I. H. "De familie van de plaatsnijder Claes Jansz Visscher." *Amstelodamum* 77 (1990): 73–82.

Van Grieken, Joris, Ger Luijten, and Jan van der Stock. *Hieronymus Cock: The Renaissance in Print*. Brussels: Mercatorfonds; New Haven, CT: Yale University Press, 2013.

Van Mander, Karel. *The Lives of the Illustrious Netherlandish and German Painters, from the first edition of the Schilder-boeck (1603–1604): Preceded by the Lineage, Circumstances and Place of Birth, Life and Works of Karel van Mander, Painter and Poet and likewise his Death and Burial, from the second edition of the Schilder-boeck (1616–1618)*. Edited by Hessel Miedema. Translated by Michael Hoyle, Jacqueline Pennial-Boer and Charles Ford. 6 volumes. Doornspijk: Davaco, 1994–1999.

Van Suchtelen, A. A. "Bol, Hans." In *Allgemeines Künstler-Lexicon: Die Bildenden Künstler aller Zeiten und Völker*, edited by K. G. Saur, 12:359–60. Munich: Saur, 1996.

Van Zuilen, Vincent. "The Politics of Dividing the Nation: News Pamphlets as a Vehicle of Ideology and National Consciousness in the Habsburg Netherlands

(1585–1609)." In *News and Politics in Early Modern Europe (1500–1800)*, edited by Joop W. Koopmans, 61–78. Leuven: Peeters, 2005.

Voges, Ramon. "Pictures and Power: The Visual Prints of Frans Hogenberg." In *Print and Power in Early Modern Europe (1500–1800)*, edited by Nina Lamal, Jamie Cumby, and Helmer J. Helmers, 300–315. Leiden: Brill. 2021.

Warren, Maureen. "Paper Warfare: Contested Political Memories in a Seventeenth-Century Dutch *Sammelband*." *Word & Image* 34, no. 2 (2018): 167–75.

Wijn, J. W. W. *Het Krijgswezen in den Tijd van Prins Maurits*. Utrecht: Drukkerij Hoeijenbos, 1934.

Zwollo, An. "Hans Bol, Pieter Stevens en Jacob Savery, enige kanttekeningen." *Oud Holland* 84, no. 4 (1969): 298–302.

NOTES

1. For this series, see F. W. H. Hollstein, *Dutch and Flemish Etchings, Engravings, and Woodcuts, ca. 1450–1700* (Amsterdam: M. Hertzberger, 1949–), 38:144–48, nos. 292–317.

2. On Bruegel's peasants, see Svetlana Alpers, "Bruegel's Festive Peasants," *Simiolus* 6, no. 3/4 (1972–73): 163–76; Walter Gibson, "Bruegel and the Peasants: A Problem of Interpretation," in *Pieter Bruegel the Elder: Two Studies*, Franklin Murphy Lectures 11 (Lawrence: University of Kansas Spencer Museum of Art, 1991), 11–52; Todd M. Richardson, *Pieter Bruegel the Elder: Art Discourse in the Sixteenth-Century Netherlands* (Farnham, UK: Ashgate, 2011).

3. This was in part thanks to the dissemination of copies and versions of Bruegel's paintings made in the workshops of his sons and other artists over the next generations. On this, see Peter van den Brink, ed., *Bruegel Enterprises* (Ghent: Ludion, 2001); Larry Silver, *Peasant Scenes and Landscapes: The Rise of Pictorial Genres in the Antwerp Art Market* (Philadelphia: University of Pennsylvania Press, 2006). The wide spread of prints after Bruegel designs was also of key importance. For recent scholarship on prints after Bruegel, see Nadine Orenstein, ed., *Pieter Bruegel the Elder: Drawings and Prints* (New Haven, CT: Yale University Press, 2001); Joris van Grieken, Ger Luijten, and Jan van der Stock, *Hieronymus Cock: The Renaissance in Print* (Brussels: Mercatorfonds; New Haven, CT: Yale University Press, 2013); Maarten Bassens, *Bruegel: The Complete Graphic Works* (London: Thames & Hudson, 2019).

4. Henk Nalis, *The New Hollstein: Dutch & Flemish Etchings, Engravings, and Woodcuts, 1450–1700, Volume 5: The Van Doetecum Family*, ed. Ger Luijten and Christiaan Schuckman, 4 parts (Rotterdam: Sound & Vision Interactive in cooperation with the Rijksprentenkabinet, Rijksmuseum Amsterdam, 1998) 1:94–135, nos. 118–61.

5. Nalis, 1:94 and 110, Fig. a.

6. See note 3 above for scholarship on Cock's publication of prints and print series after Bruegel.

7. On Visscher's biography and publishing practices, see M. Simon, "Claes Jansz. Visscher" (PhD diss., University of Fribourg, 1958); I. H. van Eeghen, "De familie van de plaatsnijder Claes Jansz Visscher," *Amstelodamum* 77 (1990): 73–82; Nadine Orenstein et al., "Print Publishers in the Netherlands, 1580–1620," in *Dawn of the Golden Age: Northern Netherlandish Art, 1580–1620*, ed. Ger Luijten and Arianne van Suchtelen (Amsterdam: Rijksmuseum, 1993), 167–200; Walter Gibson, *Pleasant Places: The Rustic Landscape from Bruegel to Ruisdael* (Berkeley: University of California Press, 2000), 45; Huigen Leeflang, "The Sign of Claes Jansz Visscher and His Progeny: The History and Significance of a Brand Name," *Rijksmuseum Bulletin* 62 (2014): 241–68.

8. For the Brussels series, see Ann Diels and Marjolein Leesberg, *The New Hollstein: Dutch & Flemish Etchings, Engravings, and Woodcuts, 1450–1700, Volume 15: The Collaert Dynasty*, ed. Marjolein Leesberg and Arnout Balis, 8 parts (Ouderwerk aan den Ijssel: Sound & Vision in cooperation with the Rijksprentenkabinet, Rijksmuseum Amsterdam, 2005–6), 5:216–32, nos. 1229–52. For the Antwerp series, see 5:233–40, nos. 1253–64. Relatively little is known about the publisher, Hans van Luyck. For his landscape prints, see Alexandra Onuf, "Hans van Luyck and the Byways of Flemish Landscape Prints," in *Tributes to David Freedberg: Image and Insight*, ed. Claudia Swan (London: Harvey Miller, 2019), 203–17.

9. Hans Bol had fled Antwerp in 1584 and, after a peripatetic period, settled in Amsterdam in 1588 for the remainder of his life and career. For an extensive survey of his print designs, see Stefaan Hautekeete, introduction to *The New Hollstein: Dutch and Flemish Etchings, Engravings, and Woodcuts 1450–1700, Volume 27: Hans Bol*, ed. Ger Luijten, 2 parts (Ouderkerk an den Ijssel: Sound & Vision in cooperation with the Rijksmuseum, Amsterdam, 2015), 1:xxvii–ci.

10. On Jacob Grimmer, see Reine de Bertier de Sauvigny, *Jacob et Abel Grimmer: Catalogue Raisonné* (Brussels: La Renaissance du Livre, 1991).

11. On the rise on the genre of landscape and its increasing specialization, see Silver, *Peasant Scenes and Landscapes*. On the development of rural landscapes in seventeenth-century Holland, see Gibson, *Pleasant Places*.

12. Peter van der Coelen estimates the size of Claes Visscher's production based on his grandson Nicolaus's stock list, drawn up sometime around 1679, which included much of the patrimony accumulated by Claes Visscher. His analysis shows that of the five thousand or more prints offered for sale in the Visscher shop, about four thousand of them were reprints and restrikes of secondhand plates. Peter van der Coelen, "Something for Everyone? The Marketing of Old Testament Prints in Holland's Golden Age," in *Patriarchs, Angels and Prophets: The Old Testament in Netherlandish Printmaking from Lucas Van Leyden to Rembrandt*, ed. Peter van der Coelen (Amsterdam: Museum Het Rembrandthuis, 1996), 37–61, esp. 38–39, 61. Nadine Orenstein's catalog of the Dutch publisher Hendrick Hondius's publications lists 284 original prints and 344 reprints from existing plates. Some plates were exchanged between Hondius and Claes Visscher, sometimes more than once, indicating the fluidity of professional and commercial exchange between these colleagues. Nadine Orenstein, *Hendrick Hondius and the Business of Prints in Seventeenth-Century Holland* (Rotterdam: Sound & Vision Interactive, 1996), 171–218. The widespread

republication of sixteenth-century prints in the seventeenth century resulted in the continuing dissemination and availability of older prints on the art market. For an analysis of this phenomenon in the Northern Netherlandish context, see Elmer Kolfin, "Amsterdam, stad van prenten: Amsterdamse prentuitgevers in de 17de eeuw," in *Gedrukt tot Amsterdam: Amsterdamse prentmakers en -uitgevers in de gouden eeuw*, ed. Elmer Kolfin, Jaap van Steen, and Jasper Hillefers (Zwolle: Waanders, 2011), 11–57, esp. 21–25. See also Orenstein et al., "Print Publishers in the Netherlands," 193–94.

13. Erika Kuijpers et al., eds., *Memory before Modernity: Practices of Memory in Early Modern Europe* (Leiden: Brill, 2013); Judith Pollmann, *Memory in Early Modern Europe, 1500–1800* (Oxford: Oxford University Press, 2017).

14. For a survey of the revolt, see Jonathan Israel, *The Dutch Republic: Its Rise, Greatness, and Fall, 1477–1806* (Oxford: Clarendon Press, 1998), 169–275, 478–546, and esp. 399–420 on the Twelve Years' Truce.

15. Jasper van der Steen, *Memory Wars in the Low Countries, 1566–1700* (Leiden: Brill, 2015), 68, with references to contemporary sources in note 14.

16. As quoted in Van der Steen, *Memory Wars*, 67.

17. J. W. W. Wijn, *Het Krijgswezen in den Tijd van Prins Maurits* (Utrecht: Drukkerij Hoeijenbos, 1934); Geoffrey Parker, *The Army of Flanders and the Spanish Road, 1567–1659: The Logistics of Spanish Victory and Defeat in the Cow Countries' Wars* (New York: Cambridge University Press, 1972).

18. Alex Cosemans, "Het Uitzicht van Brabant op het einde der 16de eeuw," *Bijdragen tot de Geschiedenis van het Hertogdom Brabant* 27 (1936): 285–351.

19. Another such print by A. van Leest illustrating Houwaert's Orangist poem "Milenus Clachte" of 1578 shows a similar scene of Belgica harassed by soldiers in front of a burning town. For a fuller analysis of these images, see Elizabeth McGrath, "A Netherlandish History by Joachim Wtewael," *Journal of the Warburg and Courtauld Institutes* 38 (1975): 196, ill. 34a–d. The painter Peter Paul Rubens was also deeply concerned about the fate of the Netherlands. Svetlana Alpers has argued that several of his paintings, including *War and Peace* (ca. 1629–1630) and *The Kermis* (1635), respond to the contemporary circumstances in the Southern provinces. Svetlana Alpers, *The Making of Rubens* (New Haven, CT: Yale University Press, 1995), 28–64.

20. Judith Pollmann, "No Man's Land: Reinventing Netherlandish Identities, 1585–1621," in *Networks, Regions and Nations: Shaping Identities in the Low Countries, 1300–1650*, ed. Robert Stein and Judith Pollmann (Leiden: Brill, 2010), 245.

21. For examples of commemorative prints, see Alexandra Onuf, *The Small Landscape Prints in Early Modern Netherlands* (London: Routledge, 2018), 154–56.

22. J. G. C. A. Briels, *Zuid-Nederlandse Immigratie 1572–1630* (Haarlem: Fibula-Van Dishoeck, 1978). See also Gustaaf Asaert, *1585: De val van Antwerpen en de Uittocht van Vlamingen en Brabanders* (Tielt: Lannoo, 2004).

23. Israel, *Dutch Republic*, 308–11. Marianne Eekhout has shown that Amsterdam's relatively late renunciation of the Habsburg regime was a source of some embarrassment in the city and within the United Provinces. Amsterdam stakeholders and civic authorities went to considerable efforts to omit recent memories of the war

from their civic self-representation, opting instead to highlight the city's mercantile and commercial success. Maria Francisca Davina Eekhout, "Material Memories of the Dutch Revolt: The Urban Memory Landscape in the Low Countries, 1566–1700" (PhD diss., Leiden University, 2014), 201–3, https://scholarlypublications.universiteitleiden.nl/handle/1887/29686.

24. Johannes Müller, *Exile Memories and the Dutch Revolt: The Narrated Diaspora, 1550–1750* (Leiden: Brill, 2016), 89–92.

25. While certainly some Catholics from the north moved south as the Northern Provinces came to be governed by Calvinist assemblies, by far the largest movement of peoples had been in the other direction, from south to north.

26. For example, Johannes Müller reports the case of the merchant Johan Thijs, whose correspondence indicates his long-standing desire to return to his native Antwerp. In 1599 he writes: "Our hope is that the war, which has endured for so long now, will soon be over and that at last we can return to Antwerp." As late as 1606 his letters reflect his hope that "finally we may see a sudden change" in the course of the war that would allow him to return home. Thijs was not unique in these sentiments. On the contrary, Müller has argued that "for many refugees keeping alive the memory of their homeland served to anticipate a return." Müller, *Exile Memories*, 65, 59–64.

27. William of Orange was a prolific propagandist. He did not argue for his cause on strictly religious grounds, but rather appealed to a communal sense of Netherlandish feeling as opposed to the tyrannical, foreign Spanish rule. By avoiding the narrower confessional tack, Orange was able to avoid association with the narrower and more militant anti-Catholic rebels who had been blamed for inciting violence and iconoclasm in 1566. Jasper van der Steen has argued that this non-confessional justification for revolt was echoed and solidified through a variety of propagandistic media, including prints, news sheets, and songs. See Van der Steen, *Memory Wars*, 42–51. Vincent van Zuilen has shown that this sentiment of Netherlandish unity was employed not only in the Northern Netherlands but in Southern Netherlandish propaganda and discourse as well, where it served to justify very different political goals. Vincent van Zuilen, "The Politics of Dividing the Nation: News Pamphlets as a Vehicle of Ideology and National Consciousness in the Habsburg Netherlands (1585–1609)," in *News and Politics in Early Modern Europe (1500–1800)*, ed. Joop W. Koopmans (Leuven: Peeters, 2005), 61–78.

28. Pollmann, "No Mans's Land," 257–58. For an analysis of the contemporary publication by the Flemish exile William Baudartius, who wrote his antipeace tract "Morghen-wecker" (Wake-up call) in 1610, see Pollmann, "No Man's Land," 256; Van der Steen, *Memory Wars*, 71–73.

29. This phrase is used in the motto or prompt for the 1596 festivities announced by the Leiden chamber of rhetoric, "De Witte Acoleyen" (The White Columbine): "Why is a just war to be praised over a crooked peace?" The local Flemish chamber, "De Orange Lelie" (The Orange Lily), wrote a response highlighting how any treaty with the Habsburgs could not be trusted. Jacob Duyms, himself a Southern exile who previously had been imprisoned by the Spanish army, later published a collection of plays about the revolt with similar sentiments in his 1606 *Ghedenck-boek*. Müller, *Exile Memories*, 66–68.

30. Pollmann, "No Man's Land," 246–47.
31. Pollmann, "No Man's Land," 260.
32. For a summary of the religious debates and their political repercussions, see Israel, *Dutch Republic*, 372–98, 433–49; and especially Jasper van der Steen, "A Contested Past: Memory Wars during the Twelve Years Truce (1609–21)," in Kuijpers et al., *Memory before Modernity*, 45–61. Maureen Warren discusses the way in which polemical prints, including a set published by Claes Jansz. Visscher, participated in this hotly contested religious and political conflict. Maureen Warren, "Paper Warfare: Contested Political Memories in a Seventeenth-Century Dutch *Sammelband*," *Word & Image* 34, no. 2 (2018): 167–75.
33. Simon Schama, "Dutch Landscape: Culture as Foreground," in *Masters of 17th-Century Dutch Landscape Painting*, ed. Peter Sutton (Boston: Museum of Fine Arts, 1987), 64–83. See also Catherine Levesque, "Landscape, Politics, and the Prosperous Peace," *Nederlands Kunsthistorisch Jaarboek* 48 (1997): 222–57; Ann Jensen Adams, "Competing Communities in the 'Great Bog of Europe': Identity and 17th-Century Dutch Landscape," in *Landscape and Power*, ed. W. J. T. Mitchell (Chicago: University of Chicago Press, 1994), 35–76.
34. H. Perry Chapman, "Propagandist Prints, Reaffirming Paintings: Art and Community during the Twelve Years' Truce," in *The Public and Private in Dutch Culture of the Golden Age*, ed. Arthur K. Wheelock Jr. and Adele Seeff (Newark: University of Delaware Press, 2000), 43–63, esp. 50.
35. Eekhout, "Material Memories," 70ff.
36. Onuf, *Small Landscape Prints*, 104–12.
37. The Roode Poort served as the fortified entrance into the northeastern part of the city until the 1550s, when the expansion of the city walls created a new gate. Even after its functional use was supplanted, the old tower remained standing until 1818. Robert vande Weghe, *Geschiedenis van de Antwerpse straatnamen* (Antwerp: Mercurius, 1977), 636–37.
38. For recent scholarship on Hogenberg's prints, see Lisa de Boer, "Hogenberg and History: Popular Imagery of the Golden Age and the Making of Dutch History," in *The Arts, Community and Cultural Democracy*, ed. Lambert Zuidervaart and Henry M. Luttikhuizen (Houndmills, Basingstoke, Hampshire: Macmillan Press, 2000), 214–32; Ramon Voges, "Pictures and Power: The Visual Prints of Frans Hogenberg," in *Print and Power in Early Modern Europe (1500–1800)*, ed. Nina Lamal, Jamie Cumby, and Helmer J. Helmers (Leiden: Brill, 2021), 300–315.
39. On the idea of "armchair travel," see David Freedberg, *Dutch Landscape Prints of the Seventeenth Century* (London: British Museum, 1980), 15–18; Catherine Levesque, *Journey through Landscape in Seventeenth-Century Holland: The Haarlem Print Series and Dutch Identity* (University Park: Pennsylvania State University Press, 1994); Walter Gibson, *Pleasant Places*, 41.
40. For a discussion of Cornelis Claesz as a print dealer and an identification of many of the prints described in the catalog he published in 1609, titled the "Const ende Caert-Register," see H. W. de Kooker and B. van Selm, *Boekcultuur in de Lage Landen, 1500–1800: Bibliografie van publicaties over particulier boekenbezit in Noord- en Zuid-Nederland, verschenen voor 1991* (Utrecht: HES, 1993), 217–25, esp.

n199. For further assessment of these series and their significance in Visscher's early publishing career, see Gibson, *Pleasant Places*, 38.

41. For the Brussels series, see Diels and Leesberg, *New Hollstein: Collaert Dynasty*, 5:216–32, nos. 1229–52. Ann Diels has written the most comprehensive analysis of these series. Ann Diels, "Hans Collaert I," in *Met Passer en Penseel: Brussel en het oude hertogdom Brabant in beeld*, ed. Véronique Van de Kerckhof, Helena Bussers, and Véronique Bücken (Brussels: Dexia, 2000), 206–10; Diels, introduction to Diels and Leesberg, *New Hollstein: Collaert Dynasty*, 1:li, n110. See also Stefaan Hautekeete, "Van Stad en Land: Het beeld van Brabant in de vroege topografische tekenkunst," in Van de Kerckhof, Bussers, and Bücken, *Passer en Penseel*, 46–57, esp. 52–53.

42. In 1591, Hans Bol had emigrated to Amsterdam, where he lived and worked until his death in 1593. While there, Jacob Savery and Frans Boels trained in his workshop. As a result, his work and reputation were widely appreciated in the Northern Netherlands. A. A. van Suchtelen, "Bol, Hans," in *Allgemeines Künstler-Lexicon: Die Bildenden Künstler aller Zeiten und Völker*, ed. K. G. Saur, vol. 12 (Munich: Saur, 1996), 359–60. Though Cornelis Claesz's stocklist also describes the series as by Bol, Visscher's attribution has been disputed by scholars who believe that the drawings related to this series are inconsistent with Bol's style. An Zwollo, "Hans Bol, Pieter Stevens en Jacob Savery, enige kanttekeningen," *Oud Holland* 84, no. 4 (1969): 298–302; Christie's, *Dutch, Flemish and German Drawings*, sale cat., Amsterdam, November 30, 1987, cat. 6, 12–18.

43. Hieronymus Cock made similar claims in his original two sets of the *Small Landscape* prints, identified on the 1559 title page as "naer dleven" (after the life) in Dutch and "ad vivum" (from life) in Latin, and in the 1561 title page as "ad vivum." For a summary of scholarship on the meaning and function of these terms, see Onuf, *Small Landscape Prints*, 20–23, with reference to further literature.

44. Diels and Leesberg, *New Hollstein: Collaert Dynasty*, 5:233–40, nos. 1253–64.

45. Forrest Clingerman, "Memory, Imagination, and the Hermeneutics of Place," in *Interpreting Nature*, ed. Forrest Clingerman et al. (New York: Fordham University Press, 2013), 250.

46. Paul Ricoeur, *Time and Narrative*, vol. 1, trans. Kathleen McLaughlin and David Pellaur (Chicago: University of Chicago Press, 1984); Paul Ricoeur, "The Text as Dynamic Identity," in *Identity of the Literary Text*, ed. Mario J. Valdés and Owen Miller (Toronto: University of Toronto Press, 1985), 175–86.

47. Clingerman, "Memory, Imagination, and the Hermeneutics of Place," 257, 259.

48. Clingerman, "Memory, Imagination, and the Hermeneutics of Place," 254. Emphasis in the original.

49. Martin Drenthen, "Reading Ourselves through the Land: Landscape Hermeneutics and Ethics of Place," in *Placing Nature on the Borders of Religion, Philosophy, and Ethics*, ed. Forrest Clingerman and Martin Dixon (Farnham, UK: Ashgate, 2011), 124–25. In this essay, Drenthen explains that the term "legible landscape" was first coined by author, poet, and activist Willem van Toorn in the 1980s.

50. Simon Schama has discussed the efforts to formulate a collective and distinctively Dutch identity in the wake of the revolt. See Simon Schama, *The*

Embarrassment of Riches: An Interpretation of Dutch Culture in the Golden Age (London: Collins, 1987), esp. 51–125. On the earlier roots of Netherlandish identity, see Alastair Duke, "The Elusive Netherlands: The Question of National Identity in the Early Modern Low Countries on the Eve of the Revolt," in *Dissident Identities in the Early Modern Low Countries*, ed. Judith Pollmann and Andrew Spicer (Farnham, UK: Ashgate, 2009), 9–55.

51. Karel van Mander, *The Lives of the Illustrious Netherlandish and German Painters, from the first edition of the Schilder-boeck (1603–1604): Preceded by the Lineage, Circumstances and Place of Birth, Life and Works of Karel van Mander, Painter and Poet and likewise his Death and Burial, from the second edition of the Schilder-boeck (1616–1618)*, ed. Hessel Miedema, trans. Michael Hoyle, Jacqueline Pennial-Boer and Charles Ford, vol. 1 (Doornspijk: Davaco, 1994), 21. For an analysis of the content and structure of this anonymous biography, see Henk Duits, "Het leven van Karel van Mander: Kunstenaarsleven of schrijversbiografie?," *De zeventiende eeuw* 9 (1993): 113–30.

52. Translation mine. The original Dutch reads: "Maer soo lustighen stadt, noch soo wel gelegen / En vant ik als Haerlem in Hollant fijn" and "vol aertse paradijsen." J. D. Rutgers van der Loeff, *Drie lofdichten op Haarlem* (Haarlem: De Erven F. Bohn, 1911), 19–20.

53. Müller, *Exile Memories*, 110–22, quotation on 116. See also Mieke B. Smits-Veldt, "'Het vaderland' bij Hollandse rederijkers, circa 1580–1625: Grondgebied en identiteit," in *Vaderland: Een geschiedenis van de vijftiende eeuw tot 1940*, ed. N. C. F. van Sas (Amsterdam: Amsterdam University Press, 1999), 83–107, esp. 87–96.

54. Pierre Nora, *Realms of Memory: The Construction of the French Past*, ed. Lawrence D. Kritzman, trans. Arthur Goldhammer, 3 vols., European Perspectives (New York: Columbia University Press, 1996), 1–20.

55. Hollstein, *Dutch and Flemish Etchings*, 38:84–86, nos. 149–60

56. The *Small Landscapes* are routinely acknowledged as the formal precedent for Visscher's *Plaisante Plaetsen* series, and several scholars have discussed the connection between Visscher's copies of the earlier series and his views of Haarlem explicitly. See, for instance, Gibson, *Pleasant Places*, 38, 85; Tanja Michalsky, "Die Natur der Nation: Überlegungen zur 'Landschaft' als Ausdruck nationaler Identität," in *Europa im 17. Jahrhundert: Ein Politischer Mythos und seine Bilder*, ed. Klaus Bussmann and Elke Anna Werner (Stuttgart: Franz Steiner Verlag, 2004), 344. Catherine Levesque also mentions Visscher's copies of the *Small Landscapes*, though she relates the *Plaisante Plaetsen* more explicitly to the *Large Landscape* series, designed by Pieter Bruegel and published by Hieronymus Cock, to place the *Plaisante Plaetsen* more convincingly within the humanist tradition of descriptive geography. Levesque, *Journey through Landscape*, 17–41.

Index

Page references for figures are italicized

Adam de la Parra, Juan, 117, 124, 125
Agincourt, 49–51, 53, 56
America, 1, 126, 135, 136, 138, 139,
    140, 141, 144, 149, 156
Amsterdam, 121, 175, 187, 199, 200,
    201, 204, 212
Anaxagoras, 108
Antwerp, 13, 167–68, 185–86, 200–206,
    208, 209, 210, 220, 226n6, 228n26
Aphasia, 72–74
Architecture, 77, 78, 80, 81, 83,
    86, 215, 219
Assarino, Luca, 124
Avesnes, 27

Barcelona, 117–22, 124–27
Barretines, revolt of the, 127, 131n12
Battle of Crécy, 23–26, 28–29, 36–38
Beaumont, Jean de, 27–28,
Becket, Thomas, 35
Bel, Jean le, 28
Belgica, 13, 170, 184–87, 196n82, 203,
    204, 227n19
Berart, Gabriel, 121–23
Bibliothèque Royale de Belgique, MS
    16604 XVIII, 27
Black Legend, 174, 206

Blessed Sacrament, 121, 122, 125
Bol, Hans, 201, 210–12, *212*, *213*,
    226n9, 230n42

The Book of the Duchess, 29
Bourbons, House of the, 119, 132n35
Bourgeois de Paris, 50
Brabant, 13, 27, 191n2, 199, 200–202,
    205, 207, 208, 210, 212, 215, 216–20
Bruegel the Elder, Pieter, 195n63, 200,
    201, 210, 225n2, 225n3, 231n56
Brussels, 13, 201, 210, 212, *212*, 213,
    215, 219, 220
By Antwerpen, 210, *214*

captivity, 50–52, 55–56, 151
Caribs, 126
Catalonia, principality of, 11,117–19,
    121, 122, 126–27, 132n35; Catalan
    constitutions, 120;
Catalan institutions, 11, 119, 120, 126;
Catalan nationalism, 118
Catalan revolt, 9, 11, 117–18, 119, 122,
    123, 126, 233
Catholicism, 100, 205; Catholic Church,
    49, 120, 125; Catholic doctrine,
    93n40; Catholic faith, 123, 127;
Catholics, 121, 126, 139
chambers of rhetoric, 175, 217, 228n29

233

Charles VI of France, 49–50, 57, 65n54
Charny, Geoffroi de, 25, 38
Charron, Pierre, 123
Chronicon majus, 27
Chronique de l'Abbaye de Saint Trond, 36
Claesz, Cornelis, 210, 230n42
Cock, Hieronymus, 83, 200, 208, 210, 225n6, 231n56
Collaert, Adriaen, 213, *214*
Collaert, Hans, I, 184–85, *185*, 187, 203, *203*, *212*, *213*
collective memory, 5–7, 9, 26, 28, 31, 38, 118, 126
Columbus, Christopher, 126
Consell de Cent, city council of Barcelona, 119, 120, 121
converso, 100, 114n18, 115n53
Corpus Christi Day, 117, 122, 124–27
Corpus Christi Day Revolt, Corpus de Sang, 118, 119, 120
Cortés, Martín, 135–37, 155, 160n1, 161n9, 161n10, 162n12, 162n15,
Counter-Remonstrant, 207
courtly love and violence. See *fin'amor*
criollo, 135–36, 138–40, 143, 145, 149–52, 154–55, 161n5, 162n20,
Crusades, 1, 5, 100
Cupid and violence, 98, 99, 102–4, 105, 106, 108, 110

dehumanization, 10, 86
Díaz del Castillo, Bernal, 134n59, 139, 151
Diputació del General, 119, 120, 131n14
Dutch Golden Age, 207
Dutch Republic, 9, 12–13, 167, 201, 202, 207–8, 216, 218, 220
Dutch Revolt, 167, 169, 202. See also Eighty Years' War

Edward III, King of England, 24, 27–28, 35, 45n40
Eighty Years' War, 1, 9, 12, 167, 169, 170, 173, 185, 188, 201, 202, 235

emigration, 12, 13, 204, 217, 230n42
emotives, 25, 31, 37
emplacement, 215–16
engraving, 12, 83, 167, 177–78, 179, 182, 183, 186
Enguerrand de Monstrelet, 50
Environs of Brussels, 210, 212–13, *212*, *213*
exile, 10, 50, 52, 54, 80, 125, 135, 142, 205–8, 212, 216–17, 220, 228n29

Fama, 25, 33, 37, 43n10
Fernández de Oviedo, Gonzalo, 134n59
fin'amor, 100–101, 110, 114n21, 115n42
Flanders, 27, 191n2, 201, 205, 217
forgetting, 8, 11, 58, 110, 216. See also *oubliance*
France, 1, 9, 10, 24, 26, 27, 28, 29, 38, 49, 50, 52–55, 56–60, 67, 69, 70, 76, 80, 85, 87, 120, 121, 122, 127, 233; French Crown, 24, 27, 132n35; French monarchy, 11, 117
Francken, Ambrosius, 185, *185*, 203, *203*, 206
Friesland, 27, 191n2

Galle, Philips, 167, 168, 183, 208
gender, 25, 32, 33, 34, 80, 82, 85, 175, 234
Gerusalemme liberata, 4
Girona, Bishop of, 120
Goltzius, Hendrick, 9, 12–13, 167–70, *168*, *169*, *170*, *171*, 172–73
Granada War, 100
Grau, Jeroni, 122
grief, 24, 26, 29–34, 36–37, 44n16, 109
Grimmer, Jacob, 201, 213, *214*, 226n10
grotesque, 10, 70–74, 78–79, 80, 82–87, 91n11, 91n17
Guillén de la Carrera, Alonso, 124

Haarlem, 12–13, 167, 175, 176, 177, 187, 203, 204, 217–20, 231n56; Siege of, 12, 176, 203, 204, 219

Habsburgs, Spanish court of the, 118, 119, 120, 127, 167, 173, 175, 201, 203, 227n23, 228n29
Hainault, 27–28, 32
Henry of Lancaster, 28
Henry V, 49
"hermaphrodites," 80, 85, 234
historical memory, 13, 118, 202, 218
Hogenberg, Frans, 174, *174*, 209, *210*, 229n38
Holland, 13, 27, 186, 187, 191n2, 201, 202, 208, 216, 217, 218, 220
Hook and Cod Wars, 27
Hundred Years' War, 30, 37, 38, 57

Iberia, 11; Iberian Peninsula, 100, 119, 127, 139, 233
identity, 6, 12, 13, 14, 24, 37, 51, 118, 136, 137, 138, 175, 202, 216, 217, 230n50;
collective identity, 6, 12, 118
imprisonment, 50–52, 54, 55–56, 60, 140, 176, 207, 228n29
L'Isle des hermaphrodites (*The Island of Hermaphrodites*), 70, 80–82, 84–87, 234

Jews in Spain, 100
John II, King of France, 25, 38

Koninklijke Bibliotheek, MS 72 A, 29

Lamba Doria, 108
Leiden, 175, 203
Liber de spiritu et enima, 35
lieux de mémoire, 7, 218
Lisbon, 121
Livre de chevalerie, 38
López de Gómara, Francisco, 134n59
Louis II, Count of Blois, 28
Louis XIII of Bourbon, 117, 121, 123, 125
Lucius Aemilius Paullus, 107

Madrid, 125, 142, 144

Malory, Thomas, 35
Margaret I, Countess of Burgundy, 28
Margaret II, Countess of Hainault, 27, 28
Marquès, Antoni, 121
Mars, god of war, 99, 102, 113n9
Martí Viladamor, Francesc, 121, 122, 124
Matilda of Lancaster, 28
Maurice of Nassau, 207
Medici, Catherine de, 10, 76–78, 86
milieux de mémoire, 7, 218
Moles, Leonardo, 120
Montaigne, Michel de, 72, 73–74, 87
Montjuïc, hill of, 121
mortuary roll, 9, 27
Muisis, Gilles li, 27, 28–29, 38

New Spain, 138, 139, 140, 143, 144, 146, 155
New World. *See* America
Nicopolis, 49, 50, 63n13, 65n54

Olivares, Count Duke of, Gaspar de Guzmán y Pimentel, 121, 122, 124, 125, 131n21
ornamentation, 23, 70–71, 73, 74, 77, 78, 80, 81, 82, 86, 91n11, 91n17
oubliance (forgetting), 58, 67, 68
Ovid, 78, 111, 167, 171–72, 175, 177, 179, 184, 234

parergon, 77, 79, 84, 91n17
Parets, Miquel, 122–23
Pasqual de Panno, Francesc, 125
patria, 144, 149, 206–7, 217, 220
Pearl, 29
peasants, 1, 2, 90n2, 117, 155, 185, 196n84, 200, 213
Pericles, 107, 108
Petrarch, 98, 100, 113n5
Philip II, King of Spain, 167, 173, 179
Philip III, Duke of Burgundy, 56, 57
Philip IV, King of Spain, 117, 118, 120, 121, 123

Philip VI, King of France, 24, 25, 28
Philippa of Hainault, 27
Picatrix, 99
Plaisante Plaetsen, *218*, 219–20
postmemory, 136–37, 139, 149, 151, 163n44
prints, republication of, 201, 220, 226n12
prison, 50–51, 54, 57, 140
propaganda, 120, 122, 123–27

Queralt, Dalmau de, 117

Regiunculae et Villae Aliquot Ducatus Brabantiae, 199–201, *199*, 208–10, *209*, *211*, 213
regress *ad infinitum*, 72–73
Li Regret Guillaume, 29
relaciones, 118, 119, 120, 130n5
De remediis utriusque fortunae, 98, 100
Remonstrant, 207
representation, 23, 25, 32, 51, 53, 55, 67, 69–70, 71–73, 74, 79, 84, 123, 124, 147, 204, 215
Rioja, Francisco de, 125, 126
Riudarenes, church of, 120, 121
Ros, Alexandre, 125–26
Rouen, 121
Rubí de Marimon, Ramon, 125

Sala, Gaspar, 118, 121, 124, 132n30
Salisbury, 27
Sandoval Zapata, Luis de, 136–39, 149–55
Sarroca, Josep, 122
Het Schilderboek, 217
segadors (reapers), 117, 118, 121–26, 132n25
skepticism, 71–72, 77, 91–92n20, 100
Sorel, Charles, 122, 124
Spain, 1, 11, 98, 100, 115n53, 135–36, 138–39, 140–42, 144, 146, 167, 170, 175, 187–88, 206–7; Spanish Crown, 9, 11, 12, 119–20, 135, 137, 139, 140, 142, 144, 151, 155–56, 204; Spanish monarchy, 12, 126
Suárez de Peralta, 135–52, 155, 156
suspension of judgment, 72–73, 77, 87, 93n34

temporality, 4, 91n14, 98, 103, 109
tercios, 117, 120
Terence, 103
testimony, 3, 60, 109, 118, 123, 133n40, 136, 138, 147
Thirty Years' War, 1, 2, 120
Torquato, Tasso, 4, 5, 19n20
Twelve Years' Truce, 13, 175, 201, 202–4, 206–8, 217, 220

Union of Utrecht, 13, 167, 168, 175, 186, 191n2
United Provinces. *See* Dutch Republic

Van Luyck, Hans, 201, 226n8
Van Mander, Karel, 176, 217
Visscher, Claes Jansz., 9, 13, 199–202, 204, 207–15, 216–20, 226n7, 226n12
Voeux du Héron, 28
Vopis, Francesc. *See* Gaspar Sala
Vredeman de Vries, Hans, 10, *69*, *75*, *81*, 82–83, *83*, 86–87, 93n45

War of the Reapers, 118
War of the Spanish Succession, 127
Wars of Religion (France), 1, 9, 10, 67, 70, 72, 74, 80, 85, 87, 234
William I, Count of Hainault, 27
William II, Count of Hainault, 27
William III, Count of Hainault, 28
William of Auvergne, 35
William of Orange, 173, 175–76, 186, 188, 206, 208, *210*, 228n27
wounds, 3–6, 51, 56, 98–99, 102–7, 109, 118, 138, 151

Xenophon, 107, 108

Zeeland, 27, 186, 191n2
Zwartewall, 28

About the Contributors

Nicholas Ealy is professor of English and Modern Languages at the University of Hartford. Trained as a comparativist, his research focuses on the medieval literature of France and Iberia, with an emphasis on the discourses of love, desire, and narcissism. He is the author of *Narcissism and Selfhood in Medieval French Literature: Wounds of Desire* (Palgrave, 2019) and has published in *Studies in French Cinema, Fifteenth-Century Studies, Studies in the Novel, eHumanista: Journal of Iberian Studies*, and the volume *Sexuality, Sociality, and Cosmology in Medieval Literary Texts* (Palgrave, 2013). His current research is on narcissism and testimony in medieval and early modern Spanish literature.

Ivan Gracia-Arnau is postdoctoral researcher at the Universitat de Barcelona (UB) and visiting fellow at the Centro Interdisciplinar de História, Culturas e Sociedades (CIDEHUS) of the Universidade de Évora. He holds a PhD in Early Modern History from the UB (2020) with a dissertation entitled *Textual Representations of Violence: Barcelona, Corpus of 1640*. In his research he has focused on the study of representations of popular violence in writings produced during the Catalan revolt of 1640. He is currently part of the project "Rebellion and Resistance in the Iberian Empires, 16th–19th Centuries," and of the research group Power and Cultural Representations in the Early Modern Age.

Covadonga Lamar Prieto is associate professor and Pollitt Endowed Term Chair at the University of California, Riverside. She holds a PhD in Philology (2007), a PhD in Hispanic Linguistics (2012) and a PhD in History and Sociocultural Studies (2019). Her research examines the written cultural manifestations of the first generation born after a social or political conflict: the cultural objects they produced, which historical phenomena were involved in language change, as well as the contemporary consequences of language contact.

Kimberly Lifton is PhD student in the Medieval Studies Department at Yale University. She has several forthcoming articles on the material culture of politics during the fourteenth and fifteenth centuries in journals such as *The Medieval Journal* and *Peregrinations*. Her research currently focuses on England's visual and textual responses to the rise of the Ottomans in the fifteenth century amidst the Hundred Years' War and the Wars of the Roses. She is the recipient of the Dhira Mahoney Fellowship, the Pasold Research Grant, and the A. Bartlett Giamatti Fellowship.

Kathleen Long is professor of French at Cornell University. She is the author of two books, *Another Reality: Metamorphosis and the Imagination in the Poetry of Ovid, Petrarch, and Ronsard* and *Hermaphrodites in Renaissance Europe*, and more than fifty articles and book chapters. She now focuses her work on early modern theories of gender and of nonnormative corporealities. Her particular interests are in the relationship between gender, bodily, and behavioral norms and early modern theories of political order, as well as the circulation of very different ideas concerning natural variation's crucial role in human survival and thriving. She is the editor of three volumes: *High Anxiety: Masculinity in Crisis in Early Modern France*; *Religious Differences in France*; and *Gender and Scientific Discourse in Early Modern Europe*, and coeditor for a series on *Monsters and Marvels: Alterity in the Medieval and Early Modern Worlds* (Amsterdam University Press). Her current projects include a translation into English of *The Island of Hermaphrodites (L'isle des hermaphrodites)*, a monograph on literature in the wake of the French Wars of Religion (*Bringing up the Dead*), and a study of early modern theories of disability and gender difference, *The Premodern Postnormal*.

Charles-Louis Morand-Métivier is associate professor of French at the University of Vermont. His research focuses on late medieval and Renaissance representation of massacres and war and on the history of emotions. He is the author of *The Tragedy of the Sack of Cabrières. A Critical Edition and Translation in Prose*, forthcoming with ACMRS; the co-editor (with Tracy Adams, Auckland) of *The Waxing of the Middle Ages: Revisiting the Late French and Burgundian Middle Ages* (forthcoming, Delaware), and the coeditor with Andreea Marculescu (Oklahoma) of *Affective and Emotional Economies in Medieval and Early Modern Europe* (Palgrave Studies in the History of Emotions, 2018). He has published on Christine de Pizan, Philippe de Mézières, Alain Chartier, François Villon, emotions in the Renaissance, Pierre de Ronsard, Joachim du Bellay, and French Renaissance theater.

Alexandra Onuf is associate professor and chair of the Art History Department in the Hartford Art School at the University of Hartford. She received her PhD from Columbia University in 2006. Her research focuses on the history of prints in the Netherlands in the sixteenth and seventeenth centuries, particularly landscape imagery and early modern print publishing practices. She is the author of *The Small Landscape Prints in Early Modern Netherlands* (Routledge, 2018). She has also published articles in the *Art Bulletin*, the *Print Quarterly*, and the *Burlington Magazine*, as well as essays in several edited volumes, including most recently an essay on Rembrandt van Rijn.

Rachel Wise is art historian specializing in the art of early modern Northern Europe. Most recently she has held a Belgium American Educational Foundation postdoctoral fellowship at the Rubenianum in Antwerp, Belgium. She has published on counters struck during the Eighty Years' War with *The Rijksmuseum Bulletin*.